Flowers in History

Flowers in History

PETER COATS

FRONTISPIECE: *Habit de Jardinier by Nicholas de Larmessin.*

Weidenfeld and Nicolson

5 WINSLEY STREET LONDON W1

© 1970 by Peter Coats

Designed by Jane Mackay
for Weidenfeld and Nicolson Ltd

Photoset by BAS Printers Limited, Wallop, Hampshire
Printed in Switzerland by
Imprimeries Réunies S. A., Lausanne.
SBN 297 17964 0

Contents

Introduction

There is nothing in this life pleasanter ...
than to wander through woods, plains, garlanded and adorned
with ... plants of various sorts, and most elegant to boot,
and to gaze intently upon them.
But it increases that pleasure not a little more
if there be added an acquaintance with the virtues and powers
of these same plants ...

These lines, so very suited to being the first of the Introduction of this book, come from one of the earliest herbals, *De Historia Stirpium*, written by Leonhart Fuchs and published in Basle in 1542. And to the 'virtues and powers' of plants that he mentions might well be added the history. And how and from whom plants got their names, and finally, out of the many varieties available, the kinds which an experienced gardener has found the most rewarding.

I would have liked to call this book *Plants in Person* because I think of plants as very personal things. Not only do I have as strong likes and dislikes in the plant-world as I do in the person-world – but I consider that people have played so great a part in the evolution, cultivation, naming and even creation of plants, that the man-plant relationship is an interesting one. Creation ... for, though nature produced the primrose and the cowslip, it took man – and an Englishman – to cross them and make a totally new flower, the polyanthus which is now world known and taken absolutely for granted.

But it was thought important to include the word flower in the title, and so the present title was chosen. One of the best and most descriptive names borne by any recently published book, I suggest, with some lack of modesty, was

7

Lord Wavell's Anthology – *Other Men's Flowers*; lack of modesty because it was I, when on that great and good man's staff in the war, who named it. The title derives from a quotation from Montaigne that I happened to find in the GHQ library in India, but though perfect for an anthology would, perhaps, not have been suitable for this book: for the flowers I describe are not really other men's flowers, but very much our own, and some of them are very much the flowers of certain people.

There are men and women, and I do not only mean those who have had their names given to plants, who will always be linked with certain flowers. Mary the Blessed Virgin, with the lily, is one. And the sunflower is surely the flower of Louis XIV, whose emblem it was. Sunflowers are also linked in our minds with Van Gogh. Louis XIV disliked all Dutchmen and we cannot imagine what he would have thought of Van Gogh – or of his paintings. But they share the sunflower, though Van Gogh considered that the sunflower was his alone. In America, some states are always indentified with certain flowers, such as Kansas with the sunflower, and Iowa with the wild rose.

Monet will always be thought of as painter-in-ordinary to the water lily. The names of Fantin-Latour, the Empress Joséphine and Redouté will be for ever linked with roses. The camellia is the flower of Dumas' unfortunate heroine, and there are more.

Then there are the names which occur over and over again in any books about the history of flowers – names of herbalists, botanists, gardeners, flower painters and plant hunters. Who were they, and what part did they play in the man-plant story?

Dioscorides was one of the first botanists. He was, it is believed, an army doctor at the time of the Emperor Nero, in the first century AD, and he wrote a book, in five parts, *De Materia Medica*. The parts relative to botany make it the earliest known herbal and the Byzantine version of the book, now in the Library of Vienna, is the oldest existing herbal in the world. In it are listed the names of over five hundred plants with their value and properties in medicine. The book has a romantic story: it was compiled about AD 512 for a Byzantine princess – Anicia Juliana, daughter of the Emperor Flavius, and was already over a thousand years old when it came to light in Constantinople in 1562. Its discovery was first reported by Ogier de Busbecq, Ambassador of the Holy Roman Empire, who was an enthusiastic botanist, and who, incidentally, introduced the tulip to western Europe. 'I should have liked to have bought it,' he wrote, 'but the price frightened me: ... a hundred ducats was named, a sum which would suit the Emperor's purse better than mine'. But Busbecq prevailed on the Emperor to acquire this treasure, now known as the *Codex Vindobonensis* and one of the great prizes of the library in Vienna.

Dioscorides' work, as transcribed in the *Codex*, was treated as completely authoritative until the sixteenth century. The Spaniard Nicolas de Monardes in Elizabethan days was full of praise for the soldier-botanist's writings,

'*Let him who hath two loaves sell one, and buy flower of narcissus: for bread is but food for the body, whereas narcissus is food for the soul*' Mahomet.

'Which are so celebrated in all the worlde, whereby he gate the glory and fame ... and there hath remained more fame of hym, by writing them, than although he had gotten many cities by his warlike actes'. The plant-loving army doctor's name became so identified with the study of plants that it nearly displaced the word botany itself and Doctor Agnes Arber, in her excellent work on herbals, quotes William Turner as referring to the occupant of the chair of Botany at the University of Bologna in 1534 as 'Reder of Dioscorides'.

Doctor Arber further remarks, on the subject of Dioscorides, 'It is a striking sign of the continuity of Botany' that several of the plant names he used nearly two thousand years ago should have survived – among them aristolochia, anemone and anagallis.

Though the *Codex Vindobonensis* is one of the rarest books in the world, there is a reproduction of it in facsimile which makes it available for study. A thousand years were to pass from the time that the original *Codex* was first compiled for the Princess Anicia, before an illustrated herbal of equal quality was produced.

The first herbals of modern times were illustrated with woodblocks which only provided coarse representations of the plants. Sometimes the name of the author – Rycharde Banckes, for instance, whose *Herball* was published in 1525 – has come down to us, but never the name of the illustrator. These early herbals were designed for the use of physicians and apothecaries and the illustrations were meant to be more instructive than decorative. But before herbals showed illustrations which treated plants aesthetically, two artists – two of the first names in plant painting – had appeared who depicted flowers with a sensitivity and appreciation which have never been equalled: Albrecht Dürer and Leonardo da Vinci. It is outside the scope of this book to do more than salute these two great names. A drawing of violets by Dürer is shown on page 215, and a drawing of a lily by Leonardo da Vinci on page 102.

These two giants painted flowers, as it were, by chance. They are not remembered primarily as flower painters. Artists who are famous for their paintings of flowers, such as the Flemish Ambrosius Bosschaert, will be noted later.

First household name in the history of English-speaking botanists is John Gerard – barber, doctor and gardener to Queen Elizabeth's Lord High Treasurer, Lord Burleigh. Gerard's fame derives from his herbal, published in 1597. Opinions vary as to the merits of the book, but its type and layout were a great advance on any previously printed herbal, and it contains among its many woodcuts the first representation of a potato, a plant then recently introduced from America. But Gerard's knowledge of botany was not profound and he even shows an illustration of the fabled Barnacle or Goose Tree which he actually claims to have seen. This tree, said to grow in the north of Scotland and the 'Orchades' or Orkneys, was supposed to bear fruit from which hatched barnacle geese. He had, he claimed, actually witnessed the phenomenon '... what our eies have seene, and hands have touched, we shall

LEFT *John Parkinson (1567–1650) published his famous herbal Paradisi in Sole – a pun on his name 'Park in Sun' – in 1629. For many years it was the authoritative English herbal.*

Passiflora as depicted in Parkinson's Paradisi in Sole.

declare'. He then goes on to describe this botanical and ornithological wonder, which, he believed, resulted in the hatching of a mysterious 'FOULE, bigger than a mallard, and lesser than a goose'.

Though Gerard was inaccurate in many of his plant descriptions, at the best credulous and at the worst a liar, his herbal will for ever be a classic. Anyone writing about plants should study it, for it provides countless descriptions and quotations. And the great Linnaeus himself must have looked on Gerard's weaknesses with indulgence, for he named the plant *gerardia* after him.

A revised and much improved edition of Gerard was edited by the physician Thomas Johnson (with the description of the Barnacle Tree omitted) and appeared in 1603. 1629 saw the publication of the second famous English herbal – that of John Parkinson (1567–1650). This had an impressive title, part of which was a pun on Parkinson's own name: *Paradisi in Sole* (Park in sun) *Paradisus terrestris*. 'A garden of all sorts of pleasant flowers which our English ayre will permit to be nursed up ... together with the right orderinge planting and preserving of them and their uses and vertues.' Parkinson's book – which contains cultural gardening hints as well as illustrations – was dedicated to Queen Henrietta Maria, the French consort of Charles I, with the request that she would listen graciously to 'this speaking garden'. Parkinson followed up his *Paradisus terrestris* by another work, the *Theatrum botanicum*, which had an even greater success. Though both his books were an improvement on Gerard, and Parkinson's plant descriptions are more detailed and more accurate than his predecessors, the classes into which he divides his plants are arbitrary, and make little constructive sense. One group comes under the heading of 'Venomous, sleepy and hurtfull plants – and their counter poysons'. Another section is that of 'Strange and Outlandish Plants', meaning unfamiliar and foreign plants. 'In Parkinson's classification', writes Dr Arber, 'we see Botany reverting once more to the position of a mere hand maid to medicine'.

The names of Gerard and Parkinson will always figure prominently in the story of man's relationship with plants. Parkinson's fame rests on his books, and he is further commemorated (by Linnaeus) by the parkinsonia – the Jerusalem Thorn – a tree the author once planted in a garden in Morocco where it grew with such incredible speed that it approached the Barnacle Tree in wonder.

The Tradescants – father and son – are celebrated names in botany. The father was gardener to the English royal family and was succeeded in that office by his son John. The Tradescant collection of specimen plants, mostly from Virginia, was left to Elias Ashmole and was the nucleus of the Ashmolean collection at Oxford. The Tradescants' name has been given to two very different plants – the well-known greenhouse plant *Tradescantia fluminensis* or Wandering Jew, and the old-fashioned Spiderwort, *T. virginiana*, which was introduced from the eastern states of America, and has been growing in Western gardens for many centuries. The Tradescants' story is well summed up by the inscription on their family tomb in Lambeth churchyard:

> Know stranger, ere thou pass, beneath this stone
> Lye John Tradescant, Grandsire, Father, Son
> The last dyed in his Spring: the other two
> Lived till they had travelled art, and nature through
> As by their choice collections may appear
> From what is rare, in land, in sea, in Air.
> Whilst they (A Homer's Illiad in a nut)
> A world of wonder in a closet shut
> These famous antiquarians that had been
> Both gardeners to the Rose and Lily Queen
> Transplanted now themselves, sleep here and when
> Angels shall with their trumpets waken men
> And fire shall purge the world, these hence shall rise
> And change the garden for a Paradise.

John Tradescant the Younger (1608–62) was the son of James I's Dutch gardener. His collection of specimen plants was the nucleus of the Ashmolean Collection.

RIGHT *Robert Morison (1620–83), a Scottish botanist, born in Aberdeen. He was an ardent royalist, left England during the Commonwealth, and became gardener to the Duke of Orleans. Charles II made him his 'Botanist royal'. A thistle surmounts his coat of arms.*

The Rose and Lily Queens are the very English Elizabeth I and the very French Henrietta Maria.

As a herbalist Nicholas Culpeper (1616–54) hardly deserves the fame that he has achieved, for what he wrote on the subject of herbs and medicine sometimes verges on complete nonsense. His *Physical Directory* was published in 1649, and he introduced the work as 'an ASTROLOGO-PHISICAL DISCOURSE OF THE VULGAR HERBELS OF THIS NATION …'. Culpeper was convinced that there was a mystic link between certain herbs and certain stars, and that, for instance, wormwood was ruled by the planet Mars. 'I prove it thus', he writes, 'what delights in Martial places is a Martial herb … wormwood delights in martial places (for about Forges and Ironworks you may gather a cart load of it). Ergo it is a Martial Herb.'

He was also very conceited, and criticized his predecessors as being 'as ful of nonsense and contradictions as an egg is ful of meat'. Yet Culpeper's name is still a household word and would be, for his herbal is still regularly republished, even if the various Herbalist Societies and Culpeper Houses with their tisanes and herbal pills were not there to keep his memory as green as camomile tea.

No outstanding names in botany have come down to us from the late seventeenth century. John Evelyn had a famous garden at Deptford, London, (and cannot have been pleased when his tenant, Peter the Great, amused himself by being pushed through the beautifully clipped yew hedges): he had a collection of dried and pressed flowers which impressed Pepys.

It is not until the early eighteenth century that we read of the name which will always resound in the world of plants – that of the Swede, Linnaeus. Linnaeus' great career can be said to have started after a chance meeting with the astronomer Anders Celsius in the garden of the University of Uppsala. Little can the learned Celsius have realised that the poverty-stricken student, in his paper-patched shoes, was one day to become so famous. For it was Carl Linné, born in 1707, the son of a poor pastor in Smoland in the south of Sweden, who was to be the founder of modern botany and fix the nomenclature of plants as it is universally recognized today. Hailed as Dioscorides

John Evelyn (1620–1706). The diarist lent his house at Deptford to the visiting Peter the Great who amused himself by being pushed through the topiary hedges in a wheelbarrow.

Secundus and Princeps Botanicorum, Linnaeus must have been a delightful man, with his sharp brown eyes and long nose. His motto was 'All for the love of flowers'. He was courageous too, and in pursuit of his favorite study undertook a plant-hunting expedition to Lapland, which was fraught with discomfort and at times with great danger. Yet such was Linnaeus' gentle disposition that he was always able to find good in evil. 'The enthusiasm with which his imagination retraces every idea of his Lapland expedition turns the wild scenes of that country, even in the minds of his readers, into a paradise inhabited by all that is innocent and good …' wrote Sir James Smith, who after Linnaeus' death acquired his priceless collection for England.

Linnaeus had the gift of getting on with people, and though he never learned any other modern language than his native Swedish he made many friends in Holland, France and England. In England especially was he appreciated. (It was in England that the first Linnaean Society was formed.) The learned Philip Miller, Peter Collinson, Sir Hans Sloane, founder of the British Museum, were his friends. Linnaeus loved the wild flowers of England, and is said once to have fallen on his knees in rapture, on Putney Heath, at his first sight of the golden flowers of the native gorse. Linnaeus' reaction to flowers was always immediate and he was once cured of an attack of gout by the arrival of a case of new and interesting botanical specimens.

Many of Linnaeus' friends and contemporaries are commemorated in the names he gave to plants. One of his most dearly loved pupils was the German Johann Bartsch, whom Linnaeus described as 'a genteel, handsome, ingenuous and well behaved youth'. Bartsch died on an expedition to Surinam. Linnaeus suffered deeply, but assured his friend's fame by giving his name to the bartsia. Better-known plants commemorate Linnaeus' fellow Swedes. The Mountain laurel, or Calico Bush, of North America received its name Kalmia from Linnaeus' most promising pupil, Peter Kalm. Kalm held the theory that an infusion of the roots of lobelia, also an American plant, might be a cure for syphilis – hence *Lobelia siphilitica*. The bright yellow cone flower – rudbeckia – commemorates a kindly Swedish family in which Linnaeus was once tutor

FAR LEFT *Matthias de L'Obel (1538–1616) botanist and physician to King James I. Linnaeus gave his name to the lobelia.*

Joseph Pitton de Tournefort (1656–1708). His system of plant grouping as set out in Institutiones Rei Herbariae *was superseded by that of Linnaeus.*

Fame, flora and medicine crown Linnaeus – Princeps Botanicorum.
The frontispiece of Robert Thornton's well-known Temple of Flora *published in 1799.*

and the alstroemeria (of which the Ligtu hybrids, from Chile, are such popular plants with connoisseurs) was named after the botanizing Baron Alströmer. Sometimes Linnaeus' christenings were tinged with humour, as when he named a family of desert plants, which dislike the damp, tillandsia, after a friend Ellias Tillands who was terrified of the sea.

Linnaeus, with characteristic modesty, gave his own name to a very unspectacular plant – *Linnaea borealis*. The humble flower he chose as his own he found flowering in West Bothnia in 1732. It is by no means rare, but it is difficult to find, as it grows only among other wild plants, and its delicate twin flowers are often hidden by stronger growing leaves. Did Linnaeus note a resemblance between this humble Lapland flower and himself? His nine-teenth-century biographer, C. L. Brightwell, writes that in the early days of his career, he, like the flower, unfolded

> in a remote northern region ... unknown and overlooked, without the advantages of fortune or place. The world thought not of him, while in poverty and obscurity he pursued his scientific researches: few knew or valued this solitary wanderer ... who explored the recesses of nature, and culled the treasures of the mountain and glen, the forest and the moor ... which in due time, he presented, arranged ... to the delight and astonish-ment of kindred minds in every region ...

Linnaeus, towards the end of his successful career, was famous throughout the world. Among his devoted women admirers were the Queen of Sweden – who actually allowed him to catch her during the royal game of Blind Man's Buff, an unheard-of honour – Lady Ann Monson, an Englishwoman, after whom he named a shrubby relation of the geranium, monsonia, and an American, Jane Colden, 'perhaps the first lady to have studied perfectly the Linnaean system'. Miss Colden's industry was also rewarded with a plant, the coldenia.

But Linnaeus' success involved him in public life to such an extent that he had little time for active botany. In a letter to Dr Haller of Göttingen he wrote, 'once I had plants and no money – now what is money good for, without plants?'

He died, full of honours, in 1778, and a drama about the disposal of his famous collection ensued. It had been left to his son who did not long survive his father; and then passed into the hands of his widow, who sold it to Sir James Smith for little more than a thousand pounds. The transaction was so speedily effected that the precious collection was on board a ship and on its way to England before the news became known in Sweden. At once there was a national outcry, and although the much told story of a man-of-war being sent by the Swedish government in pursuit of the vessel is apparently untrue, public opinion was shocked, and the King of Sweden furious.

Sweden's loss was England's gain, and the precious collection became the treasure of the Linnaean Society. This learned group obtained its Royal Charter in 1802, and is now housed in a wing of Burlington House, close to my home in Albany, Piccadilly.

I have dwelt at some length on the story of Carl Linnaeus not only because it is a favorite one, but in any book on plants and people the prince of botanists must play an important part.

Linnaeus' system of nomenclature is recognized by all except very few. Jean-Jacques Rousseau, in his *Lettres sur la Botanique* criticized it: 'Nothing could be more absurd ... than if a woman asks the name of some herb or garden flower, to give by way of answer a long tirade of Latin names which sounds like a conjuration of hobgoblins'. Perhaps Rousseau might have preferred the name of Old Man to artemisia and that of Sow-Bread to cyclamen.

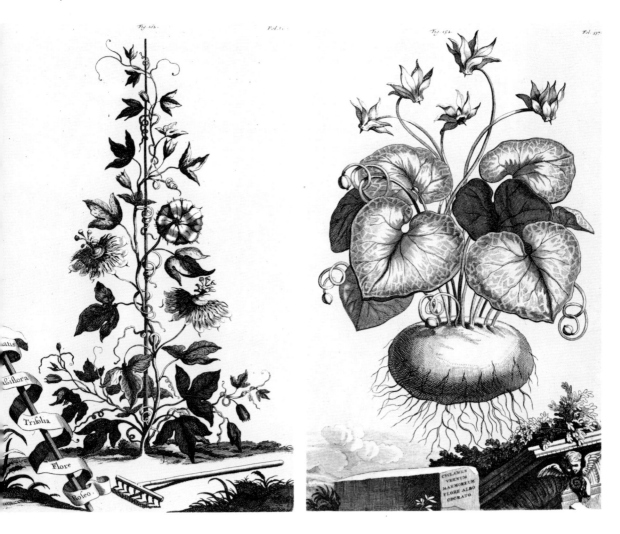

Passiflora triflolia flore roseo *and* Cyclamen vernum – Ruskin, *who questioned the use of Latin or Greek names for plants might have preferred to call it Sow-Bread. From illustrations in* Phytographia Curiosa, *per Abrahamum Muntingium, published in Amsterdam in 1713.*

Ruskin, too, disapproved of the latinization of plant names and, in his *Garden of Proserpina*, which was certainly not intended to be scientific, he writes very entertainingly on the subject of the naming of plants:

> I call the present system of nomenclature confusedly edified, because it introduces – without, apparently, any consciousness of the inconsistency, and certainly with no apology for it – names founded sometimes on the history of plants, sometimes on their qualities, sometimes on their forms, sometimes on their products, and sometimes on their poetical associations.
>
> On their history – as 'Gentian' from King Gentius, and 'Funkia' from Dr Funk ... On their qualities – as 'Scrophularia' from its (quite uncertified) use in scrofula ... On their forms – as the 'Caryophylls' from having petals like husks of nuts .... On their products – as 'Cocos nucifera' from its nuts.
>
> And on their poetical associates – as the 'Star of Bethlehem' from its imagined resemblance to the light of that seen by the Magi.
>
> Now, this variety of grounds for nomenclature might patiently, and even with advantage, be permitted provided the grounds themselves were separately firm, and the inconsistency of the method advisedly allowed,

Hosta (*formerly* Funkia) glauca marginata, *with leaves outlined in white. Ruskin questioned the worthiness of Herr Funk to have a plant named after him. The new name, hosta, derives from Nicolaus Host (1761–1834) the Emperor of Austria's doctor.*

and, in each case, justified. If the histories of King Gentius and Dr Funk are indeed important branches of human knowledge; if the Scrophulariaceae do indeed cure King's Evil – if pinks be best described in their likeness to nuts – and the Star of Bethlehem verily remind us of Christ's Nativity – by all means let these and other such names be evermore retained. But if Dr Funk be not a person in any special manner needing either stellification or florification; if neither herb nor flower can avail, more than the touch of monarchs, against hereditary pain; if it be no better account of a pink to say it is nut-leaved, than of a nut to say it is pink-leaved; and if the modern mind, incurious respecting the journeys of wise men, has already confused, in its Bradshaw's Bible, the station of Bethlehem with that of Bethel, it is certainly time to take some order with the partly false, partly useless, and partly forgotten literature of the Fields; and, before we bow our children's memories to the burden of it, ensure that there shall be matter worth carriage in the load ....

Before we can wisely decide this point, we must resolve whether our botany is intended mainly to be useful to the vulgar, or satisfactory to the scientific élite.

Ruskin would certainly not have approved Linnaeus' changing the Latin name of the sweet-smelling Mock Orange, long known as syringa (from the Greek work syrinx, or pipe, apt enough, as its hollow stems may well have been used by Greek shepherds) to philadelphus, a name taken from that of Ptolemy Philadelphus, a King of Egypt in 300 BC. Linnaeus gave the name syringa quite arbitrarily to an unrelated genus – the lilac – which has resulted in confusion and some annoyance ever since.

Linnaeus, in devising his hierarchy of plants had a weakness, if he was not borrowing the name of a favorite Swedish pupil, for giving plants the names of heroes of classical history: and he was certainly responsible for the commemoration of the obscure King Gentius which so annoyed Ruskin. In this he was following a two-thousand-year-old tradition. Ancient Greek history and legend provided names for plants from the earliest times.

'To the Greeks', Germain Bazin tells us in his *Gallery of Flowers* 'flowers were part of that cycle of metamorphoses which in myth after myth, end always in man: they spring or take their color from the blood of heroes, rise from their tears or appear at the birth of the Gods'. Venus' slipper is commemorated by an orchid, the youth Narcissus has his flower, and Daphne fills a very special place in the man-plant relationship as she not only gave her name to a Bay-tree, but actually turned into one. Plant in person, indeed.

Christianity plays less part in plant legend. There is a *Flos Jovis* – but no Flos Jesus. The Crown Imperial is said to have stared boldly at Christ on His way to His crucifixion, and for ever after has had to hang its head, weeping. The curious stamen and pistil formation of the Passion Flower has given passi-

19

LEFT Fritillaria imperialis.
*The Crown Imperial is said
to have stared boldly at
Christ on the way to His
crucifixion, and so to have
hung their flower-heads in
shame ever since.*

*The curious stamen
and pistil formation
of the Passion Flower
gave passiflora its
popular name, owing to
its likeness to cross,
nails and thorns.*

flora its popular name owing to their supposed likeness to cross, nails and thorns. Keats' 'ardent marigolds' are said to be dedicated to the Virgin but no strong thread of legend attaches them. In ancient times their name was simply Golds and they were the flowers of jealousy. Chaucer describes jealousy wearing 'of yelwe guldes a garland'. It must be understood that these flowers were what we now call calendulas, commonly called pot-marigolds in the past. They were not related to the so-called French and African marigolds of Central America, which bear the nomenclature, *tagetes*. They were probably growing in Europe long before Christianity, and such brightly colored and plentiful flowers would certainly have been used in religious festivals, whether pagan or Christian. With the establishment of the Church in England, the Mary was probably added, and by the time of Shakespeare, it was marigolds that were going 'to bed wi the sun' and 'Mary-buds' that opened their golden eyes.

Lilies are other flowers which have always been connected with the Virgin Mary – Madonna lilies, *Lilium candidum* in particular. But there is no mention in the Bible of the connexion and it is more likely that lilies have achieved this signal honour thanks to the early Italian painters, who often portrayed Mary with lilies, or being greeted by angels carrying lilies in their hands.

*Frontispiece to an early book
of flower illustrations*
Hortus Eystettensis *published in
Nuremburg in 1713.*

The First Flower Paintings. When were flowers first painted for themselves – not merely as decorative adjuncts to religious pictures or as illustrations to apothecaries' handbooks? The first herbals, as we have seen, showed pictures of plants, but these were usually factual and crude, and were designed to enable doctors who were interested in the curative or harmful properties of plants, to identify them.

The first flower 'pictures' – not in paint, but in bronze – the expert Mr David Carritt suggests, are the flowers on the gates of the Baptistery at Florence. These 'Gates of Paradise', as Michelangelo called them, were fifty years in the making, and were mainly the work of Lorenzo Ghiberti (1378–1455). Among the many exquisite decorative motifs are panels and friezes of the flowers that grew near Florence ... including hollyhocks and poppy-heads. Giovanni di Paolo used Ghiberti's bronze flowers as models for the flowers he included in panels on either side of his picture 'St John the Baptist in the Desert', which is in the National Gallery in London. Ghiberti's flowers, and Giovanni's version of them, must be some of the earliest decorative, yet precise, flower portraits. They antedate the flower piece, usually accepted to be the earliest, which Hans Memling painted in 1490 on the back of a portrait of 'A man in an attitude of prayer' in Baron Thyssen's Collection. This painting is of a Majolica vase of white lilies, blue iris and a handful of columbines. Each flower is meticulously portrayed, and its individual character stressed. Each has its own religious symbolism: the lilies purity; the iris (the *fleur de lis*) royalty but as the flower of the sky, the heavens, too, perhaps the Kingdom of Heaven itself; while columbines, with their dove-shaped flowers, symbolize the Holy Ghost.

Three-quarters of a century was to pass before three names occur which will ever be famous in the history of flower painting: Jacques de Gehn (1565–1629), Ambrosius Bosschaert (1573–1621), and Jan Breughel (1568–1625).

22

Jacques de Gehn painted the first dated Dutch flower painting – a vase of tulips and fritillaries – which was completed in 1600. It was once in a book of twenty pages of flower paintings which was bought by the Emperor Rudolf II and is now in a private collection in Paris.

Ambrosius Bosschaert painted his beautiful flower pieces, of which twenty-four are known, between 1607 and 1621. Though all Bosschaert's pictures are signed AB they are to be identified not only by the graceful arch or alcove in which his vases are usually set, but also by the placing of a large flower at the top of each composition – as can be seen in his bouquet at the Mauritshuis shown on page 28 of this book.

The Flemish Jan Breughel (Fluweelen or 'Velvet' Breughel, on account of his grand clothes, compared to those of his simpler father, Peter Breughel, the 'Peasant') lived from 1568 to 1625. He was a few years older than Bosschaert and is said to have been his tutor. Jan Breughel is famous for the beautifully executed wreathes of flowers he painted to surround portrait faces by Rubens and other artists, as well as for the rare and unusual flowers he delighted to include in his flower pieces, such as the newest double hyacinths, or the latest striped, in Dutch *gevlamde*, 'enflamed' tulips. Professor Bergström quotes an interesting letter that Jan Breughel wrote to his patron Cardinal Borromeo in 1606: 'I have commenced a bouquet of flowers for your Eminence. The result will be a success and very beautiful, both because of its naturalness and because of the rare beauty of the different flowers, many of which are unknown or seldom seen here; for this reason I have been to Brussels in order to copy from nature some flowers which are not to be found at Antwerp.' In another letter Jan Breughel writes, 'Your Eminence's picture is making good progress. I devote myself to it every day with the greatest diligence and interest. Your Eminence can be sure that I have never done anything like it before. I believe that there will be more than a hundred flowers in natural size of which the great part are rare and choice. The ordinary flowers are lilies, roses, violets and carnations; the others are unusual and have never yet been seen in this country.'

Finding models for these great portrait bouquets presented problems. All the flowers included could not be expected to flower at the right moment or to last more than a few days. Some harmless cheating was necessary – studies of the ever popular tulips, iris, narcissi, roses (the last two with flowering seasons two months apart) had to be made and carefully filed for future use. Thus in several different flower compositions of Jacques de Gehn the selfsame flower occurs in precisely the same juxtaposition.

One of the most interesting of the Dutch flower painters was a rich young lady of Amsterdam, who did not let a husband, ten children, or fifty years of married life interrupt her passion for painting, with infinite care and precision, her compositions of flowers. Bryan says of Rachel Ruysch (1664–1750), 'The labour she bestowed on her works prevented their being numerous.' And Victoria Sackville-West in her poem *The Garden* praises 'Rachel

A 'Bloempot' by
Rachel Ruysch
(1664–1750) one of the
most talented of
Dutch flower-painters.
The unusual placing
of the poppy is
characteristic.

RIGHT *Lilies, iris
and columbines,
signifying purity,
the sky (or heaven)
and the Holy Ghost
respectively. A detail
of the Portinari
altar-piece painted by
Hugo van der Goes
(1435–85).*

Ruysch – so nice, so leisurely, that seven years were given to two pictures'. These were pictures of fruit and flowers respectively – one of which, so highly was it valued, Rachel Ruysch gave to her daughter as a marriage portion.

Towards the end of the seventeenth century was born the celebrated Jan Van Huysum, the artist whom Jacobo Weyermann called the 'Fenix Aller Bloemschilders'. One of Van Huysum's first flower paintings is dated 1706. His loose, asymmetrical flower arrangements are far more sophisticated than the carefully balanced *Bloempots* of the Dutch flower painters who preceded him. He delighted in full-blown flowers – petals about to fall, and stems rakishly poised. In his paintings, irrespective of season, spring hyacinths jostle mid-summer roses. A characteristic of his foliage and fruit is their cool glaucous sheen, and the dew drops he painted with such extraordinary, eye deceiving craft.

Professor Bergström says of Van Huysum, 'He may at times seem superficial, even something of a virtuoso, but his drawing is superb, his colouration rich and his composition admirably light and free: his mature oeuvre is a shimmering reflection of the rococo style.'

Eleven years after the death in 1749 of Jan Van Huysum, last of the great Dutch flower painters, there was born in France Pierre Joseph Redouté. Redouté's name is so bound up with roses that his career is described in some detail in the chapter on roses.

But there is a direct link between the 'Raphael of the Rose' and Jan Van Huysum, which is provided by Gerard Van Spaendonck. Van Spaendonck was a flower painter of the school of Van Huysum, and attempted to rival the master in his exuberance. Towards the end of the eighteenth century he evolved a technique of using water color which Redouté, who was his pupil,

24

OVER PAGE *Water lilies by Claude
Monet (1840–1926).*

copied and perhaps perfected. Mr Wilfred Blunt, in his *Art of Botanical Illustration*, writes, 'Redouté, thanks to the patronage he enjoyed and to his tireless energy, has reaped the harvest Van Spaendonck sowed; Redouté's name is known the world over, while that of his master is forgotten.'

From the death of Pierre Joseph Redouté in 1840 there are no names of artists specially famous for their flower paintings until that of Henri Fantin-Latour (1836–1904) whose studies of flowers, and of roses especially, cast an almost magical spell. Such was his love of Cabbage Roses that a pink centifolia was named after him.

If Fantin-Latour was first and foremost the painter of the rose and Claude Monet (1840–1926) was the painter of the water lily, Vincent Van Gogh (1853–90) will surely always be known as painter extraordinary of the sunflower. Sunflowers, he would say, belonged to him. And in a letter to his brother Theo he wrote, 'I am painting now with the rapture of a Marseillais eating bouillabaisse, which will not surprise you when you hear that the subject is big sunflowers. I am working on them every morning, starting at daybreak – for they fade quickly. ...'

Van Gogh thought of decorating his studio walls only with paintings of sunflowers 'of which the pure or broken chrome yellows will sing against different backgrounds of blue. ...' And when his friend Gauguin came to stay with him at Arles, he was to find his bedroom decorated with sunflowers, 'twelve or fourteen' to the bunch.

In Van Gogh's view, suggests his biographer Frank Elgar, 'the significance of these large flowers goes beyond that of the ordinary still life ... he worships the sun and its color – the yellow color of light, health, and incessant renewal. When he exclaims, at the height of his rapture "How beautiful yellow is", he is not only speaking as a painter, but also as a man ecstatically proclaiming his desire to possess the whole of creation. ...'

The First Plant-Hunters. It was not until the end of the eighteenth century that the whole world was systematically searched for plants that were hitherto unknown in Europe. The names of the men engaged in this great work are often commemorated by the plants they brought home. One of the first of these was Joseph Banks, whose name will ever be celebrated in the annals of horticulture. Banks was a rich young Englishman, who had been educated, oddly enough, at both Eton and Harrow. At school he is described as:

well disposed and good-tempered, but so immoderately fond of play that his attention could not be fixed to his studies. At fourteen his tutor had the satisfaction of seeing a change come over his pupil, which Banks afterwards explained as follows. One fine summer evening he had stayed bathing in the Thames so long, that he found that all his companions had gone. Walking back along a lane, the sides of which were clothed with flowers, he was so struck by their beauty as to resolve to add botany to the

A vase of flowers by the Flemish artist Ambrosius Bosschaert (1573–1621).
The placing of the 'bloempot' in an arched window is typical of his work.

classical studies imposed by authority. He submitted to be instructed by the women employed in culling simples to supply the druggists' shops, paying sixpence for each material item of information. During his next holidays, to his extreme delight he found a book in his mother's dressing-room, which not only described the plants he had met, but also gave engravings of them. This proved to be Gerard's *Herball*, and although one of its covers was gone and several of its leaves were lost, he carried it back to school in triumph, and was soon able to turn the tables upon his former instructors. (*Dictionary of National Biography*.)

Banks' interest in botany never flagged – and he spent a fortune on equipping expeditions to different parts of the world to collect new plants.

In 1768, he was the moving spirit of one of the first great plant hunting enterprises in history. He was only twenty-five, but already he was a Fellow of the Royal Horticultural Society and had botanized on the inhospitable shores of Newfoundland. Though the great Captain Cook was in command of the *Endeavour* which sailed in August 1768, Banks' word was listened to with respect. Not only was he courteous and highly intelligent, but he had also put up £10,000 of his own money for the expedition.

There is no space, and it would be outside the scope of this book, to tell the fascinating story of the *Endeavour's* journey. It must suffice to record the rewards to botany that accrued. In Brazil, in spite of the Viceroy's lack of co-operation, Banks and his party made copious notes on the exotic parasitic plants growing in the forests near Rio de Janeiro, and even found rare plants in the green 'sallading' they bought in the market. In the extreme south of what is now the Argentine they went ashore on Tierra del Fuego, where Daniel Solander, a Swedish pupil of Linnaeus, literally nearly died of cold.

With its collection of plants, seeds and dried botanical specimens ever growing, *Endeavour* now made for the warmer waters of the Pacific. In Tahiti the landscape painter of the party, Alexander Buchan, died, and Joseph Banks lamented 'my airy dreams of entertaining my friends in England with the scenes I am to see have vanished' – but, as Mr Kenneth Lemmon tells us in his absorbing book *The Golden Age of Plant Hunters*, 'The ebullience of the young naturalist soon returned' and Banks was enjoying dinners of roast dog and the favors of the local beauties. On to New Zealand, where they saw many plants hitherto completely unknown. Mr Kenneth Lemmon describes them as including 'the largest buttercup in the world – a forget-me-not with leaves like rhubarb ... tree-like daisies ... mosses more than a foot tall.'

When the *Endeavour* reached Australia (which it very nearly missed) Banks and his party saw their first kangaroo – and were fascinated by giant eucalyptus trees – which Banks was the first to call Blue Gums. When, after many adventures, *Endeavour* left Australian waters for New Guinea, she carried

LEFT *Sir Joseph Banks (1743–1820)*
by Sir Thomas Lawrence.
RIGHT *Captain Cook (1728–79).*
Portrait by J. Webber.

specimens, hitherto unknown, of plants such as acacia, banksia (the Australian Honeysuckle Tree), grevillea, and of course eucalyptus. After many mishaps, near disasters, illnesses, deaths, Banks' party, after a round-the-world journey which had lasted three years, returned to England in 1771.

Joseph Banks was a very extraordinary man. In the late eighteenth century, when someone in his position who was interested in plants and gardens might be expected to devote time saved from hunting or the pleasures of London, to some gentle landscape gardening or growing camellias, Banks risked his fortune and his life in the search for new plants to enrich Western gardens and greenhouses. He was to continue to do so until his death in 1820. The great Linnaeus said of him (quoted by Kenneth Lemmon), 'I cannot sufficiently admire Mr Banks – who has exposed himself to so many dangers – surely none but an Englishman would have the spirit to do what he has done.'

The tender banksias are not plants which are found in many gardens. The banksian rose, however, a beautiful yellow Chinese rose, can be grown in most gardens on a sheltered wall. It was introduced in 1824 and called after Sir Joseph's widow.

Sir Joseph Banks' name still resounds in the history of botany. He was the first of an indefatigable group of plant hunters some, though not all, of whom are commemorated in gardens today by plants which bear their names.

Few today recall the name of Francis Masson – a protégé of Sir Joseph Banks – an indefatigable plant hunter who braved lions to send home seeds of the first geraniums and ericas to England. We also have Masson to thank for the first cineraria – *C. cruenta*.

Poor Masson. After years of devoted work in every extreme of hot and cold climate he died in Canada. His grave is unmarked; even his own plant, massonia, is seldom grown and has been dismissed as having 'little beauty'.

More fortunate in many respects was William Kerr – a young Scotsman after whom the well-known, widely-planted kerria is named. Kerr plant-hunted, again under the patronage of the all-powerful Banks, in China, where frustrating dealings with the Chinese officials drove him, literally, to drink. 31

But we owe him the sweetly scented *Daphne odora*, the first *Azalea sinensis*, and the first *Camellia sasanqua*.

Yet another young gardener – sent out into the world to risk his life collecting plants – was David Nelson, who embarked on two of the most famous voyages of history, the last voyage of Captain Cook and, ten years after, that of the *Bounty*, under the command of Captain Bligh. Nelson was on board Captain Cook's *Discovery* when its cutter was stolen by natives – and in an attempt to recover it, the great and gallant Cook was murdered.

When Nelson eventually reached England again, after adventures in the heat of Africa and the arctic weather of the Aleutians, he brought seeds and dried specimens of hundreds of then unknown plants – including his own *Nelsonia campestris*, a tender plant with mauve flowers and velvety leaves.

Nelson's next voyage was in the ill-fated *Bounty*. Few remember that the object of the voyage of the *Bounty* was exclusively botanical. The ship was to transport young bread-fruit trees from the Pacific islands to the West Indies.

> For the first time in history (Kenneth Lemmon tells us) a ship – and one of the Royal Navy's at that – was being commissioned for no other purpose than to act as a floating conservatory; to transport plants of the bread-fruit from Tahiti to the West Indies where British traders and planters had suggested to the king that this fruit would prove a cheap and most acceptable home-grown diet for the thousands of slaves in Jamaica and the other islands. Furthermore the gardener had complete responsibility and charge of the botanical side of the voyage, with permission – nay, instructions – to command captain and crew to carry out his gardening orders.

The outcome of the voyage is well known. After the bread-fruit trees had been laboriously and carefully collected in Tahiti the *Bounty* started on her long haul to the West Indies. A month later, led by Fletcher Christian, the crew mutinied and Nelson, Captain Bligh and a few other of the officers were cast adrift – as were the precious bread-fruit trees. After a nightmare voyage of nearly four thousand miles in an open boat Captain Bligh and Nelson reached the Dutch settlement of Timor, but Nelson died a few weeks after, one more in the lengthening line of victims in the cause of botany.

A further victim was to be another Scot, David Douglas, who hunted for plants, not, as most of his predecessors did, in the tropics or the Arctic, but in countries with temperate climates. A fact which, in a sense, made his task more rewarding, for the plants he discovered could be expected to flourish in the open in any garden in his native land. But his journeys were only a degree less hazardous, and poor David Douglas met a strange and horrid death when he fell into an animal trap in Honolulu and was gored to death by a bull already trapped there. Douglas' most successful journeys had been through the mountains and valleys of the western United States and it was from there that he sent back seeds and roots of plants which were to add so much to the beauty of the landscape in Europe. Douglas loved trees, and was more impressed by a rare kind of cedar which he saw growing near Niagara than he was by the falls themselves. He is commemorated by the Douglas Fir (*Pseudotsuga douglasii*), which is now completely taken for granted as a feature of European landscapes. Among the numberless other trees, shrubs and plants he introduced were *Berberis mahonia*, *Arbutus menziesii*, the first seeds of clarkia, the Tree Lupin, fifteen new penstemons and the popular *Ribes sanguinea* and *Garrya elliptica*.

The father of Benjamin Disraeli – Isaac – whose *Curiosities of Literature* was published in 1791, wrote with great truth: 'Monuments are reared, and medals struck, to commemorate events and names which are less deserving of our regard than those who have transported into the cold regions of the North, the rich fruits, the beautiful flowers, and the succulent pulse and roots of more favoured spots.'

One of the earliest plant hunters in America was a member of the Tradescant family, John the Younger. In the seventeenth century, he sent asters to England from Virginia – these became the forbears of Michelmas daisies. Later in the century, England received for the first time the American golden-rod, phlox, bee-balm and evening primrose.

In the eighteenth century, John Bartram, called by Linnaeus 'the greatest natural botanist in the world', explored the entire eastern seaboard of North America, accompanied by his son William. He corresponded and exchanged plant materials with Peter Collinson, a wealthy Quaker wool merchant of London. With the support of Collinson, Bartram introduced between 150 and 200 plants to England and Europe. Through Collinson's efforts, he was designated Botanist Royal to George III.

At the beginning of this century, the botanist E. H. Wilson, often referred to as 'Chinese Wilson', spent twelve years in China, looking for new plants. He collected first for the nursery firm of Veitch, and later for the Arnold Arboretum of Harvard College, of which he became Keeper. He enriched American and European gardens by over a thousand new plants. Especially noteworthy were sixty-five kinds of rhododendrons introduced to cultivation, and the Regal Lily.

The plant hunters of the 'Golden Age' – Banks, Kerr, Masson, Nelson, Douglas and Gibson – introduced plants to Western gardens and the Western landscape that completely transformed the horticultural scene. Their journeys were fraught with appalling hardships and danger: and it took great patience, ingenuity and luck to surmount the difficulties of transporting their discoveries back to Europe, owing to change of climate, slowness of sailing-ships, and neglect and lack of interest on the voyage. The plant hunters, and there were to be many, who came after them benefited from their experience, and from faster ships and, above all, a greater understanding of the needs of plants in transit. By half way through the last century the hard work of plant hunting had been done, and there were fewer hardy plants left growing in the wild to discover.

Robert Fortune (1812–80) who introduced the tea plant to Assam, George Forrest (1873–1932) who sent wonderful plants home from China, as did the genial Abbé David (1826–1900) whose name is borne by many good plants, and Frank Kingdon Ward, who introduced so many rare rhododendrons, all have names that will have a place, among many others, on the roll of honour of botanical achievement. But the plants they collected were more for the specialist and the connoisseur – the rare new rhododendron, the delicate pink poppy, the miniature primula. They were not the first lupin, the first penstemon, the first Douglas Fir. The dangers, and they were considerable, and the difficulties they encountered are not to be compared with the perils which beset Francis Masson who was nearly eaten by a lion, or Banks, nearly eaten by cannibals or poor David Douglas, dying horribly in an animal pit.

Early Gardeners. If the years 1770–1820 were the golden age of plant hunters, the following century certainly deserves to be called the silver. In the story of plants in that period one well-known name succeeds another: many of these names have been given to plants and so are familiar to all gardeners: a few, ungratefully, have not.

For instance, the Loudons. There is no loudonia listed in the Royal Horticultural Society's massive dictionary of plants: and yet, according to Alice Coats in *Plants and their Histories*, John Claudius Loudon (1783–1842) and his wife Jane (1803–58) 'made the most copious and erudite contributions to garden literature that were ever achieved in the space of a lifetime'. In the garden of their house in Porchester Terrace in Bayswater the Loudons formed a magnificent collection of plants. The Loudons' London was Wordsworth's London, too, 'all bright and glittering in the smokeless air' and so they were able to grow many rare and delicate species plants in their Bayswater garden, which today would not survive a month.

The literary activities and achievements of the delicate, half crippled John Claudius Loudon were impressive. He edited the first botanical magazine, and wrote an authoritative *Encyclopaedia of Plants* and several other important works. His *Suburban Gardener* and *Villa Companion* are still read. Mrs Loudon

LEFT *David Douglas (1798–1834) after whom the Douglas Fir is named. Intrepid botanist and traveller, he was killed by a wild bull in Hawaii.*

RIGHT *Reginald Farrer (1880–1920) Plant collector and author of several lively books on botanizing,* Gentiana farreri *commemorates his name.*

was no less industrious, and her four-volumed book, *The Ladies Flower Garden*, was beautifully illustrated, many of the plates being of her own drawings.

The Hookers, father and son, William (1785–1865) and Joseph (1817–1911) were important figures in the Victorian gardening scene. There is a plant hookera which is one of the Liliaceae – and there is a *Berberis hookeri*, a *Silene hookeri*, and a curious insectivorous pitcher plant *Nepenthes hookeriana*, which was collected by Joseph Hooker in Borneo. Joseph was a brilliant botanist and Director of the Botanical Gardens at Kew at the age of twenty-four. He sent many plants to the Golden Gate Park, San Francisco, in 1880. Many of his plants still flower there every spring.

The names of a man and a woman of the gardening world which will, with the greatest propriety, be ever linked are those of Gertrude Jekyll (1843–1932) and William Robinson (1838–1935). They are names which will occur throughout this book, and they are perhaps, for the amateur gardener of today, the most important names of all. For Gertrude Jekyll and William Robinson can be said to have 'invented' modern gardening as it is understood in England and America today. Their ideals, considered revolutionary at the time, are the ones gardeners of taste and imagination strive hard to reach today.

Gertrude Jekyll was born the year Loudon died and was a devoted student of his books and theories. She might well be described as the first professional woman gardener, and there are still gardens in full beauty of maturity which she laid out. Many of these were designed in co-operation with her

William Hooker (1785–1865), was director of the Royal Botanical Gardens at Kew in 1841, and had them opened to the public for the first time. His son Joseph (1817–1911) was another distinguished botanist.

Gertrude Jekyll, painted by William Nicholson in 1920.

William Robinson, author of the classic English Flower Garden, *first published in 1883. He was one of the first to plant herbaceous borders.*

great ally, the architect Sir Edwin Lutyens. Miss Jekyll's garden at Munstead – home of the Munstead strain of lavender – was a place of pilgrimage.

Gertrude Jekyll wrote at least fourteen books on plants and the theory of gardening, which are classics of their kind. In one, *Wood and Garden*, she expounds in characteristic fashion her feelings about how the thoughtful gardener, who can claim to have some taste, can achieve a pleasing effect by the juxtaposition of plants. Plants can, she writes:

> be so placed by the hand that knows, that the group is in perfect drawing in relation to what is near; while by the ordinary gardener they would be so planted that they look absurd, or unmeaning, or in some way awkward and unsightly. It is not enough to cultivate plants well; they must also be used well. The servant may set up the canvas and grind the colours, and even set the palette, but the master alone can paint the picture. It is just the careful and thoughtful exercise of the higher qualities that makes a garden interesting, and their absence that leaves it blank, and dull, and lifeless.

Many of Gertrude Jekyll's favorite plants are described later in the book: her silver-leaved artemisias, dark purple lavender, cool green-flowered hellebores. Many, because they are not members of the plant families chosen for inclusion, can only be noted here in passing. Miss Jekyll loved the contrast supplied by the cloudy flowers of gypsophila and the hard glossy leaves of bergenia. She admired yuccas – which she called the noblest plant of the English garden, and the architectural shape of *Euphorbia wulfenii*. One of her favorite planting combinations was that of *Vitis coignetiae*, with its burning autumn coloring, and the pure blue powdery flowers of the late summer flowering ceanothus.

She loved to plant borders of one color – and she was the first to do so, though John Evelyn had his garden 'of curious greenes'. Miss Jekyll was a real perfectionist, and for her gold garden she considered goldfish quite the wrong color.

Though no one deserves one more, she has no flower named after her. There is a variety of Love in the Mist, nigella, 'Miss Jekyll', and that is all.

William Robinson, a contemporary and colleague of Gertrude Jekyll, shared many of her ideas. It is he who can be said to have first had the idea of 'wild gardening' now so widely practised. He hated formality in the garden and thought the gardens of Versailles hideously contrived; for Robinson there was no middle way. For him there were but two styles:

> ... one straitlaced, mechanical, fond of walls or bricks, or it may be gravel; fond also of such geometry as the designer of wallpapers excels in, often indeed of a much poorer and less graceful kind than that; fond too of squirting water in an immoderate degree, with trees in tubs as an accom-

The herbaceous border with its bold plantings of contrasting colours and foliage was an innovation of the late nineteenth century.

paniment, and perhaps griffins and endless plaster and stone work. The other, with true humility and right desire though often awkwardly and blunderingly, accepting nature as a guide, and endeavouring to multiply, so far as convenience and poor man-power will permit, her most charming features.

In his practice of 'wild gardening' William Robinson did just that – the gifts Nature had provided, the inviting glade, the stream, the fern-grown boulder, were featured and made much of. If they did not exist, they might, if it was done with tact, be devised. Robinson aimed to create, on a small scale, what the great protagonists of the Romantic Revival – Kent, Capability Brown and Repton – had conjured across a hundred acres.

Robinson's great contribution to the flower gardener, rather than the landscape gardener, was his book published in 1883; *The English Flower Garden*. This work, with its evocative illustrations (some of which decorate the pages of this book) must surely have been a milestone in books about flowers; it is still a prized possession of many a gardener.

Gertrude Jekyll and William Robinson are given joint credit for the invention of the herbaceous border – a garden feature which must be noticed in any book about plants and flowers. For, though it is now the fashion rather to sniff at herbaceous borders, they still provide the only practical and decorative way to assemble a collection of plants. 'Mixed border' is the fashionable phrase, today, a border of herbaceous plants with a backing of shrubs, ever-green or ever-greys. But a mixed border is only the original idea, developed and made more practical for modern conditions. The old herbaceous border did need a lot of looking after.

The names of two nurserymen of the last century must be noted. The first, George Loddiges, had a nursery in Hackney which was the first in England – and in the world. Travellers came from all over Europe to see, not only his camellias, but his revolutionary methods of steam heating conservatories, and the first automatic sprinkler. George Loddiges inherited his taste and skill in gardening from his father Konrad, who came to England from his native Hanover in the reign of George II. To Konrad Loddiges is given the credit – or the reproach – of having introduced in 1756 the first plants of *Rhododendron ponticum* into England.

Second great nurseryman of the pair is James Veitch (1815–69). He was one of five generations of Veitches who ran the nursery which superseded Loddiges' about 1850. The Veitch family were dedicated gardeners and most successful businessmen, who achieved renown by sending plant hunters all over the world in search of new specimens. Although they did not have to face the dangers that awaited an earlier generation of plant hunters, they brought back hundreds of plants that are grown today. The first begonias were raised in Veitch's nursery, and in 1854 they achieved the first hybrid orchid; but

39

In the last twenty-five years flower decoration societies have sprung up
all over England and America – latest manifestations of the plant-person relationship.

the best-known introduction of the Veitch's must surely be *Ampelopsis veitchii*, the most widely planted of all self-clinging, deciduous creepers.

The author of this book can claim relationship with the dynasty of Veitch as he can with the erudite Alice Coats, author of several careful and entertaining books on plants and gardeners. Of the great Victorian nurseryman Miss Coats has rightly written, 'The nursery trade still awaits its historian, and it is to be hoped that someone will soon tackle this fascinating subject before too many of its ephemeral records disappear.'

With Gertrude Jekyll, William Robinson and the Veitches, the chronicle of people and plants reaches the time of living memory. Before ending this introduction one more name must be saluted.

In 1964, Victoria Sackville-West died at her home, Sissinghurst Castle in Kent, around which she had made a garden, considered by many to be the most beautiful garden in England. The garden is now maintained by the National Trust and is there, in all its original beauty, for all to see. It is difficult to imagine, in the annals of plants and gardens, that the name of Victoria Sackville-West will ever be forgotten. Not only was she a practical gardener who could dig and sow and prune, but her green fingers directed an exquisitely sensitive pen. No garden writer could so lovingly evoke the spirit of the garden or the appeal of flowers. She will be remembered for her books and for her poem *The Garden*. She is not commemorated by one flower, but by a whole garden.

From Victoria Sackville-West back to Dioscorides men have loved and sought to learn about plants. In the perplexities and rush of the modern world a garden can still provide, as Bacon found, 'the greatest refreshment to the spirits of man'. And though the beauty of one rose lasts but a day or two, roses last forever, and, as Emerson reminds us, 'violets renew their race like oaks'.

Soon there may be many men and women on the moon, but they will find no moon-flowers there. Perhaps John Gerard sums it up when he asks, 'who would look up dangerously at planets that might look safely down at plants?'

The Hon. Victoria Sackville-West, a great gardener of the twentieth century.
A corner of her herb garden with a fine clump of green-flowered Helleborus corsicus *is shown opposite.*

40

Camellia sasanqua
is a native of Japan
where it is sometimes
used as a hedge.
It was first grown

in England
in the celebrated
nursery of the
Veitch family.

Camellia

Flowers without scent, but of matchless perfection

Two names must always be associated with camellias, and they are of two very different people – a simple Jesuit priest, Georg Kamel, whose name was given to the plant; and a beautiful French courtesan of the 1840s, Marie Duplessis, whom Alexandre Dumas has immortalized as Marguérite Gautier in his famous romance *La Dame aux Camélias*.

George Kamel was born in Moravia, at Brno, in 1661. He went to the Philippines as a Jesuit missionary and from there to China, from where he sent back seeds of the plant that he found the Chinese growing in their gardens. Kamel was a respected botanist, and later wrote a learned account of the plants of the island of Luzon. Thirty years after his death (in 1704), his good work was recognized when his name was given to a beautiful race of plants he had introduced. 'K' became 'C' when Georg Josef's name was latinized into Camellus, since there is no 'K' in the Latin alphabet. This is how the charming word camellia came to be. Charming, and almost invariably mispronounced. The French get it right, but Anglo-Saxons persist in pronouncing the second syllable to rhyme with 'feel' instead of 'fell', which is illogical and incorrect.

Camellias belong to the Theaceae or Tea family, and the old Mandarin name for the plant was *T'e*, pronounced *Cha* which, whether one was ever in the British army or not, has an all too familiar ring. Few flowers are as sophisticated as camellias, and their lineage goes back for centuries. They have been grown in their present form for many hundreds of years, and they were, like tree peonies, the favorite plants of Chinese mandarins and monks alike. It was not until about 1740 that they were first introduced into America, by André Michaux, and at the same time into England by the Roman Catholic Lord Petre, of whom it was said, 'this Lord is a great lover of exotic plants and it is said that he is one of the best botanists in England.' When Lord Petre died the

43

Camellia reticulata '*Sung-Tzu-Lin*', *also known as* '*Pagoda*',
with crinkled pale rose flowers.

arboriculturist Peter Collinson described his death as 'the greatest loss that botany or gardening ever felt in this island'. Lord Petre was, it seems, 'a fine tall comely personage – his morals of great sobriety', who never indulged, according to Collinson, in a 'loose word or double entendre'.

It is not surprising that Dumas, in his famous book, should have chosen camellias for his heroine. Camellias were loved in the early nineteenth century, and poor Marguérite, who could not bear to have any scented flowers near her because they made her cough, always carried a bouquet of camellias. So much so that she was hurt and surprised when her admirer Arthur de Varville offered her a basket of another kind of flower: 'Si vous croyez que je ferai une exception pour vous, vous avez tort – les parfums me rendent malade.' She always wore white camellias for twenty-five days of the month and for five they were red – an eccentricity 'Que je signale' wrote Alexandre Dumas, 'sans pouvoir expliquer.'

In a story in that wonderful book, *Les Fleurs Animées* illustrated by Albert Grandville, which appeared at about the same time as Dumas' *La Dame aux Camélias*, the camellia was transformed into a beautiful woman, Imperia, the toast and talk of Venice. So beautiful and desirable was she, that the Doge himself, 'glorieux époux de la mer' was heard to admit that, had he been free to choose, it would have been Imperia and not the Adriatic who would have received his ring. However, the beauty married the eligible and sensitive Count Stenio, though love bored the cold Imperia and the marriage was an unhappy one.

Finally the Count could bear it no longer: 'Madame' he said to his wife 'you are like the flower they call a camellia – which a Jesuit brought us recently from the East. You are beautiful, Madam, but you have none of the true perfume of beauty which is known as love.'

'Vous ne vous trompez pas', replied Imperia, smiling coldly, 'je suis le Camélia', and off she went to a ball. Her coldness broke poor Stenio's heart, and forced him to suicide: and his dead body was brought, in a gondola, to the door of the palazzo. Only then did Imperia show some regret, and admit her sorrow at being incapable of affection like other women. She was, after all, a camellia. 'Femme ... on ne saurait exister sans amour. Fleur, on peut vivre sans parfum'. The story of Imperia is a sad one – as is, though in a different vein, Halévy's camellia story of the Franco-Prussion War. In one of the bitter-sweet tales in his famous Famille Cardinal series, Halévy tells the story of Paul Rivet – an enthusiast of camellias, who had devoted to his famous plants 'Vingt années de travail, de patience, de soins, d'adoration' only to find, after the Prussian occupation, that his beloved collection of camellias had been dug up to make room for the graves of five Uhlan soldiers.

Disraelian ladies wore wreathes of camellias in their hair and bonnets. They admired them in the great domed greenhouses of Syon and Chatsworth, embroidered them in beads on cushions, sketched them in water colors and fashioned them out of shells (one sugar-pink variety, 'Madame Lebois', looks in life as if it were made of shells). At Trentham, the Duke of Sutherland's palace in the Midlands, there was an avenue of camellias under glass. And Queen Victoria herself, who seldom mentions flowers in her voluminous correspondence, wrote to her Uncle Leopold from Osborne in March 1845: 'If we have no mountains to boast of, we have the sea, which is ever enjoyable; and we have camellias, which have stood out two winters covered with RED flowers. Does this not sound tempting? It seems almost wrong to be at home, and Albert really hardly is. ...'

Camellias, as we now know, stand out for a hundred winters, and are only liable to injury by freak spells of frost. But it was not until recently that gardeners realized that camellias are hardy. Reginald Farrer, a great gardener of sixty years ago, was one of the first to point the way, when he wrote the following lines:

> Camellia japonica will probably never reach the huge tree-like proportions it attains in Japan, but is an absolutely certain doer, almost anywhere, perfectly hardy and requiring no sort of care or protection. It is more, of course, a wild-wood tree than a rock-garden shrub, but when well-developed has a rare magnificence, with its grey smooth trunk, and its burden of flame-like crimson flowers, single, golden eyed, that nestle amid the dark glossy leafage.

And in the southern part of the United States, and the west coast of England, where they are warmed by the Gulf Stream, it is a recognized fact today that camellias thrive in the open, and flower as well as they do in their native Japan.

When the taste for herbaceous borders came in late in the last century, the camellia tended to be forgotten. Perhaps it was thought too old-fashioned and artificial. Miss Gertrude Jekyll has few words for the camellia, either in her *Colour Schemes for the Flower Garden* or in her *Wood and Garden*, and it can be said that only in the last twenty-five years have gardeners welcomed the camellia back, a contributing cause being, perhaps, the fact that camellias are the perfect plants for town gardens. And town gardens, since the Second World War, have come into their own. Camellias thrive in them. Their glossy leaves throw off city grime, and if they are given, and this is most important, lime-free soil, and shaded from the rays of the morning sun, they will flower five years out of six. Most camellias have a sexennial holiday. Only high wind is their enemy, so a sheltered site, facing south, west or north, should be chosen for them.

Culture. Camellias are not difficult as to soil, as long as it is acid. They will grow on any heavy loam, but appreciate an admixture of peat or leaf mould that has been well worked into the earth. But when planting camellias, the whole area to be planted should be well dug – not just a round space to accommodate their roots.

Sacheverell Sitwell, in his book *Old Fashioned Flowers*, singles out for special praise several hybrid camellias which were first produced in the early years of the Second Empire, some of which are still offered in catalogues today. Of them Mr Sitwell writes:

> One wonders why and by whom, the Second Empire camellias were raised. They are far removed from the atmosphere of Chopin, with the music of whom it is very easy to associate the more pallid and waxy camellias. These striped flowers have as their analogy more the music of Gounod. Countess Lavinia Maggi and Princess Bacciochi must remain the favourites of any collection of striped camellias. They are lovely in themselves, in their association with a forgotten world of luxury and fashion.

The two varieties named are still, after more than a century, widely planted, and can be bought from any nursery specializing in camellias.

Varieties. Earliest to flower of any camellias are the sasanquas – they are sometimes in full bloom in November. Their natural habitat is the woodland in Japan, where the leafless trees of winter offers them some protection. In the West they are better grown in the protection of a wall. 'Hiryu', 'Mine No Yuki', and 'Narumi Gata' are specially good varieties, while C. *sasanqua fragrans* is one of the very few camellias to have a faint scent.

Early in the New Year, the hybrids of the *Camellia japonica* begin to flower, and as these are very numerous it is proposed to mention only a few. The blood red 'Adolf Audusson' is a fine plant, as is the very old 'Jupiter', which is listed in catalogues of over a hundred years ago; it has small flowers, but of a vivid crimson. Any collection of camellias should include the pink 'Lady Clare', of which the only fault is a tendency to have leaves that go yellow, the white *magnoliae flora* and both the mathonianas, alba and rosea, 'Countess Lavinia Maggi' (already mentioned), which is pure white, but as Sacheverell Sitwell writes, has petals which are 'dappled with broad bands of carmine that look as if they had been painted on with a brush – a flower of incredible beauty'. One of the earliest *Camellia japonica* is the dark red 'Gloire de Nantes', while *chandleri elegans* – rose-colored, flaked with white – is another beautiful parti-colored flower.

Slightly less hardy than the many varieties of *Camellia japonica* are the reticulatas (reticulata means 'netted', from the 'netted' veins of the leaves). Particularly fine is the hybrid 'Captain Rawes'. Captain Rawes, after whom this fine hybrid was named, commanded the sailing ship *Warren Hastings*, and took many camellia plants back to his sister, Mrs Palmer of Bromley in Kent. C. *reticulata* was one of his introductions, and first reached England in 1820.

46

Camellia myrtifolia, with leaves pointed like those of a myrtle. From a portfolio of early nineteenth-century water colors in the Natural History Museum, London.

Pub. by I. Ridgway & Sy Piccadilly July 1 1827.

Camellia williamsii, *a cross between* C.C. saluenensis *and* japonica, *is one of the most beautiful of the newly raised hybrids. It has warm pink, semi-double flowers.*

49

Camellia williamsii *'Donation' is a generous flowerer.*

Lastly, for long lists of plant names can be tedious, mention must be made of the remarkable williamsii hybrids, many of which were raised at Caerhays in Devonshire by the late J. C. Williams. Of these hybrids the single flowered are perhaps the most effective, but all are fast growing and flower freely. The finest of the group is 'Donation', with its large semi-double flowers that are a clear pink, fading to a deep peach, and described by Mr Julian Williams as 'a superlative doer, and extremely generous in its flowering ... one of the most consistent camellias there is.'

Another is 'J. C. Williams', with blush pink single flowers and a splendid bosse of golden stamens in the centre. The parents of all the williamsii hybrids are *C. japonica* and the early flowering *C. saluensis* (from the Salween river).

Camellias are sometimes criticized for dying untidily, and when their flowers fade in hot weather, and the petals fail to fall, a camellia with its branches hung with browning flowers can look depressing; but some varieties, 'Donation' for instance, die like aristocrats. It must have been one of these which encouraged the Victorian poet Michael Field to describe the petals of a dying camellia flower as they

> Broke on the sudden from their mass, and all
> The action stately as a funeral.

Camellias are flowers of such perfection that the fact they do not smell does not seem to matter. After all, it was their lack of scent which made them the only flowers that poor Marguérite Gautier could bear to have about her.

Marguérite Gautier and Armand Duval
from the title page of La Dame Aux Camélias *by Alexandre Dumas.*

'Choosing' by George Watts (1817–1904) for which the model was Ellen Terry.
They were married, in 1864, but for less than a year.

The 'Double Clove Gillofloure'   *as drawn in Gerard's Herball.*

Carnation
which Rousseau called 'food for Phoebus' horses'

Sir John Falstaff 'could not bear carnation', according to Mistress Pistol of the Boar's Head Tavern in Shakespeare's *Henry IV*, but that was the color, not the flower. Perdita, in *The Winters Tale*, admired them – 'The fairest flowers of the season are our carnations and streaked gillyvors ...', though she qualified her praise by adding 'which some call nature's bastards'. The sensitive William Drummond of Hawthornden, who literally died of grief on hearing of Charles I's execution, described a girl's cheek with the words: 'A morn of bright carnations did o'er-spread her face', and in the sixteenth and seventeenth century, carnations were already loved and widely grown. Gerard acknowledges their popularity when he described them as 'well known to most, if not to all.'

But of all references in literature to clove carnations, or gillyvors, the earliest must come in Chaucer's *Tale of Sir Thopas* when he writes of

> Herbes great and small:
> The liquorice and the setewall
> And many a clove gilovre
> And nutmeg to put in ale.

Setewall is an old name for valerian. Gilovre – according to Nathan Bailey's dictionary, *An Interpreter of Hard Words* – describes 'Gillyflower as July flower, because it flourishes in that month', which seems apt enough. 'Why the good old name has gone out of fashion it is impossible to say', writes A. E. Bowles, 'for certainly the popularity of the flower has never waned'.

But it would be as affected today to refer to carnations as gilovres as it would be to call them 'sops in wine', which was another popular name for them in Chaucer's time. His Jolly Franklyn 'Epicurus' Owen Son' loved 'in the morn, a sop in wine' – elevenses in fact – and Thomas Tusser, (1520–80), in

Many modern pinks simply have feminine names: to list them would be 'like reading out the roll-call at a girls' school ...' But Doris, an outstanding Allwood pink, with salmon pink flowers, is a tough plant, having been known to survive flooding by sea-water.

his *Hundred Good Pointes of Husbandrie*, writes of sops in wine as an unusually strongly spiced variety of carnation which was used to flavor wine, as mint is used in the southern states of America to flavour juleps, or as the English use borage to enliven such drinks as Pimm's No. 1. Tusser knew a little about a lot of things – Thomas Fuller describes him as 'more skilful in all, than thriving in any one vocation'.

William Bulleine, in his *Bulwarke of Defence* published in 1562, described carnations as 'Domesticall flowers – which do kepe the mindes and spiritual partes through their heavenly savour and most sweet pleasant odour'. Bulleine's book was largely medicinal, but Edmund Spenser again linked carnations with drinking and merriment when in the *Shepherds Calender* he called for

> Columbine,
> With gillyflowers,
> Bring coronation and sops in wine,
> Worn of paramours ...

But sops in wine, though charming, is less descriptive of the flower then gillyvor.

In the days of James I, in the early seventeenth century, no summer flower was better loved in England than the carnation (its conquest of Scotland was to come two hundred years later). John Parkinson gives it a whole chapter to it-self, a rare distinction, and he praises its 'bravery, variety and sweet smell, that joyned together, tyeth everyone's affection with great earnestness both to like and to have ...'. In his *Paradisus terrestris*, Parkinson lists as many as fifty varieties of carnation that were popular in 1629; some of these have the most

53

fascinating names. One would very much like to grow, for instance, the Great Grey Hulo, which presumably had particularly silver foliage, for the flowers are described as red; or the Blue Hulo, with flowers of 'purplish murrey' which perhaps was the subtle slate color that is shown by some modern carnations, such as 'Lyric' or 'Lord Grey'. It would be pleasant to have a plant or two in one's garden of Ruffling Robin, John Witties's Great Tawny, or Pale Pageant. A carnation which is still widely grown is 'Painted Lady'; Parkinson describes a very similar one as 'Dainty Lady'. It must surely be the same plant, one of the few of Parkinson's plants to have survived down the centuries, with only a slight loss of respectability.

Sacheverell Sitwell, in his *Old Fashioned Flowers*, regrets the work-a-day and unevocative names given to plants nowadays. 'It should surely be part of the florist's art to make his flower more rare and enticing ...', and he deplores the fact that modern carnations are so often given 'a girl's name, like Elsie ..., such a system neither enhances the flower nor gives any indication of its properties or appearance'. Mr Sitwell also introduces us to the Tuggie family – Master Tuggie, who was a friend of Thomas Johnson, the eminent botanist, and 'who in 1603 revised John Gerard's famous herbal'. Master Tuggie, it seems, was an enthusiast for carnations, and several of his raising figure on Parkinson's list. 'Master Tuggie's Princess – flaked, feathered and speckled tawny, and Master Tuggie – His rose gillyvor'. Mrs Tuggie, it seems, carried on her husband's good work, after his death, for Thomas Johnson recommends anyone in search of more information about carnations to 'repair to the gardens of Mistress Tuggie, the wife of my lately deceased friend, Mr Ralph Tuggie, in Westminster, which in the excellence and variety of these delights exceedeth all that I have ever seen.'

The Carnation in History. Carnations were as popular in the seventeenth century in France as they were in England. Growing them was the pastime of poor and rich alike. An instance of carnations bringing distraction to political prisoners is provided by the story of the Great Condé, who was incarcerated in the Bastille at the time of the Fronde. To lighten the long hours of his captivity the famous soldier grew carnations. The incident inspired the sentimental Madeleine de Scudéry to end some verses dedicated to the hero of Rocroy with these lines:

> See these flowers that a famous soldier
> Tended with the hand that held a sword
> And bear in mind – Apollo built a wall
> So why should Mars not play the gardener?

In the next century carnations again played a part in the story of a famous prisoner. Their calyxes have often been used, in history, to conceal secret messages, usually of a romantic kind. But during the French Revolution the

The Prince de Condé (1621–86) – Victor of Rocroy –
passed his time in prison in the Bastille
by growing carnations.

Marie Antoinette (1755–93) painted as a prisoner
in the Temple by Kucharsky.
A message was smuggled to the queen
in the calyx of a carnation.

calyx of a carnation was used in a fruitless effort to save the life of Marie Antoinette herself. In September 1793, when she was closely imprisoned in the Temple, a would-be rescuer, the Chevalier de Rougeville, gained access to her cell and dropped a carnation, as if by accident, at her feet. The man was unknown to the Queen, whose surprise at suddenly seeing a strange face in her lonely cell betrayed the plot to her jailers. They allowed the Queen to read the hidden message – with what feelings of sudden hope one can imagine; as she had been forbidden a pen, she pathetically pricked out, with a pin, on a scrap of paper, that she had understood, and would be ready at the allotted hour. Then only did her captors pounce, and the Queen's last hope of rescue vanished. From then until her execution, she was subjected to far stricter treatment, and severer jailers replaced those who had let M. de Rougeville reach the Queen's cell.

'The affair of the Carnation' was made the subject of a sad verse by Constant Dubos in which

> A queen unfortunate
> In her cell disconsolate ...

Received a message from a faithful friend concealed in a carnation, which brought her a ray of hope. ... But only momentarily. The pathetic scrap of paper with its pricked out message is preserved in the National Archives in Paris.

A happier anecdote is that of Jean-Jacques Rousseau, the philosopher, who loved carnations, and once sent his friend De La Tourette, a fellow enthusiast, some roots of *Dianthus superbum* which he had found some cows eating in a field. In the accompanying note he wrote 'Do you grow *Dianthus superbum*? If not, I must send it to you. It is the most exquisite carnation, and deliciously scented. Only the Horses of the Sun should be allowed to graze on it'. 'Food for Phoebus' horses …' high praise even for a dianthus called superb.

Carnations as Florists' Flowers. In the early years of the nineteenth century pinks reached a level of popularity that they never achieved before or since. They were enrolled in the select list of florists' flowers. The most celebrated of all florists' clubs – and the first – was founded in Paisley in 1782. This incident in the carnation story is of particular interest to the author, for Paisley is the home town of his family. It is now a thriving industrial centre of half a million inhabitants, many of its citizens being employed by Messrs J. & P. Coats' giant cotton mills. When the carnation craze, for it was no less, was at its peak, the industrial life of Paisley had just begun. Pleasant fields and farms lay between it and Glasgow, which was then a small elegantly laid-out town, and which as late as 1844 was to remind the visiting Prince Consort, husband of Victoria, rather oddly, of Paris. It is a tradition in the author's family, so deep in the country did Paisley lie, that ladies driving into Glasgow to the theatre went armed with pepper pots as a defence against highwaymen. The industrial

Carnations as illustrated in Hortus Floridus *by De Passe, published in 1614.*

The carnation – or oeillet *– epitome of artifice, from J. J. Grandville's* Les Fleurs Animées.

lith: de E De Ligne

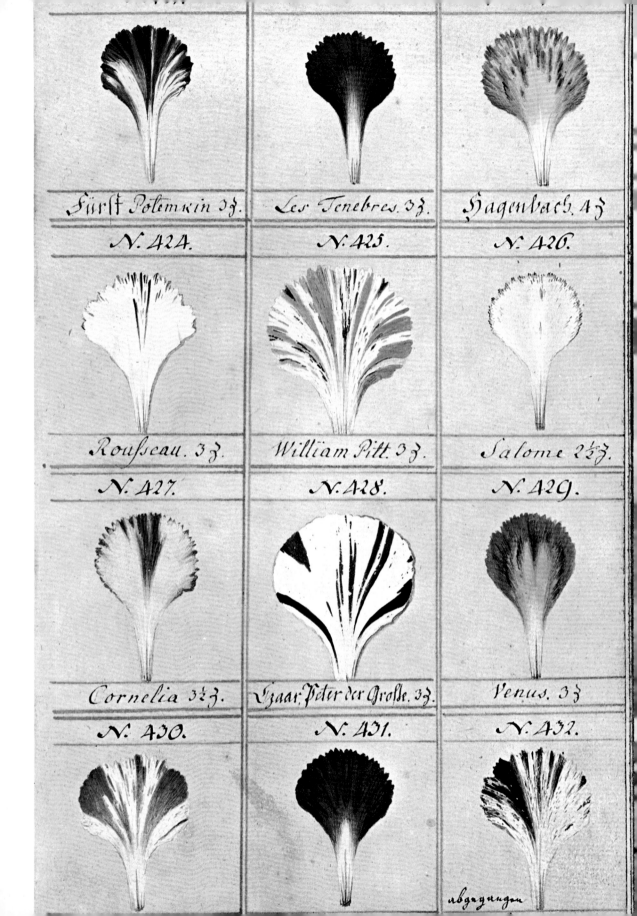

Fürst Potemkin 3ℨ.	Les Tenebres. 3ℨ.	Hagenbach. 4ℨ
N. 424.	N. 425.	N. 426.
Rousseau. 3ℨ.	William Pitt. 3ℨ.	Salome 2½ℨ.
N. 427.	N. 428.	N. 429
Cornelia 3½ℨ.	Ӡaar Peter der Große. 3ℨ.	Venus. 3ℨ
N. 430.	N. 431.	N. 432.

abgegangen

Borders of white pinks under apple-trees in the garden of Cranborne Manor in Dorset.

revolution had barely begun, the skies above Paisley were as yet unblackened by smoke, and many of the inhabitants, the Coats family included, were employed in weaving Paisley shawls in imitation of the beautiful and expensive shawls being imported from Kashmir. Their leisure was spent in growing laced pinks, and it was at this period that the list of pinks grown by the amateurs of Paisley lengthened to several hundred names – the weavers and spinners striving, as Mr Roy Genders tells us in *Garden Pinks*, 'to introduce the flower of the pink to the intricate oriental patterns of their shawls', and Mr Genders goes on to say, 'Not for these people the delights of village pub and the feel of bat and ball; the whole of their recreation was used to beautifying their tiny gardens, and at Paisley it was the pink that gave them the most satisfaction. ...'

John Loudon suggests that it was the beauty of the flowers they raised in their leisure hours which inspired the designs of the shawls they wove with such care in their working hours – and that their ingenuity was 'continually in exertion for new and pleasing elegancies to diversify their fabrics: and where such habits obtain, the rearing of beautiful flowers will easily be adopted. On the other hand, the rearing of flowers must tend to improve their genius for invention in elegant fancy muslins.'

A page from a German carnation salesman's catalogue. From the names – 'Fürst Potemkin' and 'William Pitt', the date of the book may be fixed at about 1800.

But it was only in the first half of the nineteenth century that the taste for pinks persisted in Paisley. By the 'fifties, few were being grown, and the rapid industrialization of the area may well have contributed to their disappearance. The 'Annual and Amicable Competitions', at which the prizes offered seem absurdly simple – a spade, a rake or a trowel – no longer took place. No longer were the benches at the Thursday meetings 'from the flowering of the polyanthus to the disappearance of the carnation' bright with more than three hundred kinds of carnation and eighty kinds of pink. The laced pinks of Paisley disappeared into limbo.

In the middle of the last century, however, a pink was raised with a name which is still a household word – 'Mrs Sinkins'. Its raiser was the Master of the workhouse at Slough, Buckinghamshire, who named his new flower after his wife, who probably was quite uninterested in her husband's hobby, and quite oblivious of the fame which was soon to be hers. So well known a flower is the 'Mrs Sinkins' that it was later made part of the coat of arms of the borough of Slough, an unusual honor for any modern flower.

On the armorial bearings of the city of Slough there appears 'a swan proper holding in the beak a white pink slipped and leaved ...'
It honours the first Mrs Sinkins pink which was raised near Slough.

For the connoisseur of carnations, 'Mrs Sinkins', on account of her untidy calyx, has recently been superseded by two beautiful, newly raised white flowers, 'Her Majesty' and 'Swan Lake'. But neither of these new carnations, in the opinion of the author, has the delicious evocative fragrance of 'Mrs Sinkins'.

The early twentieth century saw the carnation go up in the social scale. If it was no longer the prized flower of working class enthusiasts, it was certainly the pampered pet of the rich. Few great gardens of the period were without a house devoted entirely to carnations – and of all carnations the Malmaison was most typical of the flushed prosperity and extravagance of the time. Malmaison carnations were first raised in France in 1857 – at the time of the Second Empire – and they were so named on account of their likeness to the popular rose, 'Souvenir de la Malmaison'. But a perpetual flowering strain of carnation was not developed until the year after King Edward VII came to the throne. No flower could be more typical of his reign.

Malmaison carnations are wonderfully opulent flowers, with rich pink deeply fimbriated petals bursting from jade green calyxes, like the bosoms of Edwardian beauties, and as powerfully scented.

Today Malmaisons are very seldom grown. Few gardens have the greenhouse space to devote to carnations alone, or the garden staff to look after them. They were typical of an age of luxury and elegance that is past.

Carnations Today. Far less demanding than Malmaisons are the many carnations which can be grown in the open garden – these are plants which do not need cossetting, protection from the weather and the care of a large garden staff, and they have been greatly developed in the last half century. In the 'twenties, a particularly sensational new strain was raised from some of the surviving Laced Pinks by Mr C. H. Herbert. These new Herbert Pinks, as they came to be called, had flowers superior in form and sweetness to any that had gone before, 'Bridesmaid' being a particular favorite. But the Herbert Pinks were not perpetual flowering, and it was not until twenty years ago that they were crossed with a strain with a name which is as famous as any in the carnation story – and is almost synonymous with modern carnations – that of Allwood. It was the mating of Herbert Pinks and *Dianthus allwoodii* which produced a strain of flowers which bloomed from May until November.

Montagu Allwood devoted his whole life to the development and improvement of the carnation, and was honored by a select committee of the Royal Horticultural Society who named his own strain of hybrid pinks *Dianthus allwoodii* – Dios, divine; anthos, a flower: Theophrastus' name for a pink – so Montagu Allwood received an accolade indeed.

There are so many modern varieties of carnations that it would be tedious to list more than a few which are personally known to the author and well-proved garden plants. Indeed, so many simply have feminine names that it might be like reading out the roll-call at a girls' school. Gone indeed are the days of the evocative and descriptive names we read in Parkinson. For Lusty Gallant or Bristol Blush, we now have to put up with Joan and Doris. And 'Doris' is indeed an outstanding Allwood pink – strongly scented, with large salmon-pink flowers. And it is astonishingly tough, and is known to have survived flooding by seawater for over two hours, and flowering well the following summer. 'Joan' has semi-double flowers of coral-pink, piped with red, and a close growing, neat habit. 'Bridesmaid' has already been noted, and is a beautiful pink reared by C. H. Herbert. It makes a compact, frosty-leaved plant and shows open-faced flowers which are freely borne over a long period.

Another pink raised by Allwood is 'Loveliness', a cross between Rousseau's *Dianthus superbum* and the pink Sweet Wivelsfield, itself a cross between *D. allwoodii* and a Sweet William. 'Loveliness' is, for once, well and descriptively named, for it has shredded petals which give each flower a lacy quality like the flowers of a white Love-in-the-Mist.

The best way to grow border carnations and pinks is demonstrated by the habit of growth of the Cheddar pink *Dianthus caesius*, which grows in the rock face of the cliffs of Cheddar Gorge in the West of England. This was discovered in the eighteenth century by Sam Brewer, a Wiltshire man who

Cheddar Gorge in
Somerset, home of
Dianthus caesius,
the Cheddar pink.

had taken up botany after an unsuccessful start as a cloth manufacturer. He was afterwards head gardener at Badminton. Soon after his discovery the Cheddar pink became a great attraction for tourists, whose depredations nearly resulted in the plant's disappearance. Today the Cheddar pink is protected, but in spite of notices forbidding visitors to dig it up, the plant grows more thickly where it is out of reach.

Like all carnations, *Dianthus caesius* appreciates sharp drainage – and the poor limey soil and steep slopes of the Cheddar Gorge suits it perfectly. Canon Ellacombe noticed this characteristic of the carnation seventy years ago when he wrote in his book, *In a Gloucestershire Garden:*

> In that position it will flower freely, and increase downwards: and such plants I have on the wall of my garden, which have probably been there for more than sixty years, live and flower without any attention or protection. ... I believe the same treatment is good for all the tribe of pinks. We learn this from our own wild carnation (*Dianthus caryophyllus*), the parent of all our carnations, and the gillyflower of our ancestors; this is only found wild on our old castles, and never, I believe, in hedges or fields. To me it has always been a plant of great interest, because knowing it to be an alien, and having seen it in great abundance on William the Conqueror's own Castle of Falaise, I like to think that it was introduced either by him or some of his followers; though its seeds or some plants may have been imported with the Caen stone.

And the good Canon goes on to say that this offers an excellent hint on how to grow carnations well:

All pinks thrive in a position which is sharply drained, as on the top of this dry stone wall.

In the open border they often show as many leaves as flowers. But in Switzerland they are grown (especially the crimson cloves) in the window boxes of the chalets, and are allowed to hang down, and so grown they are very beautiful; and exactly the same treatment may be given to all carnations. They may be placed either on top of a wall, or in the chinks, and will there grow naturally with excellent effect.

No family of flowers has been so developed and improved by hybridization as the carnation; and though the carnations of today look as artificial as the *oeillet* in Albert Grandville's illustration, they have gained rather than lost by extensive cross-breeding. They are more strongly scented (though hybridization often decreases fragrance) and they are of a hundred other colors than pink. As Thomas (not John) Parkinson once wrote in his *Flower Painting Made Easy*, 'There is such an infinite variety of carnations that a particular description of them would be endless – being composed of the following colors – white, crimson, scarlet, purple and those colors so diversified that the student may take the liberty of his fancy without the danger of deviating from what may happen in Nature'. Falstaff, who did not like 'carnation', would have had a choice.

In conclusion, it is interesting to know that the word 'pink', now so universally accepted in our language as descriptive of a color, is comparatively modern. Shakespeare never used it as an adjective, but as a word which meant perfect – 'The very pink of courtesy'. Pink would seem to be a corruption of the word 'pinct' which means pinked or scalloped, which the petals of a carnation certainly are. Thus the flower gave its name to the color, not, as is generally supposed, the color to the flower.

63

A vase in the Museum of Applied Arts   *in Vienna, with a design of clematis.*

Clematis

'are as hardy as the oak … come early into flower and only cease with the approach of winter'

And that great gardener William Robinson went on to say, 'of few other flowers can this be said'.

The word 'clematis' derives from the Greek word *klema* which means a branch of a vine, or almost any kind of climbing plant. Clematis have been in cultivation in gardens for many hundreds of years, and at least one, *Clematis vitalba*, the Traveller's Joy of English hedgerows, is a British native, and was wreathing woods and copses during the Roman occupation.

Clematis vitalba was named by John Gerard Traveller's Joy '… by reason of the goodly shadow and the pleasant scent or savour of its flowers, and because of its decking waies and hedges where people travel. …' Parkinson includes a chapter headed 'Clematis, Clamberers or Creepers' which, besides clematis, describes the Passion Flower and the periwinkle. And so Gerard's and Parkinson's names take first place in the story of clematis, as they do in so many other plant histories. But if the names of those two old herbalists precede any other, chronologically, in the history of the clematis, the name of Jackman will always be linked with the hybrid clematis of today. The earliest of these hybrids was raised in Henderson's nursery at St John's Wood, London, as far back as 1835; though it was not until the introduction of *Clematis lanuginusa*, the largest of all the species, by Robert Fortune, from Ningpo in China, that it was possible to breed the beautiful large-flowered varieties of clematis we admire today. We now have crosses of *C. lanuginosa* with *C. patens*, *C. florida* and *C. viticella*, and the most famous of these crosses bears the name of the Jackman family, who were ever in the forefront of the search for new and beautiful plants. *Clematis jackmanii*, a cross between *C. lanuginosa* and *viticella*, and one of the most beautiful climbers in cultivation,

64

A group of different clematis from Crispin de Passe's Hortus Floridus *published in 1614.*

Flammula recta.

Clematis erecta

is today a household word. The first *C. jackmanii* burst on the gardening world just over a century ago and has been flowering in many gardens ever since. Many of its descendants are nearly as famous; they include such beautiful plants as the pinkest, large-flowered clematis of all – 'Comtesse de Bouchaud', as well as the shell pink 'Hagley Hybrid', the carmine red 'Ville de Lyon', the plum-colored 'Star of India', and the claret-colored 'Ernest Markham'. This last is a tribute to a devoted clematis grower, and modestly not mentioned in his authoritative book on the plant.

Mr Markham was the famous William Robinson's head gardener at Gravetye and Victoria Sackville-West, in *More for Your Garden*, has described the garden 'where they made such grandly imaginative use of clematis, and where a chance seedling of the lavender-coloured *C. macropetala* turned up pink, and was given the name *C. macropetala var markhamii* in honour of the great gardener's great head gardener. Thus Markham takes its place twice, and most deservedly, in the annals of the clematis.'

The *lanuginosa* (hairy-leaved) section of clematis is an important one, and it includes such beautiful plants as the white, black-stamened *C. henryi*, the white, yellow-stamened 'Marie Boisselot' (sometimes known as 'Madame le Coultre') and one of the most generous flowerers of all clematis – the beautiful 'Mrs Cholmondeley' which has flowers that are the color of wisteria. The flowers borne by all the *lanuginosa* group are just as fine as those of *C. jackmanii* and its descendants, but as the *lanuginosa* group flower earlier in the summer – some even in May – the plants need to be pruned back hard in January as opposed to the *jackmanii* clematis which should be cut to within a few inches of the woody stem in March. This is important, and a fact often overlooked by amateur gardeners.

The double forms of both *Clematis jackmanii* and *lanuginosa* are not favorite plants of the author – any more than they were of William Robinson ('I never plant one if I know it'). Sir Herbert Maxwell, in *Memories of the Months*, had hard words to say about them, 'let my last words about clematis', he wrote nearly a century ago, 'be to denounce all double flowered forms as abominable. No milder epithet suffices for the distortion of a perfect flower into a monstrosity that can only merit the kind of morbid attention bestowed on a two-headed calf or a four-legged chicken in a village museum. ...' Sir Herbert would not have approved of the often-planted double mauve 'Belle of Woking' or the pale pink 'Proteus' which sometimes shows double flowers if not hard pruned.

Mr Christopher Lloyd, a recognized expert on many plants, admits that his first love in the plant world was, and still is, clematis. His taste for the plant developed early in life and has lasted ever since:

At first, I was attracted, as any child would be, to the glamorous large-flowered satiny textured hybrids, such as W. E. Gladstone and Lasurstern,

The flowers borne by all the lanuginosa group are as fine as those of Clematic jackmanii.

Clematis alpina, *with pale blue flowers, growing in an old Italian oil jar.*

LEFT *Clematis montana curtains a garden gate in the National Trust garden of Hidcote Manor in Gloucestershire, originally created by the dedicated American gardener, Lawrence Johnston.*

but now I love nearly all of them, even the tiniest and most insignificant in their different ways, and for their fascinating diversity of habit, colour and flower form ...

Following Mr Lloyd's remarks perhaps we should mention just a few of the species clematis, which are less flamboyant, certainly, than the *jackmanii* and *lanuginosa* types, but which have their own very special charm.

Species clematis to acclaim include *C. alpina*, with lavender blue nodding flowers, seen flowering to perfection in an old oil jar in the illustration top right, *C. armandii*, which has large white flowers in April, and *C. montana*, a plant of the easiest good humor which is nonetheless one of the great beauties of the clematis clan. It is too well known to need any description, and how much more we would value it if it were rare.

Most exotic looking of all the species clematis must surely be *Clematis florida bicolor sieboldii* which was first exhibited at the flower show in Ghent in 1829, where it made a sensation. *C. florida bicolor* had been known in Europe for many years (an illustration of it is shown opposite) but Siebold's variety shows purple staminodes which the earlier plant did not have. It might be described as the only double clematis worth growing, and it is indeed a spectacular flower. William Robinson describes it:

The exotic species Clematis florida bicolor *was first exhibited at Ghent in 1829, when it created a sensation.*

In foliage and habit *C. florida* resembles no other species – the essential difference being in the flower which is double and bicoloured. Enriched by a collaret of larger sepals, the centre forms a corona of little violet petals which impart to the flower a certain resemblance to a Passion Flower. These petals and stamens in process of transformation turn into brown-coloured exterior anthers. The interior ones continue with the pistils after the fall of the bloom.

Miss Ellen Willmott, that passionate gardener who spent a fortune, her whole fortune, in creating a great garden in Essex which has now completely disappeared, wrote of this remarkable clematis, 'One of its peculiarities is that about one third of its flowers are absolutely double', and she described a plant in her garden as having over five hundred flowers, and added that she 'seemed only to have made some way in reckoning up the total'.

Two other unusual clematis were first raised at Gravetye Manor by William Robinson, aided and abetted by his head gardener, Mr Markham. These are *C. tangutica* Gravetye and *C. texensis* 'Gravetye Beauty'. *Tangutica* has yellow, felty petals and decorative feathery seed pods; *C. texensis*, which is more tender, has curious urn-shaped flowers of carmine red, white streaked on the sepals: as the name implies, it originates in the state of Texas.

The last species clematis we would mention is the September-flowering *Clematis flammula*. In *Colour Schemes for the Flower Garden* Gertrude Jekyll, that careful and imaginative gardener, describes a special duty in the border for this reliable and sweet smelling plant. 'Delphiniums, which are indispensable for July, leave bare stems with quickly yellowing leafage when the flowers are over.' Behind these Miss Jekyll planted, as well as *Clematis jackmanii*, *C. flammula*. When the delphiniums were over, she removed their seed pods and cut the stems down to just the right height. The clematis was then trained over them. 'But', says Miss Jekyll, 'it must not be supposed that they are just lumped one over another so that the under ones have their leafy growths smothered. They are always being watched, and, bit by bit, the earlier growths are removed as soon as their respective plants are better without them.' It took, Miss Jekyll goes on to say, several years for the two plants to become established.

They cannot be hurried; indeed, in my garden it is difficult to get the clematis to grow at all. But good gardening means patience and dogged determination. There must be many failures and losses, but by always pushing on there will also be the reward of success. Those who do not know are apt to think that hardy flower gardening of the best kind is easy. It is not easy at all. It has taken me half a lifetime merely to find out what is best worth doing, and a good slice out of another half to puzzle out the ways of doing it.

70

ABOVE Clematis patens 'Nelly Moser' has pale mauve flowers barred with carmine and striking black anthers.

Père Armand David (1826–1900) was a French missionary in China 1862–73 and collected many new plants there.

One of the great charms of all the species clematis is the feathery seed-heads which follow their flowers, and persist through the winter.

Two herbaceous clematis which are well worth growing are the sweet-scented four-foot high creamy-flowered *Clematis recta*, especially handsome in its purple-leaved form, and Père Armand David's form of *C. heracleifolia*, *C. davidiana*, which he collected, as he did so many other wonderful plants, in China about a hundred years ago; this is a deciduous sub-shrub with toothed downy leaves and indigo-blue flowers like those of a hyacinth. 'Côte D'Azur' is a particularly good form.

In the long panegyric of the clematis Anne Pratt introduces a rather different note, and tells an odd story. Anne Pratt's long life covered all but a few years of the nineteenth century and 'her delicate health rendering her unfit for active pursuits ... devoted herself to literary studies. Her works were written in popular style and were instrumental in spreading a knowledge and love of Botany, and were at one time acknowledged by a grant from the Civil List.' (Dictionary of National Biography.)

Her effort rewarded, Anne Pratt wrote a book entitled, *Poisonous, Noxious and Suspected Plants of our fields and woods*. In it she accuses the clematis of being 'acrimonious' and quotes Philip Miller, Curator of the Chelsea Physic Garden in 1722, as writing 'if one leaf be cropped on a hot day in the summer season and bruised ... it will cause pain like a flame – and the fresh leaves used in the old days to be used by beggars to cause wounds in order to excite compassion'.

It is perfectly true that the young growth of some clematis – especially the new shoots of *Clematis montana* – can cause a painful rash and red marks on the skin, which will persist for months. The writer has suffered from this, and it took him several summers of sore arms to discover which the 'acrimonious' plant in his garden was.

Cultivation. Clematis have often been described as difficult to grow successfully – 'wayward' is a word often used for them, but if a few basic rules are remembered, no garden plant can be more rewarding. There are four important rules to bear in mind: all clematis need lime in the soil, so if your soil is deficient in lime, add lime in the easily obtainable form of old mortar rubble. Clematis also like to have their faces in the sun and their roots in the shade. Ideally, they should be planted on the north or cool side of a low wall and allowed to scramble over it so that their flowers face south. The third rule is almost the most important. Clematis are almost always supplied on rooted stocks, so when they are planted, in well dug and enriched soil, it is good advice to help the plant to form new roots above the graft, by laying the new plant's rootstock flat on the ground and covering the bottom of the stem with new soil. This treatment should ensure new roots and give the plant redoubled strength of growth. These few cultural hints are given in more detail than has been done with regard to most of the other plants chosen for inclusion in this book. But clematis are not absolutely fool-proof, and when plants with special cultural needs or foibles are discussed, it would seem useful to give what advice has been found, from experience, to be of value.

One last hint on how to make clematis happy: they love tea, perhaps because they have so long been acclimatized to Britain. The author remembers, when he was a boy, being fascinated by the sight of the head gamekeeper's wife – a stately old lady in black satin – pouring the contents of the tea-pot, and emptying the tea-leaves, on to the roots of a splendid purple clematis which grew by her cottage door. 'Mr Peter Dan', she said, 'there's naething sae guid for a clematitis.' The author has never forgotten it, nor the extra syllable in clematis, and it is a cultural tip he has followed in his own various gardens ever since, with some success.

The plants mentioned in this chapter are a very few of the many clematis which today grow in Western gardens. They are plants which have been collected from the four quarters of the world, or raised by careful hybridizers, such as the Jackman family. Modern clematis, in splendor of flower and brilliance of color, have come a long way since the dusty Roman legionaries were marching over the length and breadth of Britain, and who, when they rested, must have been grateful to the wild clematis growing by the roadside, 'by reason of the goodly shadow, and pleasant scent or savor of its flowers'.

One of the beauties
of the new large
flowered hybrid
delphiniums is their

black petaloids or 'bees',
which are most
striking in
the white varieties.

Delphinium

Larkspurs provide the brightest blue of any garden plant

No two flowers would seem to be so remotely related as the delphinium and the buttercup, yet they are both members of the same great family of ranunculaceae, and the careful observer will note a similarity in their foliage, however totally different their habit, height and flower-color may be.

Delphiniums derive their name from the Greek name given to one species of the plant by Dioscorides, the Greek doctor who served in the Roman army, because he noticed a likeness, somewhat remote, between the flower's closed buds and the shape of a dolphin.

By the end of the Dark Ages, the name delphinium had come to embrace the whole genus. Though occasionally when delphiniums are meant, the name ajacis – the flower of Ajax – is used. John Gerard refers to the ajacis, small, slight and not always blue, in his famous *Herball* as 'sometimes of a purplish color, sometimes white, carnation and of sundry other colors varying indefinitely according to the soil or countrye wherein they live'.

A Greek legend, cited in an eclogue of Virgil, offers a rather far-fetched explanation why delphiniums were thought of as the flower of Ajax. A shepherd asks the riddle, 'Say in what country do flowers grow with the name of a king written on them?' The answer, it seems, is the delphinium, which is said to have sprung from the blood of Ajax who, when defeated by Ulysses, despairingly put an end to his own life. The flower bore on its petals the letter AI – the initials of his name, and 'expressive of a sigh'.

This was the flower which was the original ancestor of the splendid border delphiniums of modern gardens. The English name for the flower is Larkspur (from its horn-shaped nectary) and Gerard refers to it as such: 'In English, Larkes spur, Larkes heels, Larkes toes, Larkes clawes ... in High Dutch Ridden Spooren, that is Equitis Calcar, Knights Spur, in Italian Sperone: in French Pied d'Alouette.'

73

Delphiniums as illustrated in Parkinson's Paradisi in Sole, *first published in 1629.*

Another old French name for the delphinium was *La Dauphinelle*, and in Spanish it is known as *Espuela de Caballaro*.

The delphinium, like all flowers listed in the early herbals, was thought to have its own curative properties. *D. consolida*, a British native, was, according to Anne Pratt, 'considered a most powerful vulnerary – hence its description *consolida* – "to unite" '. And Gerard holds that the delphinium's seed and leaf 'is good against the stinging of scorpions and any venemous beast. It causes them to be without force or strength in so much as they cannot stir or move, until the herbe be taken away.'

By the mid-seventeenth century delphiniums were well established in English gardens, and there is a page of illustrations of the flower in John Parkinson's *Paradisi in Sole* which appeared in 1629. In Parkinson's day delphiniums were usually treated as annuals and grown afresh every year from seed, and the taller herbaceous kinds, such as *Delphinium elatum*, were only slowly coming into favor: as Parkinson wrote, 'the tall or upright kinds have been entertained but of late yeares'.

One of the first great breeders of delphiniums was James Kelway (1871–1952), whose family have given their names to many fine plants which were first raised in their Langport nursery. Many of these hybrids are still to be seen in gardens today. It was James Kelway who, by painstaking selection of hundreds of seedlings of *Delphinium elatum*, and laborious cross pollenization, produced plants which, though they have since been even further improved, looked much like the splendid blue spires which decorate our modern borders.

5 July 1910, has been noted as an important date in the story of the delphinium. On that date Mr Amos Perry of a well-known firm in Enfield near London staged an exhibit, at the Holland House Flower Show, which made history. It was a 'Blue Tent', entirely decorated with thirty thousand cut spires of delphiniums. The display was a sensation, and of it the *Westminster Gazette* wrote admiringly:

> The flower show that opened yesterday in the grounds of Holland House – lent for the purpose by Mary, Lady Ilchester, will long be remembered as one of the finest shows held by the Royal Horticultural Society. The area under canvas is much larger than at any previous show, and the exhibits maintain a uniform excellence ... Messrs Perry's group of delphiniums being especially noteworthy, ... and it aroused the admiration of a group of Japanese gentlemen visiting the show – the delphinium being little known in their country.

For their exhibit Messrs Perry's gained a gold medal. Holland House is now a memory – having been destroyed by bombs in 1940 – but many of the delphiniums which so impressed the visitors to that flower show nearly sixty years ago, Japanese gentlemen included, are still in commerce.

About six years before the 'Blue Tent' at Holland House two other names became associated, as they still are, with delphiniums – Blackmore and Langdon. Among the famous strains they raised in their nursery at Bath, many of which were scions of plants imported from France, were 'Daniel Osiris' and the celebrated 'Statuaire Rude' which, when first shown, bore the largest single flowers yet seen.

In the early twenties of this century another name, that of Thomas Carlyle of the Loddon Gardens, Twyford in Berkshire, became well known in the world of delphiniums.

Mr Carlyle's two most famous introductions were 'Norah Ferguson' and 'Belladonna Wendy', the Belladonna strain having been for many years a favorite plant of English gardens, but one which was considered sterile until a Mr Gibson of Leeming Bar in Yorkshire, after many attempts, induced it to set seed. It was from Mr Gibson's three precious seed pods that all the Belladonna delphiniums of today descend. Gertrude Jekyll, in *Colour Schemes for the Flower Garden*, described the flower half a century ago, as 'the lovely Belladonna delphinium, with flowers of a blue purer than that of any other of its beautiful kind. It never grows tall, nor has it the strong, robust aspect of the larger ones, but what it lacks in vigor is more than made up for by the charming refinement of the whole plant'

Recently there has been raised in the United States a new type of delphinium known as the 'Pacific Giant' strain. These splendid plants, if seed of them is planted in early spring, will flower the same year. Perhaps they lack something of the character of the earlier simpler plants, but for sheer generosity of bloom and exuberance of growth they should be welcomed by any gardener who prizes color. They are a tribute to the industry and patience of American hybridists.

There is, it must be admitted, little poetry about the delphinium. Even Victoria Sackville-West, who wrote with such a delicate touch about so many of our garden flowers, comes down to earth, with something of a bump, when she describes delphiniums in *More for Your Garden*. 'They will grow in almost any kind of soil, light or heavy, and they will do their best for us, somehow or other, but they do respond to good treatment, and who does not? It is not a question of "feed the Brute" but "feed the Beauty".'

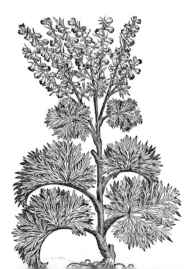

An early name for delphinium was 'ajacis' – the flower of Ajax. John Gerard refers to delphinium as such, and describes its flowers as being of colors 'varying indefinitely according to the soil or country wherein they live'.

Border delphinium 'Ann Miller' in the garden at Abbotswood in Gloucestershire.

Hellebore '*Potter's wheel*',   *a new large-flowered hybrid.*

Hellebore

'And green its glaucous leaves expand
With fingers like a mermaid's hand'

This description, by the Bishop of Down, of the leaves of the hellebore, is an apt one. There is something sinister about the plant, with its greenish flowers and glabrous curling leaves, and its honey is said to be poisonous. The Latin adjectives describing the different varieties of hellebore are, it must be admitted, faintly off-putting, *odorous, foetidus, lividus.* And the word hellebore comes from the Greek *helein*, to kill, and *bora*, food. Yet the plant has an odd fascination of its own.

Hellebore is the old Greek name used by several writers of antiquity as well as by Hippocrates, the most celebrated physician of ancient days, who practised medicine four hundred years before Christ in the island of Cos, and who gave his name to the Hippocratic Oath. But baleful as the aura of the hellebore may seem the plant was always allowed some good qualities too. In one legend, Mecampe, a cowherd, discovered that hellebores acted as a healthy purgative on his cattle. Armed with this useful knowledge, Mecampe set up as a physician, soon became famous, and was called in by Proetus, King of Argos, to cure the madness of his daughters who were suffering under the delusion that they had been changed into cows. The treatment succeeded, and Mecampe was rewarded with the hand of one of the princesses in marriage. Hence, an alternative name for hellebore was mecampodium, to mark its good qualities rather than its reputation as a poison. In Greece the finest mecampodiums, or hellebores, grew in Anticyra, which gave rise to the proverb, 'He ought to be sent to Anticyra' as we might say someone should be sent to a lunatic asylum. And an old French poem ran:

L'ellebore est la fleur des fous
On l'a dedié à maints poètes.

79

Helleborus corsicus, *from* Monographia Helleborum *by Schiffner, published in Germany in 1890.*

Old English names for hellebore are setterwort, oxheal and bear's foot, which, less fancifully than Bishop Mant's description, refer to the shape of their leaves. But the most popular name for one variety of hellebore is the Christmas Rose. Hellebores are referred to by Gerard by yet another name, neesewort, and recommended as a cure, not surprisingly, for 'Phrensies', but with the advice that it should not be administered to 'delicate bodies ... but may be more safely given unto country people which feed grosly and have hard tough and strong bodies.'

Hellebores, however they are named, are more popular with discerning gardeners today than they have ever been before. To have several varieties of hellebore in your garden is the sign of maturity of taste, of garden one-upmanship; they have become, in the gardening fraternity, a status symbol.

Some hellebores, though not as many as are grown today, have been features for many years in Western gardens; and in Victorian times, and indeed up to the present day, while labor was available, the most prized flowers were those that were carefully protected in winter by glass bells, or in miniature greenhouses which were specially built for the purpose. Not because Christmas Roses (*Helleborus niger*) are delicate – they are bone hardy – but because their stems are short and their white flowers, which are so cheerful in the depths of winter, can easily be spattered with mud in wet weather.

Situation. Though it is their reputation to like a shady position, hellebores are surprisingly good natured as to site, as long as the soil they are to grow in is thoroughly well prepared beforehand. The conscientious gardener should provide them with a good deep loam, which is sharply drained. Hellebores have long fleshy roots, and so prefer soil that has been cultivated to a depth of two or even three feet. An addition of well-rotted farmyard manure, well below the roots, at planting time, is advisable. Good drainage is important, for the fleshy roots of the hellebore rot easily if the soil is too wet. Hellebores are one of the few plants which look better planted singly than in beds and drifts; planted alone the architectural value of the plant as a whole can be appreciated; but this effect is lost when several plants are massed together.

The finest plants the author remembers were some he saw growing years ago at Kew where they flourished among ferns in the light shade of some high trees. The fronds of the ferns, some still green, some brown, made the perfect setting for the pure white flowers of the Christmas Rose and the thick layer of fallen leaves with which the ground was covered protected the petals from soil splashing up in heavy rain.

Why is it that hellebores have not, up to the last few years, been more often grown by amateur gardeners? There would seem to be two reasons. The first is that hellebores flower at a time when there are not many flower-shows – and even if there were, in the depth of winter, hellebores would be difficult plants to display; they do not like being grown in pots, and greatly dislike

Helleborus niger, *the Christmas Rose, which Reginald Farrer described as 'one of the candours of the world'. The description 'niger' comes from the color of its root.*

Helleborus foetidus, *a rare British native, has drooping clusters of jade green flowers and dark green palm-like leaves.*

disturbance. The second reason is their reputation for being difficult. Though they are plants which certainly do not like being moved, success very much depends on when this is done. If hellebores are transplanted at the right time, in August or September, after their seed has set, not in late winter when they are coming into flower; if their soil requirements are met, and if, most important of all, their roots are damaged as little as possible, hellebores will move quite satisfactorily, and will soon settle down happily in their new home.

Though every year new varieties of hellebore are listed in catalogues (twenty years ago there would have been but five or six) it is proposed only to describe the few kinds which have been proved from experience to be first rate garden plants.

Varieties. First on the list must be *Helleborus niger*, the Christmas Rose, a plant of which the pearly white flowers and general air of innocence and courage belie the slightly sinister quality of the rest of the genus. The Christmas Rose is the hellebore which that zestful writer Reginald Farrer once described many years ago as 'one of the candours of the world, in all its forms, of a white and unchangeable flawlessness ... *Helleborus niger*, so called because its heart, or root, is black, while its face shines with a blazing white innocence ...'

H. foetidus is a rare British native plant, of which the pale green buds tipped with purple start to open in the middle of January, developing in beauty through the early morning of the year until they are at their best in March. *H. foetidus* ('foetidus' refers to the plant's disagreeable smell) grows about two feet tall. When its stems are crowned with their clusters of pale jade flowers it is an exquisitely beautiful plant, and one that E. A. Bowles, the friend and fellow plant collector of Reginald Farrer, enthused over in his book *My Garden in Spring*.

> *H. foetidus* is so handsome all the year round, and especially when the central bud of the flower-shoot begins to break away from the palm-like crown of black-green leaves, that I must insert a plea for its wider cultivation.
>
> It has the darkest green leaves of any low-growing plant that I can recall, and they are so beautifully cut up into long tapering fingers that their interlacing mass is a wonderfully telling object, especially among such plants as megasea and funkia, whose large entire leaves make a striking contrast with the elaborate design of the Bear's Foot. Also it is such a good tempered plant that it will grow almost anywhere, even under a yew ... (and he goes on to say, optimistically) Some day, then, I hope to astonish my garden visitors with a planting of *Helleborus foetidus* each a yard across, their leafy, lower halves dark as night and their heads of flowers above, a clear yellow-green like that of a midsummer sky after nearly all sunset colour has faded and only the cool light is left.

Third on the list of favorite hellebores is *H. orientalis* – the Lenten Rose of which, in its different varieties, the flowers can be the purest white, white flushed with pink, or a rich dusky purple. One of the great charms of the flowers of any of the darker colored hellebores is the opalescent bloom that their petals wear, and the darker varieties of *H. orientalis* are outstanding examples of this.

Helleborus corsicus *flowers early in the year and 'Its period of interest and beauty in the garden is a longer one than that of any other plant.'*

Helleborus orientalis, *the Lenten Rose. Its flowers can be the purest white, white flushed with pink, or a rich dusty purple.*

Helleborus corsicus is a plant which lately has become the darling of garden connoisseurs. Its period of interest and beauty in the garden is a longer one than that of any other plant the author knows. And in *The Winter Garden* Mr M. J. Jefferson Brown, that expert on flowers which brighten the winter scene, has said of *H. corsicus*, 'Some plants are spectacular for a month and non-descript for eleven. Other plants look well at all times. It is the hallmark of good breeding' – such is the rare distinction of *H. corsicus*. Often it is in full flower in January, showing bunches of pale green bells on stems that grow eighteen inches to two feet high. These last for many weeks, to be followed by decorative seed capsules which can persist until June. Only then do the woody stems die back, to be immediately replaced by a panache of glistening young leaf shoots which spring from the centre of the clump. *Helleborus corsicus* is a great favorite with flower arrangers, and some years ago, when the author was a judge at the Paris Floralies, a winning flower decoration was a vase in which the young dark red shining shoots of *Paeonia officinalis* were arranged most effectively with the acid green flower of *H. corsicus*.

Recently another hellebore has been much discussed – *H. torquatus*, a plant which, after much cajolery, it was possible to procure, some years ago, from a nursery in Shropshire. It had, it seemed, dark blue flowers! – and its first flowering was awaited with impatience. But the first year, pheasants ate all the young growth, and there were no flowers at all. The second year was no better – and in spite of wire-netting, the young shoots were eaten to the ground once more, by rabbits. Third year lucky, and the plant, undeterred by the previous years' setbacks, produced ten magnificent flowers – not exactly blue, admittedly, but a rich bloomy plum color which fairly warmed the heart. *H. torquatus* is still little known but it is a plant to be cherished, cos-setted, and when it flowers, acclaimed.

The hellebore is the first flower of the year to blossom, with the exception of the daisy, which flowers all the year round, and the chickweed which can hardly be dignified by the name of flower at all. For that reason alone, hellebores should find a place in every garden.

> Within the moist and shady glade,
> What plant, in suit of green arrayed,
> All heedless of the winter cold
> Inhabits? Foremost to unfold
> Though half concealed its bloom globose,
> Whose petals green, o'erlapped and close,
>   ... etc., etc.

Bishop Mant was not a very good poet, but he loved flowers and he first thought of the leaves of a hellebore as having 'fingers like a mermaid's hand ...'.

L. Iris Susiana
maior.

Iris roots were among the botanical booty Pharaoh Thutmosis I brought back to Egypt in 1950 BC. *They are commemorated on this marble panel from Karnak.*

Iris

The flower of the rainbow

Iris was the Goddess of the Rainbow, and in Greek mythology she is hardly distinguishable from the natural phenomenon itself. On occasions she seems to have acted as messenger from the gods, as a link between Olympus and mortals below, in that she touched both sky and earth. Iris, the flower, may surely be said to have borrowed its various colors from the sky. There are few iris in cultivation which are, in color, different to the tints the sky can show, and there are few skies, of untroubled blue, thundery purple, fresh primrose or dying pink, which might not find their colors reflected in the petals of the modern iris. Only bright red is lacking, and that shade, one feels, is only just outside the busy hybridist's reach, for the advances made in recent years in the development of the iris have been very great and today gardeners can have iris in shades which were undreamt of even thirty years ago.

The story of the iris begins many years before the birth of Christ, and it is said that among the spoils of war that the Pharaoh of Egypt, Thutmosis I, brought back from his Syrian wars in 1950 BC, was an important collection of medicinal roots, dried herbs and seeds. Only a few were meant to be grown as flowers, and most of the collection was put at the disposal of the court physicians and sorcerers, for research and the production of love philtres. But Thutmosis thought highly of his botanical booty and had it commemorated on a carved marble panel which can still be seen on the walls of the temple of the Theban Ammon at Karnak. The carving includes several different flowers – among them, Egyptologists claim, a representation of *Iris oncocyclus*.

There are several English names for iris – Flag (*Iris pseudacorus*, the Yellow Water Flag), Gladdon or Gladwyn (*Iris foetidissima*). Orris, or iris root, was a household word in the Middle Ages and earlier, and was a powder which smelled of violets, made from the dried roots of *Iris florentina* or *Iris pallida*. It was used in medicine and as a scent. In France, as well as iris, the plant was

85

Iris susiana, the mourning iris, is one of the strangest of flowers, but difficult to acclimatize. Reginald Farrer once described it as 'A Troade in weeds of silken crêpe … sullenly resigned to exile …'

called 'Fleur de Luce', though there has always been some doubt whether the heraldic 'Fleur de Luce' means an iris or a lily. Gerard certainly thought of the 'Fleur de Luce' as an iris, for in his *Herball*, he wrote:

> There are many kinds of Iris or Floure de Luce, whereas some are tall and great, some little, small and low. Some smell exceeding sweete in the roote, some have no smell at all. Some floures are sweet in smell, and some without: some of one colour, some of many colours mixed: vertues attributed to some, others not remembered: some have tuberous or knobby roots, other bulbous or onion roots, some have leaves like flags, others like grasse or rushes ... the common floure de luce hath long and large flaggy leaves like the blades of a sworde ...

But in spite of Gerard, or of Randle Cotgrave who published the first French dictionary in 1611, and described iris as 'the rainbow; also a flower de luce', and of Philip Miller who describes *Iris purpurea* as the common purple 'fleur de lys', there still remains some doubt: though to anyone who has not studied the question, the 'Fleur de lys' will always mean the Royal emblem of France.

But whatever the poets or historians may say about the similarity or dissimilarity of the iris and the lily, the two flowers are related, though there is one definite technical difference between them – no iris has more than three stamens, while all lilies, without exception, have six.

The iris is the flower of Florence and Tuscany and, judging by the frequency of its representation in the art of Japan, the iris might have as good a claim to be the national flower of Japan as the chrysanthemum or the peony.

The iris, ever since Thutmosis, has played an important part in medicine, and it was used to cure a variety of complaints – the ague, shivering, the falling sickness (epilepsy), headache, falling teeth or the bite of an adder.

In poetry Milton, though he did not know a lot about flowers, Byron and Tennyson all used the iris to symbolize the colors of the sky, the last splendors of the sunset, or the prism of the rainbow. In Milton's *Masque of Comus*, the kindly 'attendant spirit', before assuming a simple disguise, says,

> But first I must put off these my sky robes
> Woven out of iris woof
> And take the weeds and habits of a swain.

86   While in his poem, *Childe Harold*, Byron proclaims,

A Japanese woodcut by Hiroshige
of the Iris Gardens at Horikiri, dating from 1857.

... Heaven is free
From clouds but of all colours seems to be
Melted to one vast iris of the West, –
Where the day joins the past Eternity.

Varieties. Earliest of all iris to flower is *I. histrioides*, which was first collected in Asia Minor eighty years ago. This is one of the few species iris which can be relied on to show its bright azure flowers every January. It likes a warm sheltered position, for wind can damage it severely, where it is dry in summer. It is the rich, sky-blue of *I. histrioides* which takes the heart.

Following *I. histrioides* (and, incidentally, the word means that the plant originated in Istria) is *Iris reticulata* – which flowers in February, and, like *I. histrioides*, as regularly as clockwork. *Iris reticulata* loves lime, and cannot have too much of it. There are several differently colored varieties, such as the purple 'J. S. Dijt' and the smoky mauve 'Hercules', but it is the well-known bright Cambridge blue 'Cantab' which is the most popular and most frequently planted of the group.

A great favorite of every gardener is *Iris stylosa*, the Algerian iris. This can flower as early in the year as *I. histrioides* and *reticulata*, if planted in its preferred position, poor dry soil at the foot of a south-facing wall, where it will get a real baking in summer. To help to ensure this, it is as well to cut down the all-enveloping leaves in June, to allow in maximum light and air. The flowers of *I. stylosa*, which are a deep lilac, last well in water; but they must be picked while still in close bud – like tightly rolled umbrellas – and allowed to open in the warmth of indoors. A particularly good, lighter-colored, variety is the slightly scented 'Walter Butt'. This, if it is happy, can show even more flowers than the type. Recently the name of *Iris stylosa*, as the great botanist Desfontaine called it in 1798, and which is so elegantly descriptive of the plant with its long, slender style, has been officially changed to the more cumbersome *I. unguicularis*.

There is a white variety of *I. stylosa* which is rarely grown, and when it is, is displayed with great pride by its owner. But it is far less effective, and seems to be more easily damaged by wind and weather than the better-known mauve variety.

One of the most attractive of all species iris is the 'Little Widow', known as 'La Vedovina' in Italian gardens. Robert and Elizabeth Browning used to pick handfuls of this intriguing little flower in the Euganean hills, during the idyllic days they spent together in Asolo – for which Browning invented a special verb, 'asolare'. 'La Vedovina' was a favourite flower of Mr E. A. Bowles, who in *My Garden in Spring*, deplored the fact that the 'Little Widow' was not only suddenly told by the experts that she was not an iris at all, but that she had undergone a change of sex – from *Iris tuberosa* to *Hermodactylus tuberosus* – 'hermodactylus' because her roots looked like

89

Iris germanica 'Golden Alps'. Almost all iris need full sun and sharp drainage.

Hermes' fingers. However her roots look, it is the flowers of the 'Widow' iris that are unique. 'I love this weird little flower,' writes Mr Bowles, 'made up of the best imitation I have ever seen in vegetable tissues of dull green silk and black velvet – in fact it looks as if it had been plucked from the bonnet of some elderly lady of quiet taste in headgear ...'.

If *Iris tuberosa* (to give the plant the name it was known by for centuries) is the most attractive species iris, *Iris susiana* must be the most fascinating, with its almost sinister coloring of grey petals veined and streaked with black. 'One of the most singular of all flowers', as William Robinson described it, *I. susiana* has a reputation for being almost impossible to grow in conditions different to those of its native Asia Minor.

Mr Geoffrey Taylor, in his study of *Some Nineteenth-Century Gardeners*, quotes a typically purple paragraph by Reginald Farrer about this most difficult plant – and the similar iris of the oncocyclus group, the iris Thutmosis brought from Syria to Egypt:

> They are a doomed and lonely race of irreconcilable Troades in weeds of silken crêpe, sullenly and grandly unresigned to exile and captivity, passing out of their captor's hands in a last defiant blaze of dark and tragic magnificence. They are chief mourners in their own funeral pomps, wistful and sombre and royal in an unearthly beauty of their own, native to the Syrian hills that have seen the birth of gods, but strange and hostile to the cruder colder lands. They are the maidens that went down into hell with Persephone, and yearly in her train they return to make a carpet for her feet across the limestones of the Levant. But not for ours – their loyalty to their mistress holds only good in Syria; they do not recognize her in the rain-cloaks that she wears in the West, and lands of younger divinities shall never twice re-greet such children of mystery as these.

Iris unguicularis, *until recently known as* I. stylosa, *shows lavender, yellow-splashed flowers in earliest spring, and like most iris, it appreciates sharply drained soil.*

'In other words, but who would substitute those other words', comments Mr Taylor, 'The Oncocyclus irids may survive in your garden for one season, but not for two.' But for any gardener who has seen *Iris susiana*, well named the mourning iris, in full panoply of sombre flower, the temptation to try to grow it for himself is irresistible.

A British native iris is the Gladdon or Gladwyn iris – *Iris foetidissima*. This has unexciting flowers of a faded mauve and grows in wide-flung groups in several parts of the country, particularly on the Sussex Downs in southern England. There is a yellow form, *I. foetissima lutea*, which is more showy and makes a good plant for a corner in half shade in the wild garden. But it is not for their flowers that the discerning gardener grows the Gladdons – but for their spectacular seed capsules. These split open in autumn to reveal brilliant red seeds within. Sometimes the whole seed capsule remains intact on the plant throughout the winter, and can provide useful indoor decoration for months on end.

Pacific Coast Iris. Recently the attention of discerning gardeners, especially those with gardens on acid soil, has been drawn to the fascinating Pacific Coast species iris. These, unlike most iris, actually refuse to thrive in alkaline conditions, so they offer an opportunity for effective planting schemes in which iris can be combined with azaleas and rhododendrons. The Pacific Coast species are found not only in California (except in the Great Valley) but in Oregon and Washington too. There they are in beauty from March to June. A few of the best of the Pacific Coast iris are: *I. tenax*, which shows flowers of all the usual iris-colors and has leaf bases that are stained a rich red (I. N. Gabrielson in *Western American Alpines* thought '*I. tenax* ... the most appealing of all native iris ...'); *Iris hartwegii*; the large flowered *Iris munzii*,

LEFT Iris xiphium – *the Spanish iris, has been grown in Western gardens for centuries. Its flowers are either blue, violet, yellow or white, and the only care the plant needs is to be left undisturbed.*

Iris paradoxa – *a rare species iris from the Caucasus with flowers that are a deep amethyst overlaid with black silky hairs.*

which flourishes in Tulare County, California; *Iris fernaldii*, with cream colored flowers, which flourishes in the neighbourhood of the Petrified Forest; and the very popular Oregon iris, *I. innominata* with deep gold flowers.

The Pumila group. These are free flowering and easy to increase, and include some of the smallest of all iris, and some of the most beautiful, such as the richly scented blue 'Cyanea' and pretty 'Mist o' Pink'. It also includes one of the ugliest – *I. pumila gracilis*, an iris which is pathetically generous with its unattractive flowers – and in *My Garden in Spring* E. A. Bowles devastatingly describes these as 'about as lovely as the waistcoat of a defunct toad, being a pale buff bun-bag shade, mottled irregularly with smoky grey'.

After that it would be a courageous gardener who planted *I. pumila gracilis*, in spite of its misleading names (*pumila*, small – *gracilis*, graceful).

Japanese Iris. An impressive group of iris are those that originate in Japan – *Iris japonica* or *kaempferi*, after Engelbert Kaempfer (1651–1716), a German doctor who travelled in China, and wrote of the flora of Japan.

The Japanese iris, like the Californians, dislike lime – their favorite situation, and where they flower best, is beside water. In *Alpine and Bog Plants* Reginald Farrer set forth his strong ideas as to where they should be planted, and was of the firm opinion that they should be planted alone.

> A proof of the brilliant scornfulness inherent in the Japanese iris may be found in the undeniable fact that it will never tolerate being mixed with other plants.
> The Japanese iris has no place in the garden, no place in the companionship of the bog. It must have a tract to itself; it is always fatal and ridiculous to plant it in individual crowns among commoner neighbours. The Japanese themselves fully recognize this, and in all gardens, public or private, *Iris kaempferi* has a broad bed to itself away from other things. There is one exception, of course, to this rule, and that is that a lonely clump of the iris is allowed to look superb, to strike the keynote of the whole composition, when set by itself, in a commanding position on the edge of some lake, at the bend of some stream. But even here the rule holds good, and the effect depends on the complete isolation of the iris.

A design of Iris japonica *by a pool, painted on a screen by the Japanese artist Koria (1661–1716).*

92

Iris sibirica is another plant which is of the greatest value for growing by the side of an ornamental pond or by the side of a stream. *I. sibirica* needs the minimum of care and will grow imperturbably for years in the same position. All iris of the Siberian group present slender tufts of slim straight stems and foliage, and provide an architectural accent which contrasts well with the lower-growing rounder-shaped foliage of other waterside plants. Three excellent varieties are the large-flowered china-blue 'Perry's Blue', the creamy white 'Snow Queen' and the sky-blue darker-veined 'Dragon Fly'. Three newer names are the dusky violet 'Caesar's Brother', paler 'Cool Spring' and the excellent 'White Swirl'. The one drawback to the Siberian group of iris is their short flowering period, sometimes for only two weeks or less, and the small size of their flowers in comparison with the height of their stems. But this possible weakness is amply made up for by the plant's striking form throughout the spring and summer.

Bearded Iris. By far the largest and most highly-prized group of iris are those that flower in May and June – *Iris germanica*, the bearded iris, the flowers that make the glory of the garden in early summer. The bearded iris has been developed in the last quarter of a century, in form, quality and color, to give a whole range of spectacular new plants.

The new iris are utterly different, and for once, for hybridization does not always mean improvement, they are infinitely superior to the plants our fathers and mothers knew in their youth. Many of them are more strongly scented than before and their color range has been extended to include brilliant yellows and golds, sophisticated browns and bronzes, and a shade which once was unknown to iris – pale pink. The form of the flowers themselves has also been improved. Instead of loose, heavy falls, like a spaniel's ears, the falling petals of modern iris almost seem to dance, and are protected from heavy rain and wind by a central midrib as strong as wire. All this has happened quite lately. Sacheverell Sitwell writes in *Old Fashioned Flowers*:

> It may be that the iris fancier, owing to the comparative newness of his subject, has worked with something of the pristine enthusiasm of a hundred years ago. He has conformed, unconsciously, to the rules of taste. The wonderful color faculty of the iris, which possesses in its species, or primitives as they could be called, such depth and brilliance, such texture and translucency, made a sure guide, we may think, to the dormant proclivities of the flower. This is another instance, in process of proving before our eyes, of the superiority of first invention. It is nearly always true in questions of aesthetics, and never in matters of machinery, The last engine, or motor, or aeroplane, is always the best, until the next one is made. But in music, in painting, or in the art of the florist, which should have its place among the lesser arts of human hands, the first is nearly ever the best. Nothing that comes after is so good.

93

These are the names of some of the best of the newest iris:

Blue – 'Arabi Pasha', first raised by Gwendolyn Anley; 'Blue Ensign', with almost horizontal falls; 'Blue Sapphire', with ruffled petals.

White – 'Cleo', with chartreuse green lights and scented; 'Rosamund', veined with violet; 'Starshine', which has been described as 'Mother O' Pearl'; and 'Cliffs of Dover'.

Mauve – 'Deputé Nomblot', with smoky purple standards and deep plum falls; 'Maisie Low', a clear violet.

Pink – 'Alastor', a cyclamen pink; the blossom pink 'Cloud Cap'; 'Party Dress', pink and ruffled; the striking 'Pink Formal'; and 'Rose Garland'.

Yellow – 'Charmaize', chartreuse yellow with green lights; 'Solid Gold', with extra-large flowers; and the beautifully moulded 'Zantha'.

Brown and buff – the flaring, ruffled 'Russet Wings'; the autumn-tinted 'Sulgrave'; golden-brown 'Bill Brown'; and the copper-colored 'Bryce Canyon'.

There are a few almost black-bearded iris, such as the splendid 'Black Hills' and 'Black Forest' and, darkest of all, 'Black Taffeta'.

Tennyson precedes what must be some of the most often quoted words in all poetry – 'In the Spring, a young man's fancy lightly turns to thoughts of love' – with the lesser known line: 'In the Spring a livelier iris changes on the burnished dove ...'. And, so that their gardens may be the homes of 'livelier iris', careful growers must bear a few simple rules in mind. These apply to most iris but more especially to the bearded iris, which are the beauty of the border in May, just before the peonies, delphiniums and roses have taken over. *Planting.* New iris roots should be planted, or replanted, directly after they have flowered – in early July. If you wait until the time often recommended, they will have made foot-long new roots, and so will suffer a severe check. Second rule to remember – do not plant iris roots, or rhizomes, too deep. They should sit on top of the soil like boats on a lake. The old withered roots can be used to anchor them, and they will soon form new ones. Third rule – iris, of all plants, like good drainage, well-prepared soil, a 'feed' of good vegetable compost and a dressing of old mortar rubble. Fourth rule – all iris like to have their roots baked by the sun, so they should never be planted in shade. In time they will grow together into such a tight, waterproof mass that in some parts of Turkey peasants' shacks are roofed with iris – hence *Iris tectorum*, 'of the roofs'. But that is for shelter, not a show of flowers – and iris in the garden, when their rhizomes become too closely entangled, should be broken up and replanted; this may have to be done every three or four years.

Iris are occasionally still found growing on the roofs of houses in Japan – this follows a tradition that the Japanese were once forbidden to grow in their gardens any plants other than those ordered by the Emperor. As orris root played a vital part in making face powder, Japanese women got round the Imperial edict by growing iris – not in their gardens, but on their roofs.

White iris, such as Gudrun and White City have a very special appeal. These are growing, with silver-leaved plants, in the garden of sixteenth-century Hush Heath Manor in Kent.

Saints bring vases of lilies to the Virgin and the infant Jesus,

more lilies make the surrounding wreath. Luca Della Robbia (1400–82) Florence.

Lily

'The dying lily puts the rose to shame'

Of all flowers, after the rose, the lily has received most acclamation in literature. It seemed to Joseph Joubert that the lily had a soul; Shakespeare mentions the lily many times; Tennyson was obsessed with it. Lilies symbolize purity, chastity, pallor, and the ancient Royalty of France. To gild a lily is to attempt, foolishly, to improve on perfection. Oregon is the lily state – and in the United States in recent years, the lily has been most spectacularly developed.

An early reference in literature is in the Bible, in which, for once, the lily is mentioned more often than the rose, and in the Sermon on the Mount, Christ told his listeners: 'Consider the lilies of the field, how they grow: they toil not, neither do they spin: and yet ... Solomon in all his glory was not arrayed like one of these.' Though some think that the flowers referred to were not lilies, but tulips, which grow wild in the Holy Land; lilies do not. Or perhaps 'the lilies of the field' were asphodels, graceful but remote relations, and not particularly glorious ones.

One of the first mentions of the lily in England comes in Gerard's *Herball*, in which he tells us that in Latin the lily was known as Juno's Rose – *Rosa junonis* –

beautiful as it is reported, it came up of her milke that fell upon the ground. For the poets feigne that Hercules, who Jupiter had by Alcumena, was put to Juno's breast when she was asleepe: and after the sucking, there fell away abundance of milke, and that part was spilt in the heavens, and the other on the earthe; and that of this sprang the liley, and of the other the circle in the heavens called *Lacteus circulus* or the Milky Way or otherwise in English, Watling Street. Saint Basill in the explication of the 44th psalme, saith that no flower so lively sets forth the frailty of mans life as the

'Of all flowers, after the rose, the lily has received most acclamation in literature';
Lilium regale, *one of the easiest of lilies to grow.*

liley. It is called in High Dutch Weiss Gilgen, in Italian Giglio, in Spanish Lirio Blanco.

In Gerard's time (1545–1612) lilies were certainly widely cultivated in many gardens; the most popular variety being the Madonna, *L. candidum* (its descriptive name was given it by Virgil), a native plant of southern Europe. This is said to have been first grown in England in 1596, though it must have been known by sight from Italian paintings many years before that. In 1596, William Shakespeare would have been thirty-two, at the height of his powers. In that year he was engaged in writing *Romeo and Juliet*, and the first sight of a Madonna lily must have been inspiration indeed to someone who loved and felt for plants as Shakespeare did. Or it may have been the martagon – the Turk's Cap lily – which Shakespeare saw when he was a boy in Warwickshire, as there is a theory that the martagon, alone among lilies, is indigenous to England, as it is to northern Spain, Italy and Asia Minor.

Until the last century, there were only a few types of lily cultivated in Western gardens and it is remarkable in the annals of the flower that the appearance of new varieties in Western gardens always coincides with the discovery and development of distant and little-known parts of the world.

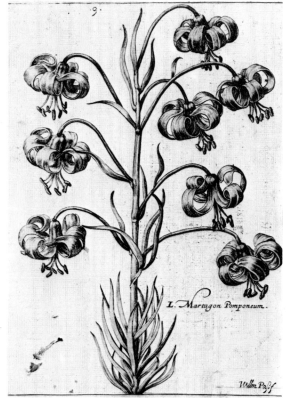

LEFT Lilium aurateum, *the giant golden-rayed Japanese lily, in the garden of Glenveagh Castle in Co. Donegal.*

Lilium martagon – *the Turk's Cap lily – from the shape of its flowers – may possibly be indigenous to England. From Crispin de Passe's* Hortus Floridus *1614.*

99

William Goldring, seventy years ago, wrote describing the introduction of new lilies from all over the world to cultivation.

> We owe much to the men of the last century, to those especially who, in the early 'forties and 'fifties down to the present time, explored the wilds of California, or the garden treasures of Japan which had existed unknown to Western peoples, probably for centuries. These men, at the risk of their health and often their lives, did their utmost to enrich our gardens with the flower treasures of other countries. Not only have botanists, who explored and collected for the sake of science and commerce, added to our Lily treasures, but also all sorts of conditions of men, including the opposite extremes of soldiers and missionaries, devoted themselves to this interesting work.

Today it may be taken for granted that the four quarters of the globe have almost been ransacked for the finest forms of lily, just as they have been for so many other plants. And with the iron and bamboo curtains so uncompromisingly drawn, it is unlikely that the foothills of the People's Republic of Ulan Bator or the slopes of Outer Mongolia will yield us any startling new species for many years to come. It is ironical that over a century ago, European botanists such as the Dutch Philipp Franz Von Siebold, could travel at will through Russia and China in peaceful search for new plants. Today, such journeys would be hazardous, if feasible at all.

But for gardeners in search of new lilies for their gardens, one light still shines, and that from the West – from Oregon – which well deserves its name of the Lily State. Here Jan de Graaff – great-grandson of Cornelis de Graaff, who was the first of the family to hybridize lilies in Holland in 1790 – bought the Oregon bulb farms in 1934. This is now the most important lily breeding nursery in the world, and has provided some magnificent new strains.

The Culture of Lilies. The gardener who wants to grow lilies must remember that the zone in which lilies grow wild is a narrow one, bounded by Siberia and Canada to the north, and the Nilgherry hills of India to the south. It is a belt which stretches from Japan, through China, northern India, and central Russia, to Canada and California – so to grow even a small selection of lilies successfully, the cultivator must do his best to reproduce in his garden in Kent or Connecticut the soil conditions of those widely different countries. He must also bear in mind three all-important cultural hints which are often forgotten, even by experienced gardeners. The first is that lily bulbs, unlike tulip or daffodil bulbs which are packed like onions in tight moisture-retaining skins, are dressed in scales. On no account must these be allowed to dry out. Sir Thomas Hammer, writing in the mid-eighteenth century, knew what he was about: 'They all love a good rich earth, and not wett, and as all skaly rootes, endure not to bee long kept out of the earth ...'.

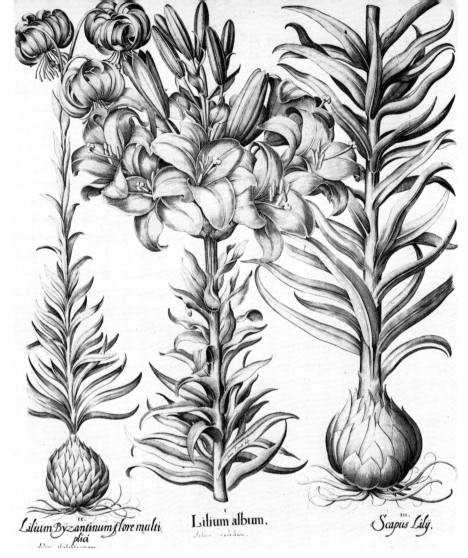

II.
Lilium Byzantinum flore multi
plici
.

Lilium album.

III.
Scapus Lily.

An engraving of Lilium byzantium (chalcedonicum), L. album (candidum) *and a lily bulb showing its scaly covering. From* Hortus Eystettensis, Nuremburg 1613.

The second point for would-be lily growers to remember is that many lilies are stem rooting and so must be planted at least six inches deep in well drained soil. There are exceptions to this rule (*L. candidum* and *L. giganteum* are two) but, generally, it is best to plant all lilies deep.

Third, lilies like their roots in shade, their heads in the sun, and Victoria Sackville-West liked to see the lilies in her garden 'piercing up between low grey foliaged plants such as artemisia, southernwood, and santolina, and rising above some clouds of gypsophila, for there is something satisfying in the contrasting shapes of the domed bushes and the belfry-like tower of the lily; an architectural harmony' – which is not only aesthetically pleasing, but sound gardening practice.

The lilies listed below are a few of the plants which the author, in his gardening experience, has found the most rewarding. None is very rare and all, with care, can be grown in the average garden.

Everyone's favorite lily must be the Madonna – *L. candidum*. This would seem to be the liliest of all lilies, the flower of the paintings of Fra Lippo Lippi and the Italian masters. *Lilium candidum* is a paragon of beauty, purity, scent and, if any flower can be, of soul. It has an endearing quality of succeeding better in village gardens, probably because it is seldom disturbed there than in larger, more cultivated borders, and Victoria Sackville-West refers to 'the notorious inverted snobbishness of the Madonna Lily' which apparently refuses to flourish except in cottage gardens. Lately it has been established,

Lilium candidum *drawn by Leonardo Da Vinci (1452–1519) from the collection at Windsor Castle and reproduced by gracious permission of H.M. the Queen.*

unfortunately, that *L. candidum* is a bearer of the dread botritis – the lily fungus which can kill a healthy clump of lilies in a week. So, lovely as they are, it may be advisable for the amateur gardener to eschew Madonna lilies, and concentrate on the easier and healthier kinds, from which there are many to choose.

L. chalcedonicum is a bright scarlet lily, and comes from Asia Minor. Gerard reports that it was sent from Constantinople 'among other bulbs of rare and daintie flowers – by Master Harbran, Ambassador there, unto my honourable good Lord and Master the Lord Treasurer of England, who bestowed them on me for my garden'. It was the parent, with *L. candidum*, of *L. testaceum*. The cross is believed to have come about by chance, for *L. candidum* is notoriously difficult to breed from, and has no other descendants.

L. testaceum is the Nankeen lily – outstandingly beautiful and of the easiest cultivation. Its color – a clear apricot – is unlike any other shade in the lily world. It grows gracefully to the same height as a martagon, but though its flowers are similarly shaped they smell more sweetly. Like *L. candidum* it is not stem rooting, and so should not be planted too deep.

Next on the list of the author's preferences is *L. auratum*, the giant golden-rayed lily from Hokkaido in Japan. First introduced into Western Europe in 1862, by that great nurseryman John Veitch, this has been one of the best loved of lilies ever since. Edward Hyams, in his definitive book *Lilies*, which he wrote in collaboration with the great Jan de Graaff and which is a mine of information, writes of its flowers that they 'are neither Turk's Caps, nor bells, nor trumpets but great flat wide open starry bowls'.

L. auratum is quite distinct from any other variety, both in splendor and size of flower, coloring and scent, but it is not the easiest to cultivate. It demands a well-drained, sandy soil, which is full of peat to retain moisture. And it likes to be planted where it can be sheltered from cold winds early in the year, and hot sun, when its flowers – and what flowers! – are opening in July. Among the recently raised descendants of *L. auratum*, both beautiful lilies, are *Lilium auratum var pictum* and *Lilium auratum* 'Crimson Queen'.

L. brownii is a splendid plant, and particularly aptly named. (It was called after Dr Robert Brown, the English botanist.) *L. brownii*'s characteristic leaves are suffused with brown, and its flowers, while still in bud, are a rich brown, too. When they open they are trumpet-shaped, with strong waxy petals. *L. brownii* was one of the first lilies to reach Europe from China (1835), and its only fault is its almost total lack of scent. This did not deter Sir Herbert Maxwell, who wrote so sensitively about all plants, in his devotion to *Lilium brownii*. He thought it '... the loveliest of all lilies – relying for effect not upon brilliant colour but on a quiet scheme of ivory white and purplish maroon, punctuated by heavy anthers of rich russet. It is the perfect form of the flower that makes it priceless ...'

If *L. brownii* came from the Far East, one of the first lilies to reach Europe from the Far West was *L. canadensis*, the Canadian lily. This differs from most lilies in having rhizomes instead of roots, a root formation rather like that of an iris, and it is one of the few lilies which prefer a damp situation. The flowers of *L. canadensis* vary from a rich red to pale yellow, and are funnel-shaped and pendant.

In the space of a few pages, it is impossible for the writer to give a list of more than a few of his preferred lilies. But any devoted lily grower's favorites must include *L. croceum*, the Orange Lily which is a native of Switzerland and the cool northern provinces of Italy. At one time the Orange lily was much planted in Ulster, for it flowers in July, and so was popular at the annual celebrations of the Battle of the Boyne by the Orangemen on 12 July.

Another outstanding flower is *Lilium henryi* (called after Augustine Henry, who sent it to Kew from central China in 1890). This is a great lily which has always been popular, thanks to its strength of growth, general good humor and toleration of bad weather. The dark orange of its flowers is particularly well set off by the extraordinarily rich green of its foliage. Once planted in a situation that it likes, half shade and sheltered from the wind, *L. henryi* goes from strength to strength each year. Its bulbs, grown under ideal conditions, will, in due course, measure eight inches across. It is a parent, with *L. sargentiae*, of the applauded Aurelian strains which were raised in 1934 by a great French botanist, E. Debray of Orleans, and named *aureliense* after his native city (Aurelia, in Latin). It is from the Aurelian lilies that Jan de Graaff hybridized many of the great modern lilies, among them the transcendent golden 'Clarion', which well merits Victoria Sackville-West's description of a lily, 'gallant as a ship in sail'.

L. longiflorum comes originally from the Ryukyu Islands, and until the entire lily crop was wiped out by disease, was much grown in Bermuda. In the author's youth, Easter or Bermudan lilies, as they were then called, were used by the thousand for party decoration, and in the 'thirties, white lilies, with blue Echinops Ritro, the Globe thistle, arranged in square glass accumulator jars, were as popular as floral decoration as hosta leaves and *Alchemilla mollis* are today. *L. longiflorum*, as classic a lily as the Madonna, with its perfectly proportioned flowers with delicious scent, is still an appropriate flower for any occasion.

L. martagon (the word comes from the Turkish *martagan*, a special form of turban adopted by Sultan Muhammed I) is sometimes thought, as has already been noted, to be an English native; but the Turk's Cap lily is more likely to have been brought by early travellers from Italy, Spain or Turkey. It is a tall graceful lily, with many small flowers in pyramidal clusters, each with reflexed petals, which give the individual flowers their likeness to a turban. In color the martagon is usually a rich freckled purple, an unusual mahogany red or waxy white. All, unfortunately, are disagreeably scented. Its hybrids include the robust Paisley strain, also raised in Oregon by Jan de Graaff.

104   A fine pair of lilies, *L. monadelphum* and *szovitzianum*, comes from the

Caucasus. They are yellow, with stamens tipped with golden anthers and petals that are spotted. *L. szovitzianum*, a popular lily among connoisseurs, has larger flowers than the type, and scarlet anthers. When established, *L. monadelphum* is one of the earliest lilies to flower, and sometimes comes into bloom at the end of May – but it is a slow starter and new plants often show no top growth at all their first summer. Of these two flowers, Reginald Farrer once wrote:

> The twin lilies, long confused, monadelphum and szovitzianum ... are very splendid people, far too seldom grown, very stalwart and perennial, when once established in good light loam, in the companionship of trees or bushes. In style they are tall and leafy, with abundance of brilliant, big yellow flowers, like very large canary-coloured martagons. They bloom early, too, before the other great lilies are showing bud.

Lilium speciosum, from Japan, has always been admired, though it is not one of the author's favorite lilies. There seems to be something unsympathetic about its coloring – white spotted with rose pink and crimson. A frequently grown variety is called Melpomene and one does not know what the Muse of Tragedy can have done to have such an ordinary looking lily named after her.

Tiger lilies (*L. tigrinum*) come from the Far East and grow wild in Korea. They are the lilies that everyone has known from childhood. One comes startlingly to life in *Alice Through the Looking Glass*. ' "Oh, Tiger lily", said Alice to one which was waving gracefully about in the wind, "I *wish* you could talk" ... "We can talk", said the Tiger lily, "When there is anybody worth talking to".' When Alice has got over her surprise, she asks 'almost in a whisper, "Can all the flowers talk?" "As well as you can", said the Tiger lily, "and a great deal louder".'

Lilium speciosum, *with flowers that are strongly scented and sometimes flushed with carmine, growing in tubs in the garden at Nymans in Sussex. This species was introduced from Japan in 1832.*

Lilium monadelphum
*is tall and leafy
with brilliant yellow
flowers. It is slow
to start into growth,
but once established
in good light soil is
a faithful perennial.*

RIGHT Lilium regale
*border a path
in a London garden.*

106

Last on the author's list of lilies is one that made a great impression on him when he was little older than Alice. This is the largest of all lilies, *Lilium giganteum*, and he first saw it growing in the woodland garden at Newton Don, in Scotland, many years ago. Everything – almost – is splendid about this glorious plant: the glossy heart-shaped leaves, the white green-tinged flowers, the noble height which is sometimes ten feet or more. But *Lilium giganteum* has one fault which the discriminating eye of that great gardener, the late Edward Bunyard, was quick to notice. Lady Rosse describes the incident in some notes she wrote on her family's garden at Nymans in Sussex:

> My father was particularly proud of his display of *Lilium giganteum;* and one day, shortly before the war, when it was at its zenith, Mr Bunyard, that fascinating epicure and gardener, was staying with us. There was no greater connoisseur or enthusiast than he, whether of plants, food or wine of quality; no one more appreciative, illuminating, or sympathetic to entertain. But he was choosey. After a day of lavish praise, my father and I were a little nettled when he strode past our lilies without a word, rather obviously so. 'Won't you admire our giganteum lilies?' said I. 'No, I cannot bear to look at them', he answered, 'they are like very beautiful women, utterly ruined by thick ankles'. How I wish I could get that harsh judgment of this lovely flower out of my mind!

And it is true that the base of the stems of *Lilium giganteum* can measure four or five inches across, as strong and stiff as steel. But when its 'ankles' are hidden by ferns, *Lilium giganteum*, growing in woodland, its spire of flower towering overhead, is an impressive sight indeed.

The Lily in Legend. As the Tiger lily comes to life in *Alice Through the Looking Glass*, another lily comes romantically to life in Grandville's *Les Fleurs*

Tiger lilies – Lilium tigrinum – *as seen by Walter Crane in one of the illustrations for* Flora's Feast, *published in 1889.*

When lilies, turned to Tigers, blaze
Amid the garden's tangled maze

Animées, and becomes a very grand person indeed – the Queen of France. But before she reaches that elevated state, she is depicted as a simple lily, living 'aux bords d'un lac solitaire, dans un petit castel' with only a white ermine for company. The lily gives shelter to a storm-bound huntsman who falls in love with her, and woos her so ardently that, in telling her story, the lily sighs 'Je n'étais plus fleur, j'étais femme. Ma faiblesse était celle de ma sexe', and succumbs to the huntsman's plea. Her lover turns out, in the best fairy-story style, to be a prince, the future King of France, and the lily, now a woman, has to leave her little 'castel' and go to live in a grand but dusty palace. So dusty that her old friend, the ermine, although accorded 'ses grandes entrées', does not like visiting her there for fear of getting dirty.

> How I regret the day when I was the symbolic flower of innocence – messengers from Heaven would present me to those to whom they brought good news. ... In those happy days I lived on air, on sun-shine and on light. My nights were passed in contemplation of the stars ... but now ...'.

And the Lily-queen ends her story in tears.

The lily in Grandville's story was surely *Lilium candidum*, the first of all lilies, the flower of the Madonna and the royal lily of France. It is the flower which Maurice Baring certainly had in mind when in his poem *Phèdre* he wrote, 'the dying lily puts the rose to shame'; and it is the flower of which Longfellow was thinking when he wrote of Giotto's Tower as 'the lily of Florence, blossoming in stone'. The two loveliest of flowers are always compared – the rose of England and the lily of France. Their place in the garden is unchallenged. The author is grateful to Edward Hyams for introducing him to yet another instance in literature of the rose and lily mentioned in one breath. 'Walafrid Strabo (1809–49) abbot of the monastery at Reichenau in Germany,' writes Edward Hyams, 'is very eloquent on the subject of roses and lilies, which he brackets together in a curious and pleasing antithesis:

> Better and sweeter are they than all the other plants and rightly called the flower of flowers. Yes, roses and lilies, the one for virginity with no sordid toil, no warmth of love, but the glow of their own sweet scent, which spreads further than their rival roses, but once bruised or crushed turns all to rankness. Therefore roses and lilies for our church, one for the symbol in his hand. Pluck them, O maiden, roses for war and lilies for peace, and think of that Flower of the stem of Jesse. Lilies His words were and the hallowed acts of His pleasant life, but His death re-dyed the roses.

These lines, which occur in a poem entitled *The Little Garden*, make a fitting ending to this chapter on lilies.

Magnolia grandiflora 'Goliath' is the most spectacular variety of magnolia originating in *America. Its glossy green leaves – rusty felted beneath – are very handsome.*

Magnolia

Most beautiful of flowering trees – Magnolias originate in America and the Orient

Who was the French doctor who had the extraordinary honor of having magnolias named after him, and why? Pierre Magnol was a respected horticulturist who was born in 1638 and died in 1715. For many years he was the director of the botanical garden at the pleasant town of Montpellier in France. But it was not only for his services to horticulture that Linnaeus named magnolias after the good doctor in 1753. It was because Pierre Magnol 'conçut l'idée féconde du classement des plantes par famille'. Fecund indeed, for the whole structure and theory of Linnaeus' method of nomenclature of plants stems from Doctor Magnol's thought.

Before being re-christened, magnolias were known as Laurel-Tulip Trees, and they originate either in the United States or in the Far East. The American magnolias, which have grown in European gardens since the early eighteenth century, are, generally speaking, less satisfactory plants in northern gardens than their oriental cousins, as their natural habitat is in the southern states, where they flower very early in the spring. In colder gardens, they are liable to be cut by March and April frosts. But it is the habit of magnolias from China and Japan to flower later, which gives their flowers, in colder climates, a better chance of survival.

Oriental Magnolias. In China, magnolias were never regarded with the veneration and affection that we are told the high-class Chinese had for tree peonies – indeed, though it is said that magnolias were cultivated for centuries in China, it seems that it was not for the beauty of their flowers that they were grown, but for the supposed aphrodisiac quality of their powdered bark.

The Asiatic magnolias are some of the finest plants growing in gardens today, and one of the first to be imported was *Magnolia denudata*. This

110

Magnolia denudata, *showing its white flowers on almost leafless branches.*

shows its flowers on naked branches in early April. It is one of the several plants that we owe to Sir Joseph Banks, Captain Cook's friend and patron. Originally called *M. conspicua*, it was first grown in England in 1789, and it is one of the fastest growing of the magnolias. Chief danger to *M. denudata*, or Yulan Tree (it was first discovered in the Yulan hills of China), is an early spell of warm weather. Should this happen, as it sometimes does, in late February or early March the unsuspecting tree rushes into bloom, only to have its flowers spoiled by frost or high wind a few days later. And once the flowers of *M. denudata* have been frosted, any chance of a later show of blossom is lost for that season. But when it does flower, there can surely be no more beautiful sight, for its pure ivory-colored, heavily-scented flowers are perfectly displayed and in striking contrast with its leafless branches. The Yulan Tree flowers when quite young, an advantage for gardeners who do not want – or have the time – to wait.

A hybrid of *M. denudata* is one of the most famous of all magnolias – *soulangeana*, a cross with the lily-flowered *M. liliflora*. *Soulangeana* was raised, in his garden at Froment near Paris, by Etienne Soulange-Bodin. Soulange-Bodin (1774–1846), having trained to be a doctor, became, under the Empire, Chef du Cabinet to Prince Eugène. It was probably due to this connection that after the death of Prince Eugène's mother, the Empress Joséphine, Soulange-Bodin was made curator of the gardens of Malmaison. But his fame, to gardeners, will always be the fact that he raised the splendid magnolia which bears his name. If one could only plant one magnolia, *soulangeana* it should be. It lacks the almost incredible purity and whiteness of *M. denudata*, its sire, as it has inherited some of *M. liliflora's* purple coloring.

But it flowers a little later and so, as Victoria Sackville-West wrote in *More for Your Garden:* 'Seldom suffers from frost unless it has extremely bad luck at the end of April, or when those three mischievous ice-saints hold their festival in the middle of May.' Another hybrid of *M. denudata* is *M. lennei*. This can make a good-sized spreading tree, branching low down and bearing, quite early in its long life and while still quite small in stature, deep purple cup-shaped flowers. It is called after Herr Lenne, gardener to the King of Prussia.

Magnolia campbellii from Bhutan, that remote Himalayan kingdom on the very roof of the world, unlike *M. lennei*, is not a tree for impatient gardeners to plant. It seldom flowers before it is twenty years old, and when it does, it shows its blossoms so early in the year that they are often frosted. But when all goes well *campbellii* makes a tall tree, often twenty feet high, with its branches dressed overall with sculptured rose-pink flowers, and it provides one of the most beautiful sights in the gardening world. There are several fine specimens of this exquisite tree in the garden at Nymans in Sussex, and also at Leonardslee. Both gardens, open to the public for the greater part of the year, *vâlent bien le détour*, to quote the Michelin guide, and at no time is the garden pilgrim more generously rewarded than when the season has been kind and *M. campbellii* is in full rosy flower against the blue Sussex sky.

M. stellata – the starry flowered – is a magnolia from Japan, where it flowers in the wild in the woods which clothe the slopes of Fuji-Yama. It was first introduced to Europe via America in 1877, and has several good qualities – it flowers while quite young, and though it grows painfully slowly, achieves a picturesque and mature look quite early in life. The many-petalled flowers of *M. stellata* are sweetly scented, and there is an attractive pink variety, *rosea*, found near Kyoto by Mr Charles Maries, who collected so many good plants for the Veitches. Though the flowers of *M. stellata* are often damaged by frost, unlike most magnolias it seems to have the ability to go on producing new ones; so the yearly crop is never entirely lost.

Both *M. stellata* and *stellata rosea* have a passion for peat, and the more peat that can be dug into the soil at planting time, the happier they will be.

Mr E. A. Bowles, in his *My Garden in Spring*, recalls how he once had to prune a bunch of *M. stellata* which was growing too low over a rock garden path. It seemed a dreadful thing to do, 'but if done early in the season, just after the flowers have gone, the vigor of the new growths resulting from air and space and an extra allowance of sap quite makes up for the removals, and the increase ... adds to the beauty and size of the specimen'.

Oddly enough, for the scent of *Magnolia stellata* is its great charm, its fragrance was for years lost on Mr Bowles, until, 'in 1912, I realized for the first time how strongly scented the flowers are; a delicious whiff of beanfields reached my nose and set me sniffing around to locate its odor, and I tracked it down to the magnolia'. The pruning incident taught Mr Bowles that it is not only the flowers of the magnolia that are scented.

The slow growing Magnolia stellata *makes an attractive shrub of medium size and bears its starry white flowers in earliest spring.*

The bruised bark emits quite a different scent; you might shut your eyes and think Homocea was being used to touch some injured spot. One day when sawing off a rather large bough to clear the legs of the bush I was struck by the resemblance of the scent of the wood to the peppery fragrance peculiar to wooden Japanese cabinets, and I can believe it possible that magnolia wood may be employed in their construction.

Magnolia mollicomata (the name means soft-tufted, for its early shoots are downy), is a favorite magnolia. It flowers later than *M. campbellii*, always an advantage for magnolias in northern gardens, and it flowers at an earlier age, sometimes even in its twelfth year, from seed. But that is at Bodnant, the great garden in north Wales where three generations of Aberconways have had eighty years to create one of the great gardens of the world. Reginald Farrer describes *M. mollicomata* growing in the lofty valleys near Hpimaw in upper Burma, where it flowers and flourishes at a height of 9000 ft.

It abounds in the higher jungle glades going up to Hpimaw pass and down on the other side, in China. No trees bear flowers of the same shade, and the pure whites are more beautiful than the rest.

Before leaving the glorious Asiatic magnolias to describe the less spectacular North American ones, one more should be mentioned, *Magnolia parviflora* (the small-flowered) from Korea. This is a tree which should find a place in every connoisseur's garden, for it seems to have every quality. Its small stature, seldom reaching four feet, lacquered dark green leaves, and miniature flowers, each one centred with a bosse of crimson stamens, make it completely irresistible. Unfortunately, *M. parviflora* is not quite hardy, so should be planted on a sheltered spot in peat-enriched soil, but it rewards this care with a fine show of flowers in May, followed by the occasional blossom all through the summer. It is also called *M. sieboldii* after Philipp Franz Von Siebold (1796–1866) who has had his name given to many excellent plants from Japan and the Far East, *Clematis sieboldii*, among them. *Magnolia parviflora*, or *sieboldii*, was discovered growing in the wild in Korea, in 1865.

American magnolias. Magnolias from North America have been grown in Europe for longer than those from the Orient. Of these the most impressive tree by far is *Magnolia grandiflora:* and there has always been some doubt when this fine tree first reached Europe.

Mr Neil Treseder, who grows many fine magnolias in his celebrated nursery near Truro in Cornwall, and is an authority on the tree, is of the opinion that the first specimen was a young tree which was planted in a garden in Nantes in 1711. This tree became famous as the Maillardière magnolia, and it had an eventful and interesting history, which Mr Treseder discovered in the Nantes *Journal of Historical Research* for the year 1849. A naval officer, it seems, brought the magnolia over from Louisiana – then a French colony – and gave it to the owner of the manor of La Maillardière, René Darquistade, who was Mayor of Nantes in 1735. Mr Treseder takes up the story.

> The date of this original introduction was thought to be 1731 but this report sets out to prove that it was, in fact, as early as 1711, the young tree having been grown for twenty years in the orangery at La Maillardière without flowering. By this time it had grown too large for the greenhouse and the gardener would have destroyed it in his master's absence had not his wife intervened and persuaded him to let her replant it near the mansion beside the dove-cote, where it would be sheltered from the north winds.
>
> Although the gardener was convinced, as most people were at that time, that plants from the New World could not succeed in the open in that climate, he reluctantly gave in to his wife's pleadings and let her replant it in the place which she had suggested.
>
> A few years later it commenced to flower and details of the beauty of its great blossoms and their delightful perfume spread far and wide so that it was visited each season by botanists and horticulturists from all over Europe. (*Royal Horticultural Society Journal*, 8–68.)

Magnolias were originally known as Laurel-Tulip Trees, and originate either in America or the Far East. M. grandiflora, *an American native, flowers in late summer.*

Magnolia conspicua

Pl. 79.

Magnolia Campbellii HOOK. F. ET THOMS.
Sikkim Himalaya (Fleur nr.)

ILLUST. HORTICOLE.

LEFT Magnolia campbellii *originates in Bhutan and seldom flowers before it is twenty years old.*

LEFT Magnolia conspicua, *(synonym for* M. denudata*) bears its flowers in early spring on its still leafless branches.*

RIGHT *A magnolia, with a carpet of fallen petals beneath, and an ilex for background at Nymans in Sussex.*

Years later, during the revolutionary wars and the rising in La Vendée, the famous magnolia of the Maillardière was damaged by gunfire and by being partially burned and smothered with lime rubble (the worst mulch for magnolia) from falling masonry. Mr Treseder then notes that the gardeners of Nantes realized what a botanical treasure they had nearly lost and efforts, happily successful, were made to propagate the tree by layering. Thanks to this, Magnolia La Maillardière was saved to flower in French gardens for generations. The original tree, veteran of La Vendée, survived its ordeal and lived on for another sixty glorious years. It was still flowering in 1848.

In the wild, a tree of *M. grandiflora* can attain a height of 100 feet, but in gardens it is usually planted in the shelter of a wall: and how many old red brick façades are embellished with its shining dark leaves and scented goblets, growing upwards to the eaves! Even without the protection of a wall, and in the open if the garden is in the warmer parts of country, *M. grandiflora* can reach an imposing height and scent the air for yards around it with its flowers in July.

A magnificent hybrid raised from *Magnolia grandiflora* is *M. grandiflora exoniensis*, the popular and widely planted Exmouth variety. If Mississippi is the magnolia state of America, Devon might be described as the magnolia county of England, so well do magnolias grow in its gentle climate. The

LEFT *Magnolia denudata, the Yulan Tree, has flowers which bloom on the naked branches. Imported in 1789, it was one of the earliest oriental magnolias to reach Europe. A fast grower, it flowers early and is often spoiled by frost.*

Magnolias were originally known as Laurel-Tulip Trees. They were re-named after the botanist Pierre Magnol (1638–1715) by Linnaeus.

LEFT *The soulangeana variety of magnolia commemorates Etienne Soulange-Bodin (1774– 1846) curator of the gardens of Malmaison. 'If one could only plant one magnolia, soulangeana it should be.'*

Exmouth variety of *M. grandiflora* is an altogether rewarding plant, flowering while quite young and for many months every summer. Like the 'Mrs Sinkins' pink which figures on the coat of arms of Slough, *M. grandiflora* is shown on the arms of the city of Exmouth. This distinction was granted by Letters Patent in 1947. The coat of arms is surmounted by a crest of a castellated town. On either side are branches and flowers of magnolias. Exmouth's motto is *Mare ditat flores decorant* (The sea gives riches – the flowers decorate).

The Exmouth variety of magnolia both enriches and decorates the garden of Michael Haworth Booth, a connoisseur of shrubs and trees, who describes the tree in his book *Effective Flowering Shrubs*, as having:

> large, rather pale green, shiny leaves, foxy-red beneath, ... flowering when quite young and, indeed, at all times with remarkable freedom. In my old garden a plant of 'Exmouth' had grown up to 20 feet and produced hundreds of flowers before a seedling form of the common type planted near had not grown above 6 feet or ever produced a flower. ...

Magnolia acuminata is called the Cucumber Tree, from the shape of its rarely-borne fruit, and there is a very fine specimen in the park at Syon, near London. *M. acuminata* is not a tree to plant for its flowers, which are small, poor, and a dirty yellow. But it plays an important part in the magnolia story, as it is used as the stock on which many of the finer species are grafted.

Cultural Notes. Gardeners planning to plant magnolias must always remember that they are woodland trees, and in the wild they grow in half-shade and shelter provided by taller trees. Magnolias, especially the Chinese varieties, like rhododendrons, much appreciate a rich leafy woodland soil. The ground where they are to grow must therefore be well prepared, and have leaf mould and peat added to it. And it is important to provide all magnolias, especially in their early growing years, with a thick mulch of dead leaves to protect and feed their roots. In the wild this would naturally happen every year when the leaves of surrounding trees fall. In gardens, where magnolias are often planted in turf or in borders which are kept clear of fallen leaves, they do not receive this natural nourishment. And yet we are disappointed if they do not produce a fine show of flowers every spring. Under most garden conditions, if magnolias flower poorly it is because they are half starved and, as Michael Haworth Booth observes, 'rather than die the tree husbands its resources. At the best a bad habit of intermittent flowering is initiated. Feed well, then, and regularly; prune to induce a shapely sapling ... and keep the soil over the roots mulched at all times with leaves, like the forest floor.'

One of the most beautiful gardens in the world is in South Carolina, close to Charleston. It is quite simply called Magnolia Gardens, and is famous not only for its magnolias, but also for its very colorful azaleas.

Peonia wittmaniana *as shown in the* Botanical Register *for 1836. Reginald Farrer acclaimed it as 'a* rarity – a herbaceous species with big sulphur yellow flowers'.

Peony

Peonies are said to take their name from a successful doctor in Greek legend

The French for peony is 'pivoine' – the German, unimaginatively, 'pfingstrose' (Whitsun Rose) – and the Chinese, 'Sho-Yo' (the beautiful), and it was from China that the most magnificent variety of all, the tree peony, was first sent to Europe.

How did the peony, centuries ago, achieve its mellifluous name? There is a legend that the name derives from that of Paeon, who was a young pupil of the God of Medicine, Asclepias. Paeon, it seems, while walking on the slopes of Mount Olympus, was told of a mysterious root growing there. His informant was the pregnant Leto, mistress of Zeus; Leto, the Goddess of Fertility, was known as Kourotrophos ('The carer for young men') and the root was one that she must have found useful, as it had the power of palliating the pains of women in childbirth. Once in possession of the root, Paeon's success as a doctor was assured; so much so that his mentor, Asclepias, became jealous and threatened to kill him. To save her protégé's life – did she not 'care for young men'? – Leto, now safely delivered of twins (Artemis and Apollo, no less), interceded with her lover, Zeus, who turned Paeon into a plant. Perhaps Zeus felt safer with the enterprising Paeon out of the way. Hence peony – from, as Gerard tells us, 'that excellent physician of the same name, who first found out and taught the knowledge of this herbe unto posteritie'.

Since the earliest times peony roots and seeds have been prescribed for pregnant women; Dioscorides recommended them. The plant he described was almost certainly the European native peony, *P. officinalis*.

Later, in Banckes' *Herbal*, the peony is recommended as being good for women in diverse sicknesses:

TOP Peonia obovata *originates in Siberia, has white (or rose-purple) flowers with bosses of gold filaments.*
BOTTOM *A tree peony in the famous American garden at Winterthur in Delaware, where there is a fine collection of the new hybrids raised by the late Professor Saunders.*

Peony seed when it is black – it makyth... deliverance of the child in the womb, and at every time when she shall use to drink it, she must drink fifteen seeds at one time. Also, for a man or woman who has the falling sicknesse [epilepsy] eat it and drink it with wine, also hang the root about his neck and it will save him without doubt within fifteen days. ...

So from the earliest days peonies have been cultivated, if not for their flowers, then for the medicinal value of their roots and seeds. The jolly 'Brew wif' in the *Vision Concerning Piers Plowman*, written by William Langland in 1362, tempted Gloton from his church-going, and boasted, in those days of expensive spices, that she had 'pepper and Peony seed and a pound of garlic and a farthings worth of fennel seed for fasting days' – an offer Gloton was unable to refuse.

Both Gerard and Parkinson have words for the peony. John Gerard writes of it growing well near Gravesend in Kent and quotes Apuleius as saying ...

that the seeds or graines of Peionie shine in the night time like a candle, and that plenty of it is in the night season found out and gathered by the shepheards. ... Moreover, it is set downe by the said Author, that of necessitie it must be gathered in the night; for if any man shall pluck off the fruit in the day time, being seene of the Wood-pecker, he is in danger to lose his eies. The like fabulous tale hath been set forth of mandrake. But all these things be most vaine and frivolous: for the root of peionie, as also the mandrake, may be removed at any time of the yeare, day or houre whatsoever.

Parkinson, writing half a century later than Gerard, is more down to earth. No 'vaine and frivolous' tales for him. And he dismisses *Peonia officinalis* as being 'so frequent in every garden if not through every country that it is almost labour in vain to describe it'. But he admits to the flower being 'endenizened in our gardens where we cherish them for the beauty and delight of their goodly flowers as well as for their physical virtues'. But after that he has done with peonies – and he certainly does not linger over his descriptions of them, as he does over other flowers. Perhaps he just did not like them, and in his days the raw red *P. officinalis* was about the only peony grown, except, perhaps, for *P. corallina* about which, had he seen it, Parkinson might have been more enthusiastic; for the pink *P. corallina* (syn. *P. mascula*) though not a native, might possibly have been growing, in Parkinson's day, on the English mainland as it did on the remote island of Steep Holm in the estuary of the River Severn, in the west of England, where it was found in 1803. Its discovery was a great event in the botanical world. 'Here', records Geoffrey Grigson, in *The Englishman's Flora*, 'was a plant new to the British flora –

which lived in this one unique isolated station, Steep Holm,' which, according to William Lisle Bowles:

> Abrupt and high and desolate and cold
>   and bleak uplifts
> Its barren brow – barren, but on its steep
> One native flower is seen, the peony
> One flower which smiles in sunshine or in storm
> There sits companionless, but yet not sad.

Whether the lonely yet smiling peony was a true native to Britain is uncertain. It may be that it was a survival from the physic garden of an order of monks who are known to have lived on Steep Holm in the Middle Ages.

Shakespeare mentions peonies in the fourth act of *The Tempest*, when, in the masque, Iris greets the Goddess of Plenty, Ceres, with a description of her 'Banks with peonied or lilied brims': two centuries later the doomed John Keats makes a touching reference to peonies in his *Ode to Melancholy*:

> But when the melancholy fit shall fall
> Sudden from Heaven, like a weeping cloud
> Then glut thy sorrow on a morning rose
> Or on the wealth of globed peonies.

Poor Keats had the premonition that he would die young, and on him the 'melancholy fit' fell often.

Varieties of Peonies. Peonies can be divided into three groups: species peonies, which grow for us as they did in the wild, and have been collected by plant hunters from the four quarters of the world; herbaceous peonies, many of which are hybrids of *P. lactiflora* and *P. officinalis*, with an admixture of blood from some species peonies; third, and most spectacular group of all, are the tree peonies, which were brought in the last hundred and fifty years from the Far East to flower in Western gardens.

In the life story of the peony, the species are the oldest known varieties, at least in Europe, so it is fit that some of these should be described first.

P. officinalis is still grown in gardens today as it was a thousand years ago. Its early shoots, often of a dark claret color, are the harbingers of new life in the herbaceous border, and it has cup-shaped ruby red flowers. It is the parent of many of the fine new varieties of garden peonies. It is typical of most peonies in that it has foliage which comes into full beauty not only in the early spring but again in the autumn, with each 'deep cut leaf, like a medieval axe', as Victoria Sackville-West aptly wrote in her poem *The Garden*.

P. obovata is a beautiful species peony, which has white flowers centred with a bosse of golden stamens. It comes from Siberia.

P. emodi (after Mount Emodus, in northern India), which was collected in the foothills of the Himalayas in 1868, is a specially delicate and beautiful   123 plant. It has deeply cut, almost lacy, foliage, and white papery flowers veined with violet. It likes the protection from wind provided by low shrubs.

P. peregrina lobata comes from the uplands of Bulgaria and has lacquered flowers of shining carmine. It is low growing – not more than two feet high, and a plant of great character. Two good named varieties are 'Fire King' and 'Sunbeam', and both prefer half shade.

P. tenuifolia has even more finely cut leaves than those of *P. emodi*, and small crimson flowers. Its natural habitat is the Caucasus.

Two favorites of that discerning plantsman Reginald Farrer were *P. P. whitleyi* and *wittmaniana*. The latter is, he claims, 'a rarity – a herbaceous species with big sulphur yellow flowers, which like all the peonies only wants rich soil and neglect'. The single *P. whitleyi major* was the most beautiful peony he knew, with a flower 'like a huge water lily of pure white silk, and the heart of it is a tassel of fine gold. No one ever imagined a lovelier thing ...' *Wittmaniana* is a specially hardy plant. It comes from the Caucasus and is reported to have survived the winter in Leningrad without cover.

If those two peonies were Reginald Farrer's favorites, *mlokosewichii* is the preferred species peony of the author of this book. Everything, except perhaps its temperament, seems to him perfect about this transcendent plant. It was collected by the Russian botanist, G. Mlokosewich, near the village of Lagodekhi in the eastern Caucasus in 1900.

From the day the velvety mauve shoots show their heads above ground in April, to the day in September when its seed pods split open to reveal crimson seeds, *P. mlokosewichii*, colloquially, 'Molly the Witch', casts an extraordinary spell. The flowers are a clear yellow – the author has described them elsewhere as looking like sophisticated buttercups – and their anthers are an iridescent tourmaline in color. The plant's only fault is its disappointing habit of sometimes decreasing in size, year after year, until it disappears altogether. But when it does succeed, *P. mlokosewichii* is a very lovely thing.

Peonies, iris and delphiniums in a luscious flower piece by Leonard Philpot (born 1877).

If Claude Monet loved to paint water lilies, Edouard Manet chose peonies for this flower-piece in the Louvre, Paris.

宮粉牡丹

These are a few of the more desirable species peonies – which grow and blow in gardens as they grew and blew in Japan, China or the Caucasus. They are, perhaps, plants for the connoisseur. Less sophisticated gardeners may well prefer the hybrid herbaceous peonies, descendants of *P. lactiflora*, from China. These comprise some of the most spectacular plants in the gardens of England and America; but the difference between the hundreds of varieties available is so slight – only of color and size and shape of bloom – that individual descriptions would be tedious. It is enough to list a few, in colors, which would seem, from thirty years' garden experience, the most rewarding.

First pick of pink herbaceous peonies might include 'Lady Alexandra Duff'; 'Reine Hortense', which is almost lavender in shade; 'Sarah Bernhardt', a later flowerer than most; and 'Albert Crousse', a peony which has pink flowers with a crimson centre.

Of the darker herbaceous peonies, 'Felix Crousse' is a fine flowerer, and a brilliant crimson. 'Martin Cahuzak' is a deep garnet red and *P. officinalis rosea plena* has flowers which are bright rose red.

The best white border peonies are 'Duchesse de Nemours', 'Festiva Maxima' and both 'Emilie' and 'Marie Lemoine'. Lemoine is a great name in the history of peony culture.

Single herbaceous peonies have great appeal, and one, 'Antwerpia', in spite of its ugly name, is a beautiful flower with its rose-pink blooms and lemon-yellow anthers. 'Lemon Queen' has white flowers tinged with yellow, and 'Victoria' magnificent crimson flowers with showy golden centres.

Tree Peonies. Tree peonies, or Moutans, originate in the Chinese mountains of Mou-Tan, which means 'Male Vermilion' – the Chinese for peony. For a thousand years or more these were the favorite flowers of the nobility of China and it is recorded that the T'ang Emperor Hsuan Tsung so revered tree

Moutan peony painted in China by a Cantonese artist for John Reeves (1774–1856). Reeves was Inspector of Tea for the East India Company, and a specialist in the flora of China.

Peonia lutea – the yellow peony from which, crossed with P. suffruticosa, such great tree peonies as 'L'Esperance' and 'Chromatella' have been hybridized. 127

peonies that he had built a special pavilion of scented aloewood, from which to view the imperial collection. This was in the eighth century, and it was not until the eighteenth that tree peonies were introduced into Europe. They come in three categories – Chinese, Japanese and hybrids. The late Sir Frederick Stern, in his great work *A Study of the Genus Peonia*, published in 1946, groups the Chinese and Japanese tree peonies as *P. suffruticosa*, and the hybrids as the Delavayi group – Delavayi after the Abbé Jean Delavay (1834–95) who collected so many fine plants in the western provinces of China, including the splendid and robust plant which bears his name, *P. delavayi*, destined to be the parent of the majority of our modern tree peony hybrids. It was only sent to Paris from China in 1884. Sir Frederick includes *P. lutea* (yellow) in the Delavayi group. This was found in China as recently as 1900. *P. lutea* is the peony that M. Lemoine of Nancy crossed with *P. suffruticosa*, which has provided modern gardeners with beautiful peonies with flowers of lemon, gold and butter yellow, such as the famous 'L'Esperance', 'Chromatella' and 'Souvenir de Maxim Cornu'.

But before describing some of the best and most interesting varieties of tree peony, both oriental and newly raised in Europe and America, a word of warning about modern hybrid tree peonies, from Reginald Farrer. After describing the love that tree peonies inspire in the Oriental gardener, he goes on to say:

> But, remember, only the Japanese and Chinese tree peony can claim the true Japanese ecstasy of affection. Where the West has touched the products of the East a disastrous degradation has resulted; and Europe now swarms with truly horrible European tree-peonies – lumpish, double, semi-double, in tones of washy lilac and magenta. Of these Western creations let us hear no more; away with all the Mrs Erasmus Potters, the Madame Hector de Telle-Quelles, the Frau Oberhofgärthnerin Schlagenbuschenheims. What can you expect of creatures named like this? The tree peony of the East has a loose arrogant splendor; the flowers are vast, satiny in texture and sheen, sometimes torn and fringed at the edges, sometimes double, sometimes single but always of the most imperious yet well-bred loveliness, in every pure shade of color, from the white snows of Fuji at dawn, through faintest shades of pearl and pale rose to the growing ardors of coral, salmon, scarlet, vermilion, sanguine; and so on, into the deep tones of crimson, claret, and a maroon that deepens almost to black. All these marvels of gorgeousness did I mark down and collect when I was in Japan, and now, through June, the rows of Japanese tree peonies make my garden a blaze of bewildering color.

It is only fair to stress that Mr Farrer was writing sixty years ago, and that since then there has been much improvement. But it is true that some of the fine hybrid tree peonies raised in Europe by Monsieur Lemoine and others still suffer from a general weakness of stem which has yet to be bred out. These are plants which 'favor' their Moutan forbears in that they show magnificent heads of flowers which their weak stalks, legacy of *P. lutea*, have difficulty in supporting. This results in hanging top-heavy flowers hidden by foliage. A new hybrid, *P. lutea ludlowi*, is a welcome exception, and holds up its large yellow blossoms well.

Robert Fortune (1813–80), in his *Wandering in China*, gives a vivid description of his search for new varieties of peony. Once, in a remote Chinese village, he heard a rumor of the existence in the neighbourhood of purple, yellow and even blue peonies. Fortune, a sober Scotsman from Berwickshire, had difficulty in believing this, but a Chinese artist swore that he had seen flowers of these colors, and even made some drawings of the flowers he spoke of, from memory. Fortune showed the drawings to the Chinese owner of a flower-shop, who enthusiastically undertook to procure the plants from a village, near which he knew they grew, at least a hundred miles away. This was an expensive operation, but Fortune, tempted by the thought of a blue peony, though still incredulous, could not resist paying the high price demanded. After some weeks the peony plants arrived. As he feared, 'the blue peony was wanting, and the yellow had that tinge only in the centre of its white petals ...' Fortune paid the high price demanded, though he discovered soon afterwards that the flower-seller had procured the plants from a garden only a mile or two distant. Such are the hazards of plant collecting.

Reginald Farrer had a happier experience when plant hunting in 1914 near a village called Fu-Erg-Gai, 'The street of happy sons', in the Kansu province on the Tibetan border. It was here that he caught his first glimpse of Moutan peonies growing in the wild.

> I sat at last ... and rested ... till my eye was caught by certain white objects further along the hillside that were clearly too big by far to be flowers, yet must certainly be investigated, if only to find out what clots of white wool, or yet whiter paper surely, could be doing in the wild coppice ... perhaps they had some religious meaning? I would see ...
>
> Through the foaming shallows of the copse I plunged and soon was holding my breath with growing excitement as I neared my goal ... I was setting my eyes on Peonia Moutan as a wild plant ... the most overpoweringly superb of hardy shrubs. Here in the brushwood it grew up tall and slender and straight, in two or three unbranching shoots, each one of which carried at the top, elegantly balancing, that single enormous blossom, waved and crimped into the boldest grace of line of absolute pure white with featherings of deepest maroon radiating at the base of the petals from the bosse of gold fluff at the flower heart ... the breath of them went out upon the twilight as sweet as any rose. ...

Some years after that memorable encounter Reginald Farrer, in *Alpine and Bog Plants*, described the perfect setting for tree peonies in winter gardens.

> They will be [he wrote] far more congruous and beautiful against a mossy rock or some quiet curtain of leaves. For green (I wish this were as generally realized as it is generally ignored) is a far more enhancing background than glare. Beyond this, the only requirement of the tree-peony is repeated heavy feeding with the richest of manure – incongruous as such treatment may seem for such sylph-sounding creatures as Hope of Glory, Moonfoam, Clouds at Dawn, Fire-Flash, Leaping Lion and Bridal Dream.

Today, sixty years later, one might look in vain in catalogues for tree peonies with such romantic names.

Varieties of Tree Peonies. A choice of the best of the new hybrid tree peonies would certainly include the yellow *P. lutea ludlowi*, already mentioned, and the clear sulphur-colored 'Argosy', one of the several excellent plants raised in America by Professor Saunders, the distinguished secretary of the American Peony Society. 'Argosy', like many of the American hybrids, flowers later than most of its fellows and so has a better chance of escaping late spring frosts. 'Bijou de Chusan' is a wonderful pale pink, with opulent many-petalled flowers. 'Reine Elizabeth' is a good brilliant red and 'Prince Trubetskoy' has large flowers of a clear violet.

As Reginald Farrer stressed, many of the best and most strongly growing of tree peonies come from Japan. Four of the best plants are the mauve 'Ruri-ban', the generously flowering deep pink 'Miyo Hikari', the giant-sized 'Gessetai', with white fimbriated flowers which are sometimes a foot across, and the sweetly scented 'Ren-Kaku'.

Tree peonies are among the finest of all garden plants. They ask little in the way of special culture – only to be left undisturbed, sheltered from the early morning sun and, if possible, to be planted on a slope which will allow frosts to flow past and not settle around them and scorch their young shoots. 'Peonied banks', such as Iris in *The Tempest* spoke of, should be the thoughtful gardener's aim.

In his delightful introduction to *A Study of the Genus Peonia*, the late Sir Frederick Stern quotes a letter he received in 1938 from the American botanist Dr J. E. Rock in answer to his enquiry about a certain rare peony, *P. papaveracea*. Dr Rock replied that the peony in question had once grown in the Yamen of the remote Choni Lamasery in Tibet – but that the Lamasery had been burned by the Mohammedans and all the monks killed. However, went on Dr Rock, when he had heard that the peony had probably also been destroyed, he immediately sent seed of it back to China, so that such a beautiful plant might not be lost to its native country.

TOP *A Moutan peony – The word Moutan is the Chinese for male vermilion and the plant once proliferated on the slopes of Mou-tan-shan – or Peony Mountain. A print in Curtis' magazine, 1808.*
BOTTOM *A full blown flower of a hybrid tree peony is one of the most beautiful things imaginable.*

A wash drawing, over a thousand years old, from the Codex Vindobonensis *which was originally compiled for the Byzantine Princess Anicia Juliana.*

Poppy

The flower of slumber and forgetfulness, now a national emblem of remembrance

The key to this apparent contradiction lies in careful reading of John McCrae's famous poem, published in the dark days of the First World War, in December 1915:

> If ye break faith with us who die
> We will not sleep, though poppies grow
> In Flanders' fields.

'Though' being the operative word.

Poppies have figured in ancient legend since the earliest times. The god Morpheus made crowns of poppies for those he wanted to send to sleep, and poppies decorated the portals of his temple. Ceres is depicted holding a bunch of flowers in memory of the opium she took at the birth of her many children.

Papaver glaucum, the glaucous poppy, gets it name from the Boeotian fisherman Glaucus who, in Greek mythology, fell into the Aegean and suffered a strange sea-change, and became an ocean god. His curious story is told by Aeschylus. Now 'glaucous' is the word commonly used by gardeners to describe the bloomy blue-green color of the leaves of many plants which grow near the sea – plants such as Lyme Grass (elymus), Sea Holly (eryngium), and Thrift (armeria).

Homer, in the *Iliad*, likened the head of a dying warrior, Gorgythio, to a poppy-flower; and Pope translated the lines:

> As full blown poppies, overcharged with rain
> Decline the head and drooping, kiss the plain

133

FAR LEFT *Meconopsis wallichii ('Mekon' is the Greek for 'poppy' and 'opsis' for 'like') grows in the wild in Nepal and Szechuan. The flowers can be red, purple or blue and the beauty of the plant is the young spring growth which is covered with reddish silky hairs.*
LEFT *Tibetan poppies growing in the garden at Rowallane in Northern Ireland.*

Homer, in the Iliad, *likened the head of a dying warrior to a hanging poppy flower –*
A sculpture from the temple of Aegina.

> So sinks the youth; his beauteous head, depressed
> Beneath his helmet, droops upon his breast.

How did the poppy become for ever the symbol of remembrance for all the
warriors who 'declined the head, and drooping, kissed the plain' in two
World Wars? The story is an interesting and moving one.

Colonel John McCrae, a Canadian, after serving in the South African War,
became a distinguished professor of medicine at the University of McGill.
On the outbreak of war in 1914, he at once enlisted in the ranks of the
Canadian army, which was being sent to fight in Belgium. Soon after landing
in Europe he was made Medical Officer and it was during the second battle of
Ypres, in 1915, while in charge of a First Aid post that he wrote the poem
which was to become so famous. During a few minutes when the fighting had
died down he wrote in pencil on a page of his despatch book, these lines:

> In Flanders' fields the poppies blow
> Between the crosses, row on row,
> That mark our place; and in the sky
> The larks still bravely singing fly,
> Scarce heard amid the guns below.
>
> We are the dead. Short days ago
> We lived, felt dawn, saw sunset glow,
> Loved and were loved, and now we lie
>   In Flanders' fields.
>
> Take up our quarrel with the foe;
> To you from failing hands we throw
> The torch be yours to hold it high
> If ye break faith with us who die
> We shall not sleep, though poppies grow
>   In Flanders' fields.

The Latin name for poppy is 'papaver' – said to derive from the sound made when chewing
the seed. A drawing of Papaver rhoeas *by a Chinese artist in the Reeves collection*
at the Natural History Museum.

The British Legion records take up the story: 'The verses were sent anonymously to *Punch* who published them under the title "In Flanders' Fields", printing them in that heavy type that they rarely use'. In May, 1918, Colonel McCrae was brought as a stretcher case to one of the big hospitals on the coast of France. On the third evening he was wheeled to the balcony of his room to look over the sea towards the cliffs of Dover. The verses were obviously in his mind, for he said to the doctor who was in charge of his case: 'Tell them this, if ye break faith with us who die we shall not sleep.' That night Colonel McCrae died and was buried in the cemetery above Wimereux, 'Where the cliffs of Dover are clearly visible on sunny days'.

Colonel McCrae's poem by this time had become well known all over the allied world and an American woman, Moina Michael, wrote a moving poem in reply, which included the lines,

> We cherish, too, the Poppy red
> That grows on fields where valor led,
> It seems to signal to the skies
> That blood of heroes never dies ...

The wearing of a poppy appeared to her as the way to keep faith, and she decided to wear one always.

It was a French woman, Madam Guérin, perhaps more practically minded, who conceived the idea of making artificial poppies which could be sold to help ex-servicemen and their dependants. For the first year, 1921, the supply of poppies needed for England was made in France and profits from their manufacture were devoted by Madame Guérin to help the women and children who were returned to devastated areas over there.

In 1922 the Legion's poppy factory was opened in London and Earl Haig used to say that the work it provided for disabled ex-servicemen was just as important as the money the sale of poppies raised. He always took the greatest interest in the factory, which today employs 248 men. The yearly collection record by the sale, on Remembrance Sunday, of poppies made there, reached a record £1,180,000 a few years ago. Veteran groups in America sponsor the sale of poppies during the week prior to Memorial Day, May 30th.

Varieties of Poppy. Simplest and best known of all poppies is surely *Papaver rhoeas*, the corn poppy, that grows so generously in Flanders. It is a flower which is not a native, and it is not known when it first studded so many cornfields with its scarlet. Poppies only grow on cultivated land, and it is a fact that if land is left untilled for long poppies will wholly disappear. At least that is the view held by Professor Henslow, when he wrote, 'I question whether some, if not all the species of the genus *Papaver* would not ultimately disappear from our native flora, if the whole kingdom was abandoned to the uncultivated state from which it has been reclaimed for so many generations.   137

Meconopsis betonicifolia (*formerly* baileyi, *after its discoverer Captain F. M. Bailey*) *is one of the most beautiful and bluest of Himalayan poppies.*

I scarcely remember to have seen a specimen of a true poppy in an uncultivated district ..., and Professor Henslow goes on to say that poppies have frequently followed the Englishman in colonization, and that their scarlet flowers now wave above the fields of Australian and Canadian corn, and are just as unwelcome to the farmer there as they are in England. For poppies, for all their beauty and associations, quickly exhaust the soil in which they grow, and to have them in a cornfield is a sure sign of bad farming. But few cornfields in western Europe are totally without poppies, except in western Scotland where, for some reason, they are rare. In northern France, and especially in Flanders, they grow everywhere.

Ruskin loved poppies – and it was the flower of *Papaver rhoeas* growing in the ruins of Rome which inspired him to write in *The Garden of Proserpina*

I have in my hand a small red poppy which I gathered on Whit Sunday on the palace of the Caesars. It is an intensely simple, intensely floral, flower. All silk and flame, a scarlet cup, perfect-edged all round, seen among the wild grass far away, like a burning coal fallen from Heaven's altars. You cannot have a more complete, a more stainless, type of flower absolute; inside and outside, all flower. No sparing of colour anywhere – no outside coarsenesses – no interior secrecies; open as the sunshine that creates it; fine-finished on both sides, down to the extremest point of insertion on its narrow stalk; and robed in the purple of the Caesars.

John Ruskin (1819–1900) photographed at Brantwood in 1885, wrote of the poppy 'when the flower opens, it seems a deliverance from torture ... The aggrieved corolla smooths itself in the sun, and comforts itself as it can ...'

And Ruskin goes on '... but it remains visibly crushed and hurt to the end of its days'.

138

Papaver rhoeas – the simple corn poppy, Ruskin's 'intensely floral flower' and the poppy of John McCrae's famous poem – is the parent of many of the best of the cultivated garden varieties. Thomas Fairchild, the London gardener who published his *Catalogus Plantarum* in the early eighteenth century, describes poppies descended from the corn poppy as '... the most beautiful flowers that can be imagined ... as double as a rose, of a rich scarlet streaked with white, as fine as a carnation.' Among these garden beauties are the popular Shirley strain of poppies which were raised by the vicar of the English village of that name over eighty years ago.

Papaver somniferum, the Poppy of Sleep, is the opium poppy which was first cultivated in antiquity in Greece where its seeds were used as food. (Poppy seeds are still widely used in Central Europe, scattered on bread and cakes.) Its Latin name, *papaver*, is said to come from the noise made in chewing the seed. *P. somniferum* grew in the garden of Tarquin, and the Emperor Charlemagne, a zealous promoter of horticulture, mentioned the flower in his *Capitularies*. The baleful fame of this poppy, however, lies in the fact that opium can be made from its juice. Since the days of Charlemagne, 'How many thousands', asks Anne Pratt, the Victorian writer and flower lover, 'have been influenced by the juice of the poppy? Some lulled to the refreshing slumber in which pain was for a while soothed or forgotten; some given up to those wild visions and restless agitations, which have ended by paralysing alike all bodily powers and mental energies!'

So closely connected with the drug opium is *Papaver somniferum*, a form of which grows in gardens all over the Western world, that a few lines describing how opium is produced might be included here.

All parts of *Papaver somniferum* contain a white opaque narcotic juice, but this abounds especially in the capsules. In warm climates the whole plant attains a greater luxuriance and this white juice is far more plentiful. When grown for opium, small wounds are made in the capsules of the poppy, when about half ripe. From these wounds the plant bleeds, and during the night the juice thickens to a firm grey substance. The way in which opium is gathered in the East today is precisely the same as that described many centuries ago by Dioscorides. The cuts are made at sunset, and, according to an old account, the dews of night favor the exudation of the milky substance, which is scraped off on the following morning. After being thickened by being exposed to the sun, it is shaped by hand into cakes. A hundred years ago, in Constantinople, it was mixed with sugar and the juice of various fruits, and made into a kind of sweet: it was then formed into small lozenges, on which were imprinted the words *Mash Allah* – the Work of God. In those days the Tartar couriers of the Sultan, who travelled immense distances with astonishing speed, often took no other nourishment than a few of these small lozenges. However, the celebrated *Maslach*, or *Mash Allah*, of the Turks, sometimes contained other narcotic substances besides opium, such as the juice of the

Papaver somniferum *is the opium poppy. The drug can be obtained from the juice that comes from notches made in the half-formed seed capsules. The flowers of this annual are pink, white or pale mauve.*

hemp. 'Of the uses of opium to the sufferer from pain or restlessness, we need not speak. Many ... have blessed God for its soothing influence: but how often that blessing is perverted into a curse when the continual use of opium has weakened the limbs and shortened the life of man, and degraded an intellectual being to the state of imbecility ..' words as true today as when Anne Pratt wrote them a century ago.

After the field and opium poppies, *Papaver nudicaule*, the Iceland poppy, is the best known. It is a newcomer to Western gardens, its seed having been sent only in 1730, by J.H.Sprekelfen, as Alice Coats recounts in *Flowers and Their Histories*. Cousin Alice goes on to say, 'It is comforting that in this case the plant was not named for its discoverer'. Coming from the far north, the Iceland Poppy is bone hardy and its orange and lemon flowers are as bright as any in the garden in June. It is an annual and easy to raise from seed.

The Welsh poppy, *Meconopsis cambrica*, is a delicate plant with finely cut foliage and pale yellow flowers. Like its far grander Himalayan relations, it delights in cool shade and will grow quite happily at the foot of a north-facing wall, or in the joints of a stone-paved, almost sunless area. But unlike the Himalayan poppies, the Welsh poppy is quite undemanding as to soil, and will thrive in the most unpromising position. And when it finds soil conditions that it likes, it is difficult to eradicate.

In *My Garden in Summer* E.A.Bowles, who knew more about gardens and the culture and care of flowers than most people, offers a tip about how to use poppies for decoration indoors:

It took me a long while to learn how to cut them for the house, so that they would not flag and faint within an hour. They never flag now when cut, nor do they fail to last in full beauty for three days if I carry a jug of hot water (hot, not tepid) down to their bed in the evening, after dinner for preference, and cut the buds that have straightened up their necks ready to open on the morrow or perhaps the day after, and any flowers that have just split the calyx lobes and are showing their color. I put each one into my jug so that it is almost up to its neck in hot water as soon as I have cut it, and I put jug and all in the bathroom for the night, because I love to see them half open, bursting off the sepals, or even in freshly-escaped glory full of crinkles and folds, the first thing in the morning. Opened thus and transferred to other vases, they will generally last for three days, unless stood in a violent draught, or shaken by being moved about, and, moreover, will increase in beauty, for they grow in size daily. ...

Oriental Poppies. As well known as the annual poppies, and favorite plants for the herbaceous border, are the oriental poppies. But, to the author's mind at least, they are overrated, unless care is taken to plant the less well-known varieties. Their colors seem too harsh, and their foliage too coarse to associate happily with other herbaceous plants. Worst fault of all, their flowering period is short, and the unwary gardener is often left with a mass of hirsute, dull green leaves, to disfigure his border from June until autumn. Two modern varieties of oriental poppy might, however, be found a place in the border as long as they are planted behind something which will grow up in front of them when flowering is done. These are the shrimp pink 'May Sadler' and the excellent 'Perry's White' – the last being particularly attractive, with its blackish, purple stamens and crinkled papery petals.

It was the petals of a poppy such as 'Perry's White' which may have inspired two writers of the past to different feelings. The 'serious though affable' Nehemiah Grew, who was the first botanist to discover the existence of different sexes in plants, describes the crumpled appearance of the petals of the poppy after having been 'cramped up within the empalement by hundreds of little wrinkles and puckers, as if three or four cambric handkerchiefs were thrust into one pocket'. Ruskin, in another chapter of *The Garden of Proserpina*, was also concerned for the newly-opened poppy flowers' well-being:

Gather a green poppy bud, break it open and unpack the poppy. The whole flower is there complete in size and color – the stamens full-grown, but all packed so closely that the fine silk of the petals is crushed into a million of shapeless wrinkles. When the flower opens, it seems a deliverance from torture; the two imprisoning green leaves are shaken to the ground: the aggrieved corolla smooths itself in the sun, and comforts itself as it can; but it remains visibly crushed and hurt to the end of its days.

Tibetan Poppies. The poppies that have most appeal for the connoisseur of plants are those from Tibet or Nepal – from the wonderful country about which Reginald Farrer wrote in his book *On the Eaves of the World*, where he found poppies growing in the remote valleys of the 'enormous surge of green ranges that foams and ripples regularly across the world taking rich tones of blue and soft distant colors away in the direction of Jo-Ni in the north'.

Three of the finest Tibetan poppies, easily obtainable and not too difficult to cultivate, are *Meconopsis betonicifolia, M. dhwojii,* and *M. nepaulensis* (or *wallichii*).

M. betonicifolia – the most beautiful of all the Tibetan poppies, first astonished Western gardeners in 1924. It was discovered by Captain F. M. Bailey, the plant collector, who worked on the upper reaches of the river Tsangpo in Tibet just before the First World War. *Meconopsis betonicifolia* opens its sky-blue flowers with their delicate golden filaments in early June, and if it flowers well, it can be one of the loveliest of all garden plants. Like all Himalayan poppies it needs a cool soil which is full of leaf mould and humus, and a partially shaded site. In a hot dry position Himalayan poppies will never succeed. *M. betonicifolia* (because its leaves resemble those of betony) has been re-christened recently, and one wonders why. It was originally called *baileyi*, after its discoverer and introducer, Captain Bailey – a well-deserved reward for a splendid contribution to the gardens of the Western world.

The great beauty of *M. dhwojii* lies not so much in its pale yellow flowers, but in the exquisite rosette it makes, in early spring, of deeply-cut, fern-like leaves, all dressed with golden down, which glistens and sparkles in the morning dew. Mr Jack Drake describes the infant foliage of a similar Tibetan poppy – *M. integrifolia* – saying that its 'new growths emerge like some furry creature awakening from hibernation'.

M. nepaulensis, which grows in the wild in Nepal and Szechuan, can show flowers which are not only blue but red, purple and very occasionally, white. as well. It is also known as *M. wallichii,* taking its name from the genial Dane, Nathaniel Wallich, who was Director in 1817 of the Botanical Gardens in Calcutta. *M. nepaulensis* is monocarpic, like *M. dhwojii* and *integrifolia,* and makes similar basal rosettes covered with reddish silky hairs. It is one of the finest Himalayans to grow in woodland, though perhaps without the extraordinary grace of Captain Bailey's own poppy. These are just three of the Himalayan poppies which are within the reach of any careful gardener. There are many others, such as the lovely pure white *M. superba,* and the rare pink *sherriffii.* But the gardener who can show well-grown groups of the three poppies described here can be congratulated on his taste and skill.

Tibetan poppies are some of the most exquisite flowers which can be grown in Western gardens. It is strange to think that they were practically unknown to Europe or America a century ago; it is, perhaps, their very newness which enables them to cast such a spell on the imaginative gardener.

Tree Poppies. One other member of the genus *Papaveraceae* must be noticed, though it bears neither the Latin name of *papaver* nor the Greek one of *meconopsis*, but was called *romneya* after the Reverend Romney Robinson (1792–1882) – the Irish astronomer who made a study of plants, as well as planets, in his garden in Armagh. *Romneya* originates on the western seaboard of the United States, where it is known as the Californian Tree poppy. Its charm lies as much in its glabrous blue-green leaves, and willingness, unlike its Himalayan relations, to grow in the hottest, driest soil, as in its large white papery flowers.

Of the two varieties of *romneya* in cultivation *R. trichocalyx* is more generous in blossom than the more usually grown, smooth-budded, *R. coulteri*, a plant E. A. Bowles describes as a 'stingy old curmudgeon in its views about providing flowers'.

Perhaps his friend, Reginald Farrer, never told him the secret of how to make *romneya* give of its best, for in his *Alpine and Bog Plants* Farrer wrote:

Romneya coulteri is usually cultivated under a wall. It is so that I have always grown it, with the most persistent disappointment. Every year it came up ranker and more rank, and, in late summer, made abundance of buds, which developed sporadically into flower one at a time, producing no effect and passing away frustrate, before the advance of autumn frosts. Nothing I could do seemed of any avail. I protected the old wood, and I cut it off – with equal futility. *Romneya coulteri* was written down a failure. It was only last winter, when the key was given me, ... information received leads me to understand that *romneya coulteri* is an open-ground shrub, that it becomes bored and lazy if grown under a wall, that only in an unprotected place, swept by every wind and frost that befalls, will the great Californian Poppy show the floriferousness of its true character. Add to this a dressing of lime rubble, and you will probably be picking blooms of *romneya* from June to November.

Romneya coulteri –
the Californian Tree poppy,
was named after the
Reverend Romney Robinson
(1792–1882), the Irish
astronomer. The plant has
glaucous green leaves and
large white flowers, and
prefers a sunny well drained
site.

The field primrose,   *from Gerard's* Herball.

Primula

'A primrose by the river's brim,
A yellow primrose was to him'

And for Wordsworth's insensitive Peter Bell, 'it was nothing more'. The worldly Lord St Jerome in Disraeli's *Coningsby* considered that primroses made 'a capital salad'. 'His favorite flower' were the words that Queen Victoria wrote on the wreath of primroses that she sent to the funeral of her favorite Prime Minister. But she was probably referring to her consort, Prince Albert, whose tastes were simpler than those of Disraeli, so the Primrose League, founded in memory of Disraeli in 1883, was almost certainly named in misapprehension.

Whatever primroses meant to Disraeli, to most of us they surely mean the very spring itself. In Latin the word primula means 'little first', and to the Elizabethan playwrights the coming of primroses certainly meant the coming of spring. Fletcher in *Two Noble Kinsmen* writes of 'Primrose, first-born child of Ver' and, in Shakespeare's *A Winter's Tale*, Perdita regrets 'pale prime-roses'

> That die unmarried ere they can behold
> Bright Phoebus in his strength.

In both *Hamlet* and *Macbeth*, Shakespeare blends the youthful connotations of the primrose with a feeling of frivolity and doomed carelessness – 'the primrose path of dalliance' and the 'primrose way … to the everlasting bonfire'.

For Milton, primroses were the flowers of the morning, of early life, or youth. On the death of 'a fair infant, dying of a cough' he wrote, 'Oh fairest flower … soft silken primrose, fading timelessly', and in *Lycidas* he uses the forgotten word 'rathe', which means 'early' – pertaining to the morning – to describe the primrose.

145

Primula alpicola from the hills of Bhutan, has flowers that are white, yellow or pale violet.

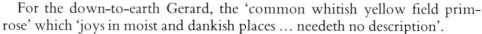

Primrose petals, from the Garden *of Proserpina*

For the down-to-earth Gerard, the 'common whitish yellow field prim-rose' which 'joys in moist and dankish places … needeth no description'.

Ruskin, in *The Garden of Proserpina*, was impressed by the unfolding, from the calyx, of the primrose's petals, and the relationship between the finished flower and the 'nursery' from which it had recently emerged.

> Look at these four stages in the young life of a primrose. First confined, as strictly as the poppy within five pinching green leaves, whose points close over it, the little thing is content to remain a child, and finds its nursery large enough. The green leaves unclose their points – the little yellow ones peep out, like ducklings. They find the light delicious, and open wide to it; and grow, and grow, and throw themselves wider at last into their perfect rose. But they never leave their old nursery for all that; it and they live on together; and the nursery seems a part of the flower.

In Germany, where primroses sometimes bear the cumbersome name of *Schlüsselblume*, for their supposed ability in Bavarian legend to open treasure chests, they are rarities. Countess Von Arnim in *Elizabeth and her German Garden* describes her attempts to introduce them.

> Primrose-roots are the English contributions to my garden. I brought them over in a tin box last time I came from England, and am anxious to see whether they will consent to live here. Certain it is that they don't exist in the Fatherland, so I can only conclude the winter kills them; for surely, if such lovely things would grow, they never would have been overlooked. But they are not going to do anything this year, and I only hope those cold days did not send them off to the Paradise of flowers. I am afraid their first impression of Germany was a chilly one.

Colored Primroses. Though the yellow primrose is a true British native and was flowering in forests many centuries ago, it was not until the early seventeenth century that the first colored primrose was grown in England. This was *P. vulgaris rubra*, and it was imported, like so many other good plants, from the Near East – Parkinson describes it in 1640 as 'Tradescant's Turkie Purple Primrose'. He goes on to say that it was valued specially for its early flowering, 'such is the lively nature of the flower that it raises its head above the snow even in the middle of winter …' and owing to its rarity 'Herbe merchants cut the root into several parts, to propagate it by that means as well as by seed'.

A hundred years after Parkinson there were many varieties of colored primroses grown, and they fast became collectors' flowers. But most of the new red, purple, blue and lilac primroses, whether they were single or double, were less hardy than the native field varieties. In *Flowers and*

146

Their Histories, Alice Coats quotes the Reverend William Hanbury's reproof to Philip Miller, when he warns 'the intelligent gardener' to disregard Mr Miller's advice to plant these rare primroses in the wild 'as if they were as hardy and durable as the other primroses: as it will soon prove the loss of the whole stock thus planted, and convince him that Mr Miller is very ignorant of their true nature and culture'.

Some of the colored, double primroses are, however, quite hardy and grow strongly enough to become naturalized. As a child, in Scotland, the author remembers a bank by the River Coil, in Ayrshire, on which a lilac-colored double primrose grew for many years. It was one of the earliest flowers to take his fancy; it may well have been either the variety 'Quaker's Bonnet' or 'Lady's Delight', both of which are double, lilac-colored and reputed to be hardy.

One of the first patches of strong flower color in spring is that shown by a primrose – the deep purple 'Wanda'. This is a flower which is apt to be sniffed at by the connoisseur. It is grown in almost every garden in the land, but in almost every garden, it is grown in the wrong place – hence the criticism. 'Wanda' must always be in shade, where its color can glow richly and mysteriously – never in full sunlight, where its color seems too strong. But in woodland or on the north side of natural rocks, 'Wanda' can look very well. One of its charms lies in its leaves, which are smaller than the leaves of most primroses, and seem to reflect the flower's colours, as they take on a purple tinge.

Cowslips. Primula veris (of Spring) is the wild cowslip of the fields – the flower that Herrick fashioned into a virgin's pall – 'Cowslips for her covering' – in the bells of which Ariel was wont to lie; and it was on Titania's pensioners, 'the cowslips velvet head' that Comus set his 'printless foot'.

Cowslips are flowers that are always favorites of children, and like many mothers before her, Countess Von Arnim taught her German children how to make cowslip balls, 'and the babies had never seen such things, nor had imagined anything half so sweet'.

The charm of cowslips – for their individual flowers are poor things compared to primroses – is their scent. The scent of the cowslip has the power given to few other flowers to transport one back over the years to childhood days. It is more evocative than the scent of roses. All one's life, or at least for much of every year, we know the scent of roses. But to smell a cowslip under perfect conditions one has to walk the meadows – which are probably wet, for it must be springtime – and one has to bend low to pick the flower. Cowslips are true country flowers, and easier to pick for children rather than for grown-ups – wet hands and wet feet go with their gathering. Few florists' shops stock cowslips.

Cowslips can be made into wine and the homely Mrs Glasse, who published *The Art of Cookery made Plaine and Easy*, in 1770, gives this recipe:

Take six gallons of water, twelve pounds of sugar, the juice of six lemons, the whites of four eggs. Beat very well, put all together in a kettle, let boil half an hour, skim very well; take a peck of cowslips, if dry ones, half a peck; put them into a tub with the thin peeling of six lemons, then pour on the boiling liquor, and stir them about; when almost cold, put in a thin toast baked dry and rubbed with yeast. Let it stand two or three days to work. If you put in before you turn it six ounces of syrup of citron or lemons, with a quart of Rhenish wine, it will be a great addition; the third day strain it off, through a flannel bag, and turn it up, lay the bung loose for two or three days to see if it works, and if it don't, bung it down tight.

But if it do, it sounds delicious.

The cowslip had a far more important function than that of making an ingredient of wine. It was to become the parent of the only variety of flower which can be claimed as a purely British creation – the polyanthus. In other countries polyanthus are frequently known as English primulas and one of the earliest mentions of the flower under the name polyanthus is by John Evelyn at the end of the seventeenth century. Polyanthus ('many-flowered') are a cross between the primrose, possibly *Primula rubra*, and the cowslip, of which varieties with red-tinged flowers are sometimes found growing wild in Warwickshire. In *Henry V*, Shakespeare, who probably saw them growing near his home, writes of the 'freckled cowslip'.

The early varieties of polyanthus raised were usually the dark purple or mahogany brown, gold-laced or white-laced types. These became favorite florists' flowers, and rivalled the tulip and the pink in the interest and affections of the working men's flower societies in northern England and Scotland. But for growing in the garden, polyanthus were soon being raised in many other, brighter shades; by the early eighteenth century they were referred to by Robert Thompson in the *Gardener's Assistant* as being 'of unnumbered dyes'. And the author, again harking back to childhood in Scotland, remembers an extemporized prayer offered in the village kirk by a visiting preacher which ran, 'Oh Lord, who painteth the petal of the polyanthus purple – shine down in all thy power'.

Some of the early polyanthus were bred from cowslips with Hose-in-Hose flowers, or from the 'Frantic or Foolish' cowslip which had a green ruff. These old flowers were the true Jacks-of-the-Green and bore such names as Galligaskins and Jackanapes. They are still occasionally grown, and stands are often devoted entirely to these old garden flowers, which attract a far greater crowd round them than those collected round the benches laden with the largest and most top-heavy begonias, and delphiniums with spikes six feet high.

Himalayan Primulas. Of primulas as a plant family Victoria Sackville-West once wrote, 'Generally speaking, the class or group enjoys a moist soil and a shady place; and as there is a constant demand for plants that will thrive in shade, the primula will be found very useful as well as beautiful.' All primulas like a damp cool root-run, and all have a great quality for any wild garden plant – that of being rabbit–proof.

The Himalayan primulas are comparative newcomers to Western gardens, but they have settled down in European and American conditions far more satisfactorily than their more particular alpine cousins, which almost always need very special treatment. One of the earliest to arrive in Europe was *Primula denticulata*, not one of the author's favorites, as he finds it clumsy and top-heavy, and the lilac of its balls of flowers unpleasing, but it was high in the favor of that discriminating gardener, Gertrude Jekyll. In her *Wood and Garden*, she enthused over some *P. denticulata* she once saw growing in what were obviously ideal conditions.

> The plants were both grouped and thinly sprinkled, just as nature plants – possibly they grew directly there from seed. They were in superb and luxuriant beauty in the black peaty-looking half-boggy earth, the handsome leaves of the brilliant color and large size that told of perfect health and vigor, and the large round heads of pure lilac flowers carried on strong stalks that must have been fifteen inches high – I never saw it so happy and so beautiful. It is a plant I much admire ...

Thus Miss Jekyll, who knew what she was speaking about.

P. denticulata was sent to Europe by the directors of the East India Company in 1837. It was first found growing on a Himalayan slope by Francis Buchanan Hamilton some years before, and Alice Coats tells us that its native name was *Neckabu Swa*, 'a name that does not transplant so well as the flower'.

After *P. denticulata*, the next oriental primula to reach Europe was *P. japonica* from Japan – a fine looking plant, which in the right situation will grow as strongly as a cabbage, which its foliage, in size, much resembles. This was first grown in Western gardens in the seventies of the last century, and is one of the best known of all the candelabra primulas. The original *P. japonica* – still often grown – has stalks that are two feet high and shows its flowers for weeks in early summer. In color it is a strong magenta, but this has lately been much improved by hybridizing, and there are now Japanese primulas in far subtler shades of pale pink, rose and salmon. One in particular, 'Mrs Berkeley', caught the fancy of E. A. Bowles who describes it in his *My Garden in Spring*, '... the spikes of flowers were in beauty for a long period. I cannot think of any name to describe their color, but I believe I could mix Naples Yellow and Rose Madder and arrive at something like its creamy flesh tint, and it shades into apricot and tawny orange in the eye which gives the flower a warm glow ...'

Rather similar to *P. japonica*, except that it has stems that are covered with a   149 mealy farina, is *P. pulverulenta*, from China, where E. H. Wilson collected seed in 1905, in the shady valleys of west Szechuan. It is from *P. pulverulenta* that the well-known Bartley strains have been raised, which now show flowers of a dozen different soft shades, from downy apricot to shell pink.

The best form of *P. sikkimensis* – native primula of the remote mountain kingdom of Sikkim – is Tilman No. 2, with oddly but agreeably scented yellow flowers, and mealy pedicels. In its native land it grows in swampy situations 17,000 feet above sea level. In the Western world it is perfectly hardy and flowers for months on end, beginning in May. It is one of the finest of all the primulas.

P. florindae – the Giant Cowslip – has been criticized for its lax heads of sulphur-yellow flower bells. But it makes up for its unalert appearance by the most extraordinary generosity of flower and seed. In the right primula soil, damp and shaded, its rosettes and heart-shaped leaves will quickly cover a large area. That great collector Captain F. Kingdon-Ward gathered the seed of *P. florindae* in south-east Tibet in 1926, and named the plant after his wife, Florinda.

Primula chionantha is surely one of the loveliest of all primulas, and it is one of the earliest of all to flower; as its name *chionantha* implies, its scented flowers are snowy white, and though they seem delicate they will bear themselves bravely for any Western gardener who does his best to reproduce the soil conditions, light, with plenty of humus, that *P. chionantha* enjoys in its native Yunnan.

These are just a very few of the Asiatic primulas which can be grown in European and American gardens. There are innumerable other kinds – varying from good-natured plants, which need little attention, to delicate and demanding varieties which will only reward the most painstaking treatment. That well-known expert on primulas, Mr Jack Drake of Aviemore, in Invernesshire, has this to say about the primulas,

> from the high places of Europe, Asia and America, they are at once, the joy, and despair of the Alpine enthusiast. A large number of them are of an easy and hearty disposition and will grow well for the majority of gardeners; some are almost impossible to grow in this country except by a few wizards, who tantalize us by bringing them to the shows year after year in perfect health: while others, although tricky and temperamental, are possible to grow and flower if treated correctly. Among these latter are some of the loveliest of the race ... and once the enthusiast has attempted them and has had some initial success, he will find himself fascinated by their jewel-like beauty ...

Primula auricula. The beauty of *Primula auricula* has fascinated plant lovers for many more years than that of the Himalayan primulas. The original plants, in the wild, were, according to William Robinson, 'one of the many charming

150

Primula florindae *'makes up for its unalert appearance by the most extraordinary generosity of flower and seed'. This primula has sulphur-yellow flowers.*
FAR RIGHT Primula japonica – *the Candelabra primula 'shows its flowers, tier upon tier of them, for weeks in early summer.' Its color has been much improved by hybridizing.*

primulas that rival gentians, pinks and forgetmenots in making the flora of Alpine fields so exquisitely beautiful and interesting.' (*The English Flower Garden*). And he goes on to say that, as the auricula was strong growing and possessed of the tendency to 'sport' into innumerable varieties when raised from seed, it soon became a favorite flower of the hybridizer.

But before telling the story, and it is quite a long one, of the auricula – what of the name itself? The word *auricula* means 'small-eared', and popular names for the plant are Dusty Miller, or Bear's Ear, which the leaves much resemble – a similarity also noted in France, where they are called *Oreille d'ours*. Louis XIV is said to have been fond of auriculas, and it was during the reign of his successor Louis XV that a book was published, *Traité de la Culture Parfaite de l'Oreille d'ours ou Auricole*. The anonymous author recommended growing auriculas as a source of spiritual satisfaction – seeing the plant as the embodiment of simplicity and innocence, and holding that the cultivation of auriculas invited its grower 'to lead a saintly life – free from all reproach'. In those early days monks, priests, men of God, all engaged in the raising of auriculas, and as Kipling, in *The Glory of the Garden*, reminds us, 'Half a proper gardener's work is done upon his knees'.

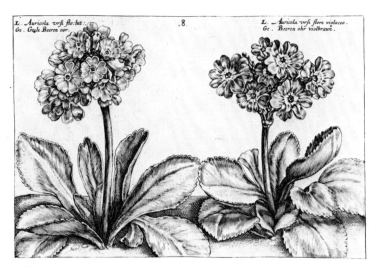

Auriculas, showing their distinctive smooth leaves. Popular names for auriculas are Dusty Miller and Bear's Ears. From Crispin de Passe's Hortus Floridus, *1614.*

The first auriculas are said to have been taken to England, like so much else, by the Huguenots, in the last quarter of the sixteenth century. Gerard gives a telling description of the plant in his *Herball* of 1597. Recognizing, like William Robinson, that the plant's home was the upper pastures of the Alps, he notes that in its native land the roots were recognized as a cure for giddiness in climbers, preventing 'the loss of their best joynte – (I mean their necke) if they take the rootes thereof before they ascend the rocks or other high places'. He calls the auricula the Mountain Cowslip and describes it in some detail:

152

A group of auriculas from Robert Thornton's Temple of Flora.
'It would seem incredible that a flower, through human skill, should attain this degree of natural or trained artificiality.'

Whatever primroses meant
to Disraeli, to most of us
they mean the very
Spring itself.

Benjamin Disraeli, Earl of
Beaconsfield, made a character
in his novel, Coningsby,
suggest that primroses
'made a capital salad'.
John Gerard (1545–1612)
wrote that the 'common
whitish yellow field
primrose ... needeth no
description'.

This beautiful and brave plant hath thicke, greene, and fat leaves, somewhat finely snipt about the edges, not altogether unlike those of Cowslips,
but smoother, greener, and nothing rough or crumpled: among which
riseth up a slender round stem a handful high, bearing a tuft of floures at
the top, of a faire yellow colour, not much unlike unto the floures of
Oxe-lips, but more open. The root is very threddy, and like unto the
Oxe-lip. They grow naturally upon the Alpish and Helvetian mountains.

But Gerard adds that most of them 'do grow in our London gardens' which
shows the good natured quality which won auriculas such popularity with
town-dwellers – whether in London or the Midlands.

Some years later John Parkinson sang the praises of the auricula in his
Paradisus, saying their flowers,

many set together upon a stalke, doe seeme every one of them to bee a
Nosegay alone of itself; and besides the many differing colors that are to

155

Primula japonica growing in front of purple-flowered Magnolia soulangeana lennei
in a half-shaded shrub border.

be seene in them, as white, yellow, blush, purple, red, tawney, murrey, or haire color, which encrease much delight in all sorts of the Gentry of the Land; they are not unfurnished with a pretty sweete sent, which doth add an encrease of pleasure in those that make them an ornament for their wearing.

Show Auriculas. The new show auriculas were the result of one of the most extraordinary developments in the history of horticulture. About 1750 a 'break' resulted in a flower which was quite unique in nature, and unique in two different ways. The color of its petals – often a clear green, was something quite extraordinary – and as if that was not enough, the centre of each flower showed a ring, or zone, of crisp white meal, known to auricula fanciers as paste. From this first and sensational break all show auriculas were descended. Prize flowers had to have certain qualities, and Thomas Hogg, in the early nineteenth century, enumerated them as follows:

> A fine green auricula may be briefly and simply described thus: Every part must be in exact proportion one to another; the stalk must be proportionate to the leaves, and the pedicles and truss to them both; the prevailing or ground colour must be bright and distinct; the eye circular, and of a clear white; the border or edging round the petal of a lively green, and all the petals or pips nearly of a size, perfectly level, and disposed in regular order; the eye, the tube, and the rim, must correspond one with another, showing an exact symmetry throughout.

Collectors exhibited their prize auricula flowers in 'Theatres' – sets of shelves, which were often elaborately painted, under a pedimented roof. A roof was essential, for a beauty of the hybrid auricula is the paste and this had to be protected, or look as if it was protected, from the rain. The new auriculas were no longer the simple plants admired by Louis XIV, for they showed colors never before seen in flowers – 'a lively green', slate blue, chamois, cinnamon, and that subtle greenish-grey that the French in the eighteenth century called so unromantically *Caca d'oie*. Special fertilizers, it was thought, were necessary to produce them. *Caca d'oie*, the real thing, was highly recommended, as were the droppings of pigeons. Some were even fed on raw meat. Mr Geoffrey Taylor, in *The Victorian Flower Garden*, quotes the Quaker James Maddock, who published a *Florists' Directory* in 1792, as recommending a compost of:

> One half rotten cow-dung, two years old; one sixth fresh sound earth, of an open texture; one eighth earth of rotten leaves; one twelfth coarse sea or river sand; one twenty-fourth soft, decayed willow wood, found in the trunks of an old willow tree; one twenty-fourth peaty or moory earth; one twenty-fourth ashes of burnt vegetables.

And Mr Taylor goes on to tell us that Isaac Emmerton, who kept a nursery at Barnet near London, advised an even more elaborate 'witches' brew' for the successful culture of auriculas. The ingredients included, as well as the essential *caca d'oie*, blood, night soil and sugar baker's scum, and reads in such a way as to turn any but the strongest stomach. The revolting mixture, according to Isaac Emmerton, would be 'the means of throwing brilliant colors into the pips or petals, and of giving life and vigor to the plants, as much as fine old Port or rich Madeira wine does to the human constitution'. But the more prosaic George Glenny, author of a book *The Properties of Flowers*, scoffed at what he called 'exciting soils' for auriculas. Today the best growing medium is considered by experts to be nothing more elaborate than a good, light potting mixture.

The stage auriculas of the seventeenth and eighteenth centuries, with their glorious colors and elaborate breeding, caught and held fast the imagination and admiration of that recognized connoisseur of the unusual, Mr Sacheverell Sitwell. In his *Old Fashioned Flowers* he devotes pages to praise of the auricula.

> In the first place, it is hardly to be conceived possible that such a plant should exist at all. There is something unreal and improbable in its edging and mealing. This latter has been stippled or dappled on to it. The white, mealy eye of the flower is a glorious and wonderful thing; but the slight and miraculous powdering upon the back of the flower is even more striking . . . This first moment of seeing a Stage Auricula is an experience never to be forgotten. It would seem incredible that a flower, through human skill, should attain to this degree of natural or trained artificiality. For the perfection of a Stage Auricula is that of the most exquisite Meissen porcelain, of the most lovely silk stuffs of Isfahan . . .

The early auriculas had splendid names. John Rea, who raised a famous collection of auriculas in his garden at Kinlet in Shropshire, and the Reverend Samuel Gilbert, his son-in-law and Rector of Quatt, were both passionately devoted to the flower. The names of some of their prizes have come down to us in Rea's *Flora, Ceres and Pomona* published in 1665, and the Rector of Quatt's *Florists Vademecum*: 'Black Imperial', 'Mistress Buggs Her Fine Purple' ('Raised in her Battersea garden near London'), and 'Mistress Austin's Scarlet'. Red auriculas – now rare – were specially highly valued, and commanded high prices. Striped auriculas were also popular and expensive, and the Rector of Quatt, who might have stepped, with the Akond of Swat, from the pages of Edward Lear, has put on record:

> ... there are two rare striped auriculas, their price bespeaks them, the one at four, the other nearer five pound, and have been sold for twenty pound, as I have been informed ... The double striped crimson and white. The

double, purple and yellow, very large and full of leaves, the two chiefest varieties in Flora's Cabinet.

In the middle of the eighteenth century the sensational break occurred, already noted, which produced the spectacular stage auriculas. Soon after, James Douglas the nurseryman wrote a book entitled *The Distinguishing of a Fine Auricula*. William Robinson notes that the auricula's 'more striking variations were perpetuated and classified and it became, like tulips, carnations and pinks, a florist's flower'. Auricula-growing soon became the pastime, not only of the wealthy connoisseurs but also of the working classes of the industrial north of England, and especially of Lancashire. Among these the spirit of competition was very keen, though the prizes striven for were modest – a trowel or a hot-water kettle being the most customary rewards.

Any flower so exquisitely designed by nature, aided by man, so odd, in colors so totally unlike any other, was quickly claimed as the perfect subject for the artist. Jan Breughel, who was painting his wreathes of striped tulips, anemones and lilies at the end of the sixteenth century, if he included auriculas at all, only painted the simple hardy varieties. It was not until the appearance of the more exotic varieties that auriculas became the popular subject for artists that they have been for the last two centuries.

The Flemish painter Pieter Casteels painted twenty-six different varieties of auricula. They were painted by the careful Georg Dionysius Ehret, and the great Redouté forsook his beloved .roses to paint several portraits of auriculas. Robert Thornton includes an auricula, in a wind-blown alpine setting, in his *Temple of Flora*.

The elegant Mrs Delaney, whom Edmund Burke considered 'the highest bred woman in the world – and the woman of fashion of all ages', often chose auriculas as subjects for her curious and finicking floral mosaics, many of which are in the Royal Collection at Windsor Castle. It was Mrs Delaney, who, in her *Autobiography* published in 1861, described her 'very pretty summer house, on the corner of it are houses built up for blowing auriculas' – another example of the stage or buffet, upon which auriculas have often been exhibited.

Auriculas Today. Today auricula plants can be bought quite cheaply, and though less spectacularly named (one looks in vain in catalogues for 'Black Imperial' or 'Mistress Buggs' Her Fine Purple'), the modern auriculas are just as fascinating as the plants which caught the eye of the *Roi Soleil* and kept the Rector of Quatt from the composition of his sermons. Some show flowers which are personally known to the author are the green-edged 'Brockenhurst' and 'Greenfinch', the grey-edged 'Grey Friar' and the white-rimmed 'White Ensign'. Of the hardier alpine auriculas – all of which can be grown in the open, in any well drained, not too sunny position – are 'Golden Gleam', 'Gordon Douglas', 'Lady Daresbury' and 'Pink Lady'.

Seed can be sown at any time of the year – but the seedlings will seldom come true. But that, perhaps, is the fascination of raising auriculas from seed. Out of two hundred seedlings there may be one prize plant, one transcendent flower such as inspired the Reverend Samuel Gilbert to write,

> With all their pretty shades and Ornaments
> Their parti-coloured coats and pleasing scents.
> Gold laid on scarlet, silver on the blew
> With sparkling eyes to take the eye of you
> Mixt colours, many more to please that sense,
> Others with rich and great magnificence,
> In double Ruffs, with gold and silver-laced
> On purple crimson and so neatly placed.

'To take the eye of you ...' of all the flowers created by the hand of man rather than conjured by nature, no flower is more calculated to do that than the auricula.

Polyanthus, entirely man-made flowers, were the result of a cross between the wild primrose, Primula acaulis *or* vulgaris *and the cowslip* Primula veris. *An early mention of the polyanthus is made by John Evelyn at the end of the seventeenth century.*

Rosa bifera pumila – *Le Petit Quatre Saisons*, *from Volume III of Redouté's* Les Roses. *This is a rose of the greatest antiquity which was certainly growing in Roman gardens. Its flowers are pink and very sweetly scented. Virgil wrote of the roses of Paestum which bloomed twice, the* biferi rosaria Paesti. *Dryden translated this as 'The Paestan roses and their double spring'.*

Rose

The most evocative and beautiful of flowers

Books have been written about the history and mystique of roses. From ancient times they have been the flowers that have been acclaimed as the very symbol of perfection, though in the Bible the rose is only mentioned twice. And whether it is a rose which was meant is debatable. The rose, like which the desert was to blossom when it received 'the excellency of Sharon', was probably that native of Palestine, the anemone. And the Rose of Sharon itself, we are now told, may well have been the workaday St John's Wort. But whatever flower was originally meant, for the translators of the Bible the flower they chose to epitomize beauty was the rose; the kind of rose which William Tyndale had seen growing in the gardens of Little Sodbury in Gloucestershire.

Roses were as acclaimed in Greece, though with more restraint, as they later were to be in Rome. Tom Moore (who wrote *The Last Rose of Summer* in the early nineteenth century) offers a translation of the great lyric poet Anacreon's account of the origin of the rose, which, it seems, sprang from Venus' blushes when observed by Jupiter, bathing.

> Then, then, in strange eventful hour,
> The earth produced an infant flower,
> Which sprung with blushing tinctures drest,
> And wantoned o'er its parent's breast.
> The gods beheld this brilliant birth,
> And hailed the Rose, the boon of earth.

Anacreon was the great lyric poet of the sixth century before Christ. He praised the pleasures of life, love, women, wine and roses and died, we are told, of choking on a grape-pip, aged eighty-five, and enjoying life to the last.

Roses in the famous garden at Sissinghurst Castle in Kent. The castle was built in the reign of Henry VIII but the garden made in the last forty years.

In the third century BC, Theophrastus, the philosopher, whose botanical work *Enquiry into Plants* was one of the first works of its kind in history, describes roses in some detail, and makes suggestions for their culture. Theophrastus was the friend and school-fellow of Alexander the Great, who would write to him with news of rare plants that he had seen on his campaigns.

Of roses Theophrastus wrote:

> Most have five petals – but some have twelve or twenty, and some a great many more than these: for there are some they say which are even called hundred petalled ... most of such roses grow near Philippi; for the people of that place get them on Mount Pangaeus, where they are abundant, and plant them ... most sweet scented of all are the roses of Cyrene ...

Bion – the bucolic poet – two hundred years later sang the rose's praise. He is one of the many poets who have suggested that all roses once were white; and that they were stained red by the blood of Adonis, the incestuous child of Myrrha by her father the King of Cyprus, when he was killed by a wild boar. Or, if it was not Adonis' blood which stained the rose, it was the blood of the amorous Venus, when she was hurrying to his assistance; and, as Moore recounts,

> Her step she fixes on the cruel thorns
> And with her blood the pallid rose adorns.

Roses wreathed the triumphant standards of the Roman armies – and the heads of Roman revellers. At the banquets of Nero, roses, five million sesterces worth, according to Suetonius in his *Lives of the Caesars*, emitted a scent that was overpowering. The Emperor Caligula, (who made his horse a Consul) walked to bed over a carpet of red roses; while the guests of Heliogabulus (who made his hairdresser Commander-in-Chief of his army) were, literally, suffocated by the scent of roses.

Thus, in Roman days, roses seem to have got into bad company. But it is not only in connection with excess that roses are remembered. Several Roman poets, in pure and lovely language, sang their praises. Ausonius was one, and for once forsook his cold analytical style, warmed a little by the rose, when he wrote his poem *De Rosis Nascentibus* ('On New Blown Roses'). His lines have been sensitively translated by Helen Waddell:

> Think you, did Dawn steel colour from the roses,
> Or was it new born day that stained the rose?
> To each one dew, one crimson, and one morning,
> To star and rose, their lady Venus one.
> Mayhap one fragrance, but the sweet of Dawn
> Drifts through the sky, and closer breathes the rose.

For the Romans, in some mysterious way the rose was connected with secrecy, and an anonymous Latin poet wrote:

> The rose is the flower of Venus: in order that her sweet thefts might be concealed, Love dedicated to Harpocrates, the God of Silence this gift of his mother. Hence the host hangs over his friendly table a rose, that the guests underneath it may know how to keep silence as to what is said.

Thus the phrase 'Sub-Rosa'; and curiously, the plaster central motif on the ceiling above the table in Victorian dining rooms was referred to as the 'rose'.

The coming of Christianity dethroned the rose. Perhaps the austere early Christians connected the flower too closely with pagan revels. But the rose's period of disfavour did not last long, and it was soon reinstated. Its five petals were taken to symbolize the five wounds of Christ, while red roses were taken to recall the blood of the early martyrs.

The Rosary is first mentioned by Thomas de Cantimpre in the thirteenth century. In a mystic sense it represented Mary's rose-garden, and the first fraternity of the Rosary was founded in Cologne in 1474.

Soon the rose motif was being incorporated in ecclesiastical architecture – and there are rose windows in many cathedrals. One of the most elaborate is in York Minster in England; and in the Chapter House at York there is an inscription which runs UT ROSA FLOS FLORUM SIC EST DOMUS DOMORUM ('as the rose is the flower of flowers, this is the house of all houses').

Fourteenth-century rose-windows such as these are to be found in the cathedrals of York and Exeter.

The Rose in Shakespeare's Poetry, and After. Shakespeare mentions the rose no less than seventy times, and the first two lines of his first sonnet run:

> From fairest creatures we desire increase
> That thereby beauty's rose might never die.

Duke Theseus, in *A Midsummer Night's Dream*, points out to the unmarried Hermia that the 'Rose distilled' was:

> Earthlier happy
> Than that which withering on the Virgin thorn
> Grows, lives and dies in single blessedness.

For the ageing Antony, young Caesar wore the rose of youth, and when Othello plucked the rose of Desdemona's life he could not 'give it vital growth again'. Oberon's bank was 'overcanopied ... with sweet musk roses and with eglantine'. For Ophelia, Hamlet was 'the rose of the fair state'. And everyone remembers Juliet's question

> What's in a name? That which we call a rose
> By any other name would smell as sweet.

163

All through the seventeenth century poets sang the rose. For George Herbert, who wrote of the rose in some of the most beautiful language ever inspired by the flower, it was, as to many others, the symbol of short-lived beauty:

> Sweet rose, whose hue, angry and brave
> Bids the rash gazer wipe his eye,
> Thy root is ever in its grave
> And thou must die . . .

and elsewhere he evokes:

> Sweet spring – full of sweet days and roses
> A box where sweets compacted lie.

Robert Herrick who loved to

> Sing of brooks, of blossoms, buds, and bowers
> Of April, May, of June, and July flowers

and wrote verses to daisies, 'not to shut so soon', to violets, and to daffodils, was obsessed by the rose. He offers yet another suggestion as to how red roses were created:

> Roses at first were white
> Till they could not agree
> Whether my Sappho's breast
> Or they more white sho'd be –.

And in an attractive and little-known poem, he describes the rose's funeral:

> The rose was sick and smiling, died
> And being to be sanctified.
> About the bed there sighing, stood
> The sweet and flowery sisterhood.
> Some hung their heads, while some did bring
> (To wash her) water from the spring.
> Some laid her forth, while others wept
> But all a solemn fast there kept.
> The Holy sisters, some among
> The sacred dirge and trental sung.
> But ah, what sweets smelt everywhere,
> As heaven had spent all perfumes there.
> At last, when prayers for the dead
> And rights were all accomplished,
> They, weeping, spread a lawney loom,
> And closed her up, as in a tomb.

One of the best known of all rose quotations occurs in the rose-addicted Herrick's poem *To love*:

Gather ye rosebuds while ye may
Old Time is still a-flying
And this same flower that smells today
Tomorrow will be dying.

Andrew Marvell wrote a poem in a different mood, when he describes how he kept a pet fawn in his garden which was overgrown with roses and lilies;

Upon the roses it would feed
Until its lips e'en seemed to bleed ...'

but such a rich diet proved fatal, and the fawn died. Its lily-bordered home was deserted. Marvell philosophically concludes:

Had it lived long, it would have been
Lilies without, roses within.

In *Old Garden Roses* Wilfrid Blunt suggests that, 'As there are "good" and "bad" years in the rose garden, so are there fruitful and barren ages in the literature of the rose. The seventeenth century was prolific: the poets of the eighteenth century sadly neglect the Queen of Flowers', but Mr Blunt offers 'at least a button-hole' in Alexander Pope's 'Die of a rose – in aromatic pain'.

The early nineteenth century saw the rose restored to favor, and Keats, Blake and Shelley were all loud in its praises. Blake, in one of his most often-quoted poems, describes the rose being menaced by a very odd insect of his own imagination – 'the invisible worm that flies in the night'. The ailing Keats too loved roses, and when thanking a friend for sending him some, once wrote in gratitude:

But when, oh Wells, thy roses came to me
My senses with their deliciousness was spelled
Soft voices had they, that with tender plea
Whispered of peace and truth and friendliness unquelled.

Elsewhere Keats enquires, wistfully:

What is more tranquil than a musk rose blowing
In a green island, far from all men's knowing?

Shelley heaped roses for his sweetheart's bed, and for Thomas Moore the last rose of summer was left blooming alone. Tennyson could scarcely hear the sound of rose petals falling, and Maud kept her roses waiting in the garden. For Browning's patriot it was 'Roses, roses all the way', which must surely be one of the best-known quotations in all poetry. But how many people know how the poem goes on – or what it is about?

It was roses, roses all the way
With myrtle mixed in my path like mad:
The house roofs seemed to heave and sway,
The church-spires flamed, such flags they had,
A year ago on this very day.

Browning wrote *The Patriot* in 1849 when he was in Italy, a sympathetic observer of Italian efforts to shake off the Austrian yoke. The poem reflects the changing loyalties of the time, and how from one year to another a popular leader could lose his following, be denounced and even executed; it was the story of the twelfth-century hero, Arnold of Brescia, that inspired the poem.

Many people today complain that modern roses, the new hybrids, lack the character and especially the scent of the roses of a hundred years ago. A poet of the last century, and one of this, seem also to be of this opinion. Christina Rossetti thought that that the roses she remembered were brighter:

Oh lost green paradise
Were the roses redder there
Than they blossom other where?

While George Moore pompously proclaimed:

The Rose of the past is better
Than the rose we ravish today
T'is holier, purer and fitter
To place on the shrine where we pray.

George Moore died in 1933 soon after a famous American writer, Gertrude Stein, had 'coined' a phrase about a rose which at once became famous: 'Rose is a rose is a rose'. The simple rhythmic phrase reminds us that a rose, for all the legends and symbolism, is after all a flower – 'whose simple doom is to be beautiful'. Gertrude Stein had her famous phrase printed in a circle – and made it her own symbol, to conjure the color, fragrance and very shape of the most beautiful of flowers.

Four widely different roses from the Hortus Eystettensis.

The Rose in French Literature. The rose plays its part in French literature as it does in English, and 'Le Roi des Rimes' – Theodore de Banville – in three famous lines sings lightheartedly:

> To study well the cons and pros
> Should be our duty, I suppose ...
> Only words. Lets pick a rose

suggesting that gathering roses is more fun than examining the whys and wherefores of life. The philosophical Antoine Arnault knew that eventually he was fated to disappear:

> Where everything one day goes
> The petals of the rose
> And the wreath of laurel

And Jacques de Cassaigne's soldier tells the rose:

> One day you will die: but perhaps
> I will die sooner than you
> For the death that my soul so fears
> May come at any time.
> You will take a day to die
> I may only take a moment.

Perhaps the most moving reference to the rose in all French poetry occurs in François de Malherbes lines to his friend Duperrier, on the death of his daughter.

> On earth, the best things
> Have the saddest fates
> She was a rose, and lived, as roses do
> A morning only.

There are innumerable references to the rose in French poetry, and most of them equate the rose's fleeting beauty with the passage of youth, or sometimes of life itself.

It is Fontenelle, in his *La Pluralité des Mondes*, who suggests that if roses – which only last a day – were to write history, each of their interpretations would be the same. For in the short life of a rose, it must seem that nothing ever changes. For roses, the gardener is always the same: within the rose's memory – 'he has always been there ... certainly ... he does not die like we do. ...'

Fontenelle's remark became famous, and Diderot quotes it in his *Réve D'Alembert*. The Doctor Bordeu, in conversation with Mlle de L'Espinasse refers to 'a transitory being which believes in immortality', whereupon the erudite Mlle de L'Espinasse takes him up with, 'Like Fontenelle's rose, which thought that gardeners never die', and the Doctor replies 'Exactly – it is light yet profound'.

A hundred and more years later Henry Austin Dobson put the story into 'a random rhyme' in his *Fancy from Fontenelle*:

> The Rose in the garden slipped her bud,
> And she laughed in the pride of her youthful blood,
> As she though of the Gardener standing by –
> 'He is old – so old! And he soon must die!'
>
> The full Rose waxed in the warm June air,
> And she spread and spread till her heart lay bare;
> And she laughed once more as she heard his tread –
> 'He is older now! He will soon be dead!'
>
> But the breeze of the morning blew, and found
> That the leaves of the blown Rose strewed the ground
> And he came at noon, that Gardener old,
> And he raked them gently under the mould.
>
> And I wove the thing to a random rhyme,
> For the Rose is Beauty, the Gardener, Time.

Richard Folkard, in his *Plant Lore, Legends and Lyrics*, mentions the festival of Salency which was instituted in the sixth century by St Médard, the Bishop of Noyon, when a crown of roses was placed on the head of the most virtuous girl of the village. Madame de Genlis, who had a passion for all flowers, heard by chance of the old custom from the Bailli of Salency, who was complaining at having to leave a pleasant house-party, and travel 'dix ou douze lieues dans des chemins de traverse abominables', to award a rose to the most virtuous girl in the village of Salency. 'The word rose at once interested me', writes Madame de Genlis, who, far from finding it, as the Bailli did, 'une vraie bêtise, ... établie dans les temps barbares', took her whole party to witness the ceremony.

168 Madame de Genlis was delighted with the crowning of the Rose Girl of

*'I have seen the dew-drop clinging
to the rose just newly born.'* (Charles Jefferys, 1807–65)
R. floribunda – *'Rosemary'*.

Salency, but the logical Jean François La Harpe, in his *Cours de Litérature*, pours scorn on the charming old custom. 'How absurd', he says, 'to offer a crown of roses to virtue – on this earth virtue should be its own reward ... no enlightened mother would allow her daughter this honor – which is not an honor but an insult. If the girl is all she should be, she should not know why a "crown of roses" for virtue is needed.' Which is another point of view.

Jean François La Harpe was the contemporary of two people whose names will always be linked with the rose: the Empress Joséphine, generous patron of botany and horticulture, and Pierre Joseph Redouté, 'Raphael de la Rose'.

Joséphine de Beauharnais was the attractive Creole widow whom Napoleon, then a obscure young general, married just before his campaign in Italy which 169 was to make him famous. Early in their married life Joséphine bought the Château of Malmaison near Paris. Here she created a garden which was quickly to become one of the wonders of France. Joséphine's favorite flowers were roses, and every known variety was planted in her garden. She commissioned Redouté to paint their portraits.

Pierre-Joseph Redouté was born in Luxemburg in the year 1759, and came from a family of painters. While still a boy he made a journey through the Low Countries to study the paintings of the great Dutch masters, Bosschaert, Van Os and especially the famous Van Huysum. When he was twenty-three he went to Paris, and worked at stage design. Here, by a fortunate chance, he met a rich botanist, Charles de Brutelle. Redouté had always been fascinated by flowers, and de Brutelle, quickly recognizing his talent, encouraged him to make flower-painting his career, and sent him to England to study the plants at Kew. While in England Redouté had the opportunity of studying the art of stipple engraving. This was to play an important part in enabling him to reproduce the flower portraits for which he is famous.

On his return to Paris, Redouté made the acquaintance of Gerard Van Spaendonck, the pupil of Van Huysum, whose *Fleurs dessinées après Nature* are some of the most beautiful of all flower engravings. Van Spaendonck, like de Brutelle, was quick to recognize Redouté's genius and gave him an appointment on the Royal Collections of Paintings on Vellum. Soon after, another important appointment came Redouté's way, that of drawing-master to Queen Marie Antoinette. In that capacity, he visited the captive queen in the Temple, bringing her drawings of plants, and on one occasion making a drawing of a cactus she had cultivated in prison.

It was the wife of Napoleon, Joséphine de Beauharnais, who was to be Redouté's greatest and most munificent Royal patron.

The first great book commissioned by the Empress was published in Paris in 1803, entitled *Le Jardin de la Malmaison*, with illustrations by Redouté and text by E.P.Ventenat. Its courteous dedication is quoted in part as it seems particularly evocative of the age, and of the affection in which Joséphine – who must have been a delightful woman – was held by those who knew her.

> Madame, you have decided that the love of flowers should not be a vain one ... and you have made a collection of the rarest plants in France. Thanks to you, even some from Arabia and the deserts of Egypt are now naturalized in our soil. These, studiously classified in the beautiful gardens of Malmaison, gently commemorate the conquests of your illustrious husband.

And Monsieur de Ventenat, after more tributes to Madame Bonaparte's thoughtfulness in wishing to make known to a wider public the treasures of her garden, ends his dedication with this compliment:

The Virgin in the Rose Garden by Stefano di Verona (1375–1451) at Castelvecchio, Verona.

Rosa Banksiæ.   *Rosier de Lady Banks.*

If, while preparing this book, I have lingered over the description of certain modest plants which seem to exist only to spread around them 'une influence aussi douce que salutaire' I would be unable, Madame, to deny an allusion which is obvious.

Joséphine's was not a profound character – and Napoleon, though devoted to her, once complained, 'A quoi bon vouloir que la dentelle pèse autant que l'or?' But she was a dedicated gardener, and a great lover of roses. She is commemorated by the rose 'Souvenir de la Malmaison' and, until they recently changed the name, by a very beautiful gallica rose, 'Empress Joséphine'. When she died, an obituary notice appeared in the *Moniteur* which, remembering that Joséphine had been Empress of France, Queen of Italy and wife of Napoleon, is surely a masterpiece of understatement: 'The death of Madame de Beauharnais excites widespread sympathy. This woman was unfailingly gentle, and possessed much charm and attraction of manner and mind. Extremely unhappy during her husband's reign she sought refuge from his roughness in the study of Botany.'

Joséphine died in 1814, and Redouté's most famous book, *Les Roses*, commissioned by her and containing portraits of the roses of the garden of Malmaison, did not appear till 1817. It was to have been dedicated to the Empress, but the Bourbons sat once more on the throne of France and *Les Roses* is dedicated to the Duchesse d'Orleans.

Roses in the Literature of the Last Century. In the last hundred years a rose has played the chief role in one of Oscar Wilde's most touching stories, in Richard Strauss' most scintillating opera, and in Nijinsky's most famous ballet.

In Wilde's story, *The Nightingale and the Rose*, a tale full of gentleness and compassion:

> A young student, passionately in love, is told by his wayward sweetheart that she will only dance with him, and listen to his declarations, if he brings her a red rose. In all his garden there is no red rose, so the student is cast down, and complains bitterly of his misfortune. A nightingale, 'from her nest in the holm oak tree' overhears him, takes pity on him, and offers to

Rosa banksiae, by P. J. Redouté. This Chinese climbing rose, which needs a warm wall and no pruning, was named after the wife of Sir Joseph Banks.

The Empress Joséphine at Malmaison. The Empress was a passionate flower lover and commissioned Redouté to portray some of the favorite flowers in her garden.

173

try to find him the rose he needs. But all the rose trees round about seem only to bear white roses, 'white as the foam of the sea' or yellow roses, 'yellow as the hair of the mermaiden who sits on an amber throne'. At last the nightingale does find a red rose tree, but all its blooms have been killed by frost and the nightingale is disappointed, 'One red rose is all I want – only one red rose. Is there no way by which I can get it?' 'There is a way,' said the tree, 'but it is so terrible that I dare not tell it to you.' 'Tell it to me,' said the nightingale. 'I am not afraid.' 'If you want a red rose,' said the tree, 'you must build it out of music by moonlight, and stain it with your own heart's blood. You must sing to me with your breast against a thorn. All night long you must sing to me, and the thorn must pierce your heart, and your life blood must flow into my veins and become mine.' 'Death is a great price to pay for a red rose,' cried the nightingale, 'and life is very dear to all. It is pleasant to sit in the green wood and to watch the sun in his chariot of gold, and the moon in her chariot of pearl. Sweet is the scent of the hawthorn, and sweet are the bluebells that hide in the valley, and the heather that blows on the hill. Yet love is better than life, and what is the heart of a bird compared to the heart of a man?'

So the pact is made, and the nightingale sacrifices her life to bring the love-sick student his rose.

But when the student offers his love the rose, she spurns it, saying that she prefers jewels, and the student throws the flower angrily away – and the nightingale lies dead in the long grass.

Richard Strauss – whose opera *Der Rosenkavalier* was first performed in Dresden in 1911 – sets his scene in Vienna in the eighteenth century. Ever since its opening night its lilting, nostalgic (though anachronistic) waltz music has cast a spell on opera lovers the world over. Its bitter-sweet Viennese charm, a mixture of sentiment and cynicism and almost Proustian pre-occupation with time and the changes it brings, has made it the most loved of all the Strauss' operas. In the shimming opening of the second act, 'The Presentation of the Rose', the stage instructions run:

> Oktavian's servants enter, in their liveries of white and pale green ... Footmen, heyducks with crescent-shaped Hungarian sabres, lackeys in soft white leather and green ostrich feathers. They are followed by a Negro, who carries the rose's case. Finally Oktavian enters carrying in his right hand the rose.

The handsome Oktavian is representing the very different Baron Ochs, and the rose is not a real one but is of silver, and scented with 'Persian Attar'. All, in fact, is artifice, but poor Sophie falls in love with Oktavian on the spot,

'Baroness Rothschild',
a hybrid perpetual rose.
A 'sport' which
occurred in 1868
from 'Souvenir de
la Reine d'Angleterre'.
It has flowers of
clear pink.

Henry VII united the
House of York and the
House of Lancaster
by his marriage to the
Plantagenet Princess
Elizabeth. In this
portrait he holds a York
and Lancaster rose.

and for her the rose is 'unbearably sweet – a greeting from Heaven'. But after that initial misunderstanding, all comes right in the end.

In Nijinsky's ballet, *Le Spectre de la Rose*, a rose actually comes to life. The story was inspired by Théophile Gautier's poem, and it became one of the great choreographer Fokine's most famous ballets.

A girl, coming home from her first ball, lies back in a chair and dreamingly thinks of the evening she has just passed. In her hand she holds a rose, given to her by her lover. Smelling it, and tired out by the pleasure of the ball, she falls asleep, and at once the Spirit of the Rose, a gauzy mysterious figure, enters, as if a vapor of the night – half man, half rose. With one leap he crosses the stage, gently wakes the girl, who finds in the Spirit of the Rose her half-formed dreams of love come true. They dance together and the girl recaptures the happiness of the ball, and with it a promise of love. Sinking once more into her chair she falls asleep, and the Spirit, with one breathtaking bound, leaps through the window, into the rose-scented night, and away.

Such was the *Spectre de la Rose*, Nijinsky's most celebrated ballet; and his celebrated last bound through the window became the sensation of Europe and America.

The Rose in History. An historic instance of the rose's role in history is the start of the Wars of the Roses, which raged in England from 1455 to 1485. Shakespeare sets the opening scene in his play of *Henry VI*, when a quarrel breaks out between Richard Plantagenet and the Duke of Suffolk. Lancastrians and Yorkists pick red and white roses respectively, and these became the emblems of the rival factions in the thirty years' warfare which followed. When finally peace came, it was consolidated by the politic marriage of Henry Tudor and the Plantagenet Princess Elizabeth of York. Henceforth the red and white Tudor rose became the emblem of the royal house of England, and Henry VII was painted holding one.

A white rose was the symbol of the Jacobites, and Prince Charles Edward's Highlanders wore them in their bonnets as they marched into England in 1745.

White roses, too, were worn by King George II's soldiers at the Battle of Minden in 1759, where the Lancashire Fusiliers were stationed in a rose   175 garden just before the battle and picked roses to stick in their caps. To this day they are called the Minden Boys, and wear white roses on 1 August.

The Rose in America. The rose is the adopted flower of several American states, with the District of Columbia unofficially claiming the 'American Beauty' rose and the state of Georgia the 'White Cherokee' rose. The rose is the flower of New York State, the wild rose that of Iowa and the Prairie rose the flower of North Dakota.

The White Cherokee rose – *Rosa laevigata*, is the state flower of Georgia, and there is a curious legend about it. This rose, it seems, was once an Indian girl whom the Nunnshi – the 'little people' – turned into a flower to save her when her village was captured by a hostile tribe; not only was she turned into a rose but, for further protection, her stem was covered with specially sharp prickles.

Another American rose-legend is that of the Grant rose, which is said to have sprung from the blood of Mrs Grant, wife of an early settler in Florida, who was killed by the Seminole. The Grant rose has blood-red flowers which are almost unique among roses in having a heavy, unpleasant scent.

Many of our finest roses have been raised in the United States, and it is there that the most sensational developments have taken place in rose creation in the last half century. Not so much in the field of the Hybrid Tea, as in France, or of the shrub rose, as in Germany, but in the making of many new wonderful climbing roses. 'Dorothy Perkins', the rose which is seen in many suburban gardens, is an American-raised rose; it was created in 1901 by the firm of Jackson and Perkins who worked in collaboration with their celebrated hybridizer, Gene Boerner, and are still raising good new climbing and rambling roses. 'Goldilocks', introduced in 1952, is one of theirs. The beautiful rambler, 'New Dawn', was raised in the United States in 1930 and inherited its useful late flowering qualities from its parent (another American), 'Dr Van Fleet', called after an American politician and enthusiastic horticulturist. Many of the new floribundas, too, are raised in America; some of the best, in fact, since the first polyanthas were raised in Denmark by the firm of Poulsen fifty years ago; the coral 'Fashion' was raised by Gene Boerner, who popularized the floribunda and worked with Jackson and Perkins in their important experimental nursery at Newark, where the sparkling 'Jiminy Cricket' was raised in 1954. Gene Boerner himself is commemorated by his own rose – a pink floribunda which was an all-American rose selection.

Ever since Charles Dingee opened the first American rose nursery at West Grove, Pennsylvania, in the year 1854, his successors have achieved great things: and some of the finest rose gardens in the world are in America, at Elizabeth Park in Hartford, Connecticut, Descanso Gardens, Los Angeles, California, and the Tyler Municipal Rose Garden in Texas. Finest of all is the rose garden at Portland, Oregon. Portland is known as the city of roses, and members of its Rose Society are called the Royal Rosarians.

The Origin of the Rose. In her poem *The Garden*, Victoria Sackville-West melodiously traces the history of the rose:

> June of the iris and the rose.
> The rose not English as we fondly think.
> Anacreon and Bion sang the rose;
> And Rhodes the isle whose very name means rose
> Struck roses on her coins;
> Pliny made lists and Roman libertines
> Made wreaths to wear among the flutes and wines;
> The young Crusaders found the Syrian rose
> Springing from Saracenic quoins,
> And China opened her shut gate
> To let her roses through, and Persian shrines
> Of Poetry and painting gave the rose.

And Walter de la Mare sums up the rose's mysterious ancestry in three much quoted lines:
> No one knows
> Through what wild centuries
> Roves back the rose.

Some roses originate in Persia and some in the Far East. Some have reached Western gardens from Greece and Italy, other more recently from North America. Modern roses owe most to the China Rose (*R. chinensis*) and what was probably the China Rose's close relation, *R. odorata*. Both these great roses only reached the Western world less than two hundred years ago. But for centuries before that they were grown and cherished in China, and their pictures occur constantly in oriental art, painted on screens, or preserved under the fine glaze of porcelain.

> '*Roses at first were white*
> *till they co'd not agree,*
> *whether my Sappho's breast*
> *or they more white sho'd be*' (Robert Herrick, 1591–1674).

177

From a cross between *R. chinensis* and the 'Rose de Quatre Saisons' (a Damask rose) sprang the Bourbon strain of roses – and these became in the course of time the parent of the Hybrid Musks.

R. gallica, said to have been a native of Gaul, is supposed to be the prototype of the 'old' roses, Cabbage roses and Moss roses, which are now so popular. The ancestry and origin of the roses in modern gardens is complicated indeed, and volumes rather than a page or two would be needed to elucidate the subject. In a book of this scope, space might be more usefully employed by giving a personal choice of roses. This will be found not to include the Hybrid Teas. The best of these change so quickly from year to year that any choice must be too arbitrary. Furthermore – the Hybrid Teas are roses better grown for cutting, than for general garden decoration.

The Different Groups of Roses. The next pages will be given to the twelve classic groups of roses – with some others, for some modern hybrids are difficult to classify exactly. They are the roses, in different varieties, which the author, through the years, has found particularly rewarding. First, for they will ever be the most fascinating, he will list some of his favorite shrub roses. Some are species roses, others were bred hundreds of years ago, while some others are the result of the industry of rose-breeders in the last fifty years. All are, in their own way, outstanding, but not so rare as to be impossible to find in specialist nurseries.

They have been chosen for their qualities as garden plants, not, it must be strongly stressed, for the magic of their names. Yet, as Victoria Sackville-West once wrote of the old shrub roses, 'Their catalogues do read like one long poem of names ... Reine des Violettes, Cardinal Richelieu, Nuits de Young, Rosa-Mundi ...'. Roses with such evocative names distill a powerful spell. But no one should grow flowers only for their names or associations.

ROSA ALBA. These are the roses and their hybrids which have been growing in English gardens for centuries. Their characteristics are leaves which are flushed with blue-grey, and very strongly scented pale-colored flowers. They flower in a glorious burst in June and July, and are the most labor-saving of shrub roses in that they need little pruning. They have the oval hips of the wild Dog rose.

Rosa alba semi-plena is the White Rose of York, and of the Jacobites. This will in time make an eight-foot bush, covered with strongly fragrant white flowers, which are, as its name implies, semi-double.

'*Felicitée Parmentier*' is a rose which has honeysuckle-scented flowers with pale pink centres. When in bud, its flowers are a very pale cream.

'*Great Maiden's Blush*': This has blush-pink flowers, and is the rose of which Victoria Sackville-West once wrote, 'Great Maiden's Blush has more than a touch of romance in her various names alone. She has also been called La Séduisante and Cuisse de Nymphe ... or the Nymph's Thigh. When she blushed a particularly deep pink she was called Cuisse de Nymphe Emue. I will not insult the French language by attempting to translate this highly expressive name ...'.

'*Madame Legres de St Germain*' is a rose which that great authority Miss Murrell of Shrewsbury has singled out for special praise. Its 'sumptuous' flowers are many petalled and cream-centred.

'*Queen of Denmark*': This is what the well-known rosarian Mr Graham Thomas describes as a 'pearl beyond price'. A hybrid of *R. alba* with centifolia or damask blood, 'Queen of Denmark' is one of the finest of all the old roses. Its only weakness is a slight laxness of growth. To anyone interested in the nomenclature of plants this has a particularly interesting story. Miss Murrell records that it was named and first shown in 1898. In 1898 there were two queens in Denmark, both called Louise. It is not known whether it was named for the younger queen – a great, great grand-daughter of the Empress Joséphine who so loved roses, or for her mother-in-law, the widowed mother of Queen Alexandra, wife of Edward VII, who instituted Queen Alexandra's Rose Day.

Two other desirable roses of the *Rosa alba* group are 'Celestial', of which the pale-pink flowers and jade-green leaves are in the most perfect harmony, and 'Nivea', a favorite of Miss Nancy Lindsay, whose love of roses shows in her descriptions of those she used to grow in her garden at Sutton Courtenay: 'Nivea ... the Tudor Rose, still grows in the legend-haunted Wye Valley as it has done these last 500 years, its age-old roots fast in the stones of ruined castles and abbeys. A tall bush of shining grey-green with branched clusters of large semi-double, milk-white spicy flowers, with conspicuous gold starred centres.'

BOURBON ROSES. It is said that the Bourbon group of roses stems from a chance cross, in the French Island of Réunion in the Indian Ocean, of a China and a Damask rose, the 'Rose de Quatre Saisons'. Damask roses had long been used by the farmers of Réunion for hedging, a purpose for which their sharp thorns make them very suitable. The importation of roses from China, in the eighteenth century, led to the irregular union between the two strains, and the birth of the Bourbon rose. They make a group which includes some of the most beautiful and romantic roses we can grow. Their strange, evocative names alone have a mystique of their own. There is space only to mention twelve. There are, of course, many more.

'*Boule de Neige*': This is a rose which has globular white flowers, tinged with green. The outer petals of each flower curl back to make a setting for the very sweet-scented flowers, which are born throughout the summer months.

'*Commandant Beaurepaire*' is a dashing deep pink – but its many flowers show, writes Mr Graham Thomas, 'almost every color peculiar to the "old" roses ... pale pink, mauve, purple, maroon and scarlet splashes alternate, giving a bizarre and rich effect'. 'Commandant Beaurepaire' is also known as 'Panachée d'Angers'.

179

Rosa wichuraiana 'Octavia Hesse', trained over a wire
umbrella-shaped framework. The wichuraiana group
of roses originate in China, Formosa or Japan
and have a strong scent of apples.

RIGHT The rose garden at Bampton Manor in Oxfordshire
planted in the modern way – with standard roses, trees and
floribundas in a setting of grey leaved plants.
In the foreground, long flowering Yvonne Rabier.

180   Rosa foetida bicolor. The Austrian Copper Briar bears
       its spectacular flowers of flame color in midsummer.
       It is from this rose that all the modern orange-toned
       Hybrid Teas are descended – though none have
       the natural flamboyance of their forbear.

'*Baron Girod de L'Ain*': One of the author's very favorite roses – which makes an upstanding five-foot bush covered recurrently through the summer with deep purple-crimson flowers which are oddly piped with white, a characteristic it shares with the more usually grown 'Roger Lambelin' – but 'Baron Girod' is infinitely superior in habit and health. It is among the ten best 'old' roses, though in fact it was raised barely seventy years ago.

'*Honorine de Brabant*' is a striped rose with mauve flowers slashed with deeper pink. It shows more flowers in a second flowering season than some of the other Bourbons.

'*Queen Victoria*' has an old fashioned look, as if made of shells, and is a delicate strong pink. It is deliciously scented and rewardingly generous in flower.

'*Madame Pierre Oger*' is a sport of 'Queen Victoria'. The flowers start a pearly white and need the sun to bring out their warmer flush of pink.

'*Louise Odier*' offers, writes Miss Murrell, 'the very essence of all summer roses'. It makes a fine robust bush covered with pink flowers, with the petals of each symmetrically arranged and breathing a heady scent.

'*Souvenir de la Malmaison*': The rose from which the rather similarly shaped Malmaison carnations got their name. It bears the name of the Empress Joséphine's home perhaps because the gardens of Malmaison were, unfortunately, only a 'souvenir' by 1842, when the rose named after them appeared. Grown as a shrub, 'Souvenir de la Malmaison' will show flowers till late in the summer though it is equally effective grown as a climber. Its saucer-like, quartered flowers are flesh pink and can be several inches across.

A few other Bourbon roses which must not be omitted are the purple-rosetted 'Zigeuner Knabe' (Gypsy Boy), the striking 'Variegata di Bologna' with white and purple splashed petals, and one of the best of all, 'Madame Isaac Pereire', with deep carmine flowers. This was a rose which was a great favorite of the late Mr Mark Fenwick of Abbotswood in Gloucestershire, who thought 'Madame Isaac Pereire' 'the loveliest and the latest, the largest and the sweetest rose in the garden. ...' And Miss Lindsay singles out for special praise a rose called after one of Napoleon's fieriest marshals, General Oudinot, as having flowers like 'great cabbages of bloody crimson'.

ROSA CENTIFOLIA. These are the roses which Gerard described as being 'in their braverie in June' – the roses that Van Huysum and the earlier Flemish painters painted. They are the offspring of the heavily scented *R. moschata* – the Musk rose – and *Rosa alba*.

'*Chapeau de Napoléon*': This is one of the most curious of the *Rosa centifolia* group. It takes its name from the likeness in bud of its crested sepals to the Emperor's hat. The flowers are a rich rose-pink. Any collector of 'old' roses should include this fascinating rose in his rose-garden.

'*Duc de Fitzjames*': It is impossible to say whether the Duke, for which this rose was named, was tall or short, fat or thin – but Miss Lindsay, in one of her telling descriptions, gives us an idea when she calls this rose: 'rumbustious, with portly cabbages of honeyed heliotrope-rose'. 'Duc de Fitzjames' certainly makes a vigorous bush, sometimes six feet high. Of it Miss Murrell writes: 'The cupped array of petals is another attraction; they are quartered with a green eye'.

'*Fantin Latour*' was a rose which everywhere caught the author's eye last summer, and it is certainly a rose which the great artist would have loved to paint. The flowers (fresh pale-pink), leaves (mint-green), and habit (robust yet compact) are all perfect.

'*Robert le Diable*', with parma-violet flowers merging to dark purple flowers which do not fade in the hottest sun, comes into bloom rather later than the other centifolias.

'*Tour de Malakoff*', whose name recalls the Crimean War, during which time the rose appeared, the oddly-named 'Spong', and the seventeenth-century 'De Meaux', are three other centifolia roses which should all be found a place.

THE MOSS ROSES. *Rosa muscosa* is the rose *par excellence* of the early nineteenth century, for it was not until Queen Victoria's girlhood that the Moss rose, with its flowers emerging shyly from its parsley-trimmed calyxes, came completely into its own – and flowered, not only in gardens, but on china, in painting and on the wallpaper of the young Queen's bedroom in Kensington Palace.

Six out of many which would embellish a rose garden are: 'Baronne de Wassenaer' – pink flowers and reddish moss; 'Blanche Moreau' – white flowers and dark moss, and a few flowers in the late summer; the deep plum-black 'Captain Ingram'; the well-known 'Nuits de Young', which Miss Lindsay describes as: 'rich and rare as a Chinese Jewel Tree – with . . . flowers of black velvet'; the equally well-known 'William Lobb', which is such a strong grower that it has been known to climb a wall. It has deep purple flowers which fade almost to blue. As 'William Lobb' grows so tall, it should be planted behind other shrub roses. 'Unique Blanche' is the last Moss rose we mention, and one of the oldest (1775). It flowers late, but some think it the loveliest of all white roses. Gertrude Jekyll admired it greatly.

ROSA DAMASCENA – *The Damask Rose*. These all grow into tall bushes, open in habit. Their hips are long and narrow. The Damask roses are said to have been introduced in Europe by the Crusaders, whose campaigns took them to Damascus, where the strong oil secreted in their flowers made them the ideal rose to grow as a crop for the production of attar of roses. Their flowers are usually white or pink.

'*Kazanlik*' is a rose with fresh apple-green foliage and its heady scent is one of the strongest rose-fragrances of the garden. The true attar of roses might well be pressed from their rose petals, and Mr Graham Thomas tells us: 'Two roses are grown at Kazanlik for distilling attar. Fields of *trigintipetala* are surrounded by hedges of *alba maxima* ... There is no rose to which Kazanlik is more usually attributed than the first named.'

'*Madame Hardy*' has white flowers which some consider to be the perfect white roses, flat saucer-like blooms, centred with pale green pointels. It makes a tall shrub and its leaves are a fresh clear green.

'*Rose de Quatre Saisons*': This is one of the oldest of all roses, and though its double shell-pink flowers are modest, it is worth a place in any collection for its long history – which dates from before Roman times – and for its long flowering season. Its role as parent, with *R. chinensis*, of the Bourbon roses has been noted.

'*Isfahan*': If the 'old' roses have a fault, it is that they do not last well when cut. 'Isfahan' is an exception and its warm pink flowers, if brought indoors, will scent a whole room for days on end. In the garden it is often grown as a hedge.

'*York and Lancaster*': No 'old' rose evokes the past as this most romantic of all flowers. It is the rose that symbolizes the union of the rival factions of the Wars of the Roses in fifteenth-century England, the rose which Gerard described as: 'The honour and ornament of our English sceptre, as by the conjunction it appeareth, in the uniting of those two most Royale Houses of Lancaster and York – which pleasant flowers deserve the chiefest place in crownes and garlands'.

The 'York and Lancaster' rose was named as long ago as 1551, when the Wars of the Roses were within living memory. Its petals are pink and white and the weakness of the rose is its occasional scanty show of flower, unless in rich soil. It is quite different from *Rosa mundi*, mentioned below, which is a gallica, has striped petals of raspberry and white (or pink and raspberry) and is far more free flowering. But in any garden the 'York and Lancaster' rose deserves a place.

ROSA GALLICA. This is a group of roses which would surely be the most acclaimed of all if they had a longer flowering season. But high summer is their moment of triumph, and they have no other. The French roses have been grown for centuries, and in the Middle Ages they were much cultivated in the district round Provins, near Fontainbleau, for use in cordials and simples. The Provins rose imported into England was the Red Rose of Lancaster. All the gallicas make tidy shrubs and they have branches that are clothed in stiff bristles rather than thorns. Their leaves are narrow and pointed, with serrated edges.

'*Rosa mundi*': The best known of the gallicas is described (above) with the 'York and Lancaster' rose, with which it is often confused. Other outstanding French roses must include:

'*Belle de Crécy*', which Miss Murrell describes as 'surely the most beautiful and almost the most floriferous of all the "old" roses. Exquisite buds in which rose and lilac tones compete ...'.

'*Camaieux*' is a 'young' rose – barely forty years old – but is already the most popular striped rose after 'York and Lancaster' and *Rosa mundi*.

Rosa gallica. '*High summer is their moment of triumph and they have no others.*'

Rosa gallica versicolor *or* Rosa mundi, *in an Irish garden. It has petals that are striped in raspberry and white.*

'*Cardinal de Richelieu*' is one of the first ten 'old' roses, with its purple dusky flowers which bloom in masses for several weeks in June.

'*Charles de Mills*': Miss Nancy Lindsay says of this splendid crimson purple-flowered rose, 'an exotic beauty some yards high of smooth dark jade bedizened with non-pareil, ruched, razed blooms of glowing fuchsia and purple ruby, like old Spanish velvet'.

Rosa francofurtana – 'of Frankfurt': One wonders why this workaday name has been given to a rose which some think the most beautiful rose in the world, and one which originally bore the name of that devoted rose-grower, the Empress Joséphine. If one could only grow a single gallica, this rose would be the one. The flowers are a rich fondant pink and are veined with a darker shade and the branches are practically thornless.

Five other gallicas to note are the low-growing, pink (with a tinge of azalea) flowered 'Belle Isis', the strong growing violet 'Duc de Guiche', the neat 'Du Maître d'École' and the rich 'Tuscany Superb'. And certainly the pink single-flowered rose which is so oddly named *gallica complicata*, of which Victoria Sackville-West once wrote, 'I can't think why it should be called *complicata*, for it has a simplicity and purity of line which might come straight out of a Chinese drawing'.

ROSA MOSCHATA – *The Musk Rose*

> But above all the Musk
> With classic names, Thisbe, Penelope,
> Whose nectarous load grows heavier with the dusk
> And like a grape too sweetly muscadine.

These are the roses with which Oberon's bank was over-canopied in Shakespeare's *Midsummer Night's Dream*, and it is their gift for long flowering which has won them a place in every garden. The best of the modern Musk roses were raised in England by the rose-grower and hybridizer, the Reverend Joseph Pemberton.

'*Buff Beauty*' is the rose of which the enthusiastic Miss Nancy Lindsay wrote, 'Golden as a tiger – candied as a ripe apricot, gloriously spicy – Buff Beauty holds my heart.'

'*Cornelia*' is a rose which first appeared on the market in 1925. The copper-pink flowers persist for months and its sprays of glossy dark leaves and reddish-budded flowers last well when cut. It can be used to make an effective hedge.

'*Felicia*' is a cross between the famous German rose 'Trier' – raised in 1903 by Peter Lambert – and 'Ophelia'. It is a rose with all the great qualities of the Musks: color – two shades of silver and salmon pink; sweet scent, healthy foliage, and the additional talent of making a low flower-covered hedge if severely pruned.

'*Penelope*' has creamy-pink flowers with golden anthers, followed by pale pink hips. It has all the Musk rose's robust habit of growth and Miss Murrell recommends growing it with grey-leaved plants, for which she finds it is the perfect foil.

These are just five out of a large choice of wonderful strong-growing Musk roses. Five more must be mentioned, if only in passing: 'Moonlight', with rich dark stems and ivory flowers – a rose which will quickly reach the height of twelve feet; the magenta-colored 'Nur Mahal', called after the wife of the Great Mogul; 'Prosperity', flushed mother o' pearl flowers; 'Thisbe', as strongly scented as any; 'Vanity' the child of one of the best of all climbing red roses – 'Château de Clos Vougeot' – with rich pink flowers ('Butterfly-Blooms', Miss Murrell calls them); 'Wilhelm', a bright red upstanding rose with buds as dark as garnets. In the United States it is known as 'Skyrocket'.

ROSA RUGOSA. These are called Japanese roses – though the Japanese, who dislike untidiness in any form, are not as fond of roses as they are of other flowers; they consider they die untidily. But Rugosa roses – except in very wet weather – are an exception, and let fall their petals neatly: perhaps that is why the Japanese occasionally give them valuable space in their tiny gardens. The Rugosas comprise some of the most rewarding of all shrub roses, not only for their flowers, but for their spectacular hips.

'*Blanc double de Coubert*' has papery white flowers, green ferny leaves and a scent which can waft for fifty yards. Like all the Rugosas, the foliage in autumn turns a rich butter-yellow, which gives the plant added value in the garden scene.

'*Frau Dagmar Hastrup*': Two most august authorities differ as to whether the last name of 'Frau Dagmar' is Hastrup (Mr Graham Thomas) or Hartopp (Miss Murrell), but both join in acclaiming its pale pink single flowers with creamy stamens. It also has the most imposing hips of all the Rugosas.

'*Hansa*' is one of the most generous flowers, even if the color of the flowers – a brash purple – is not to everyone's taste.

'*Roseraie de L'Hay*', which has much the same habit as 'Hansa' but richer, more velvet-textured flowers and brighter leaves. It is called after a famous rose garden near Paris.

The crimson 'Mrs Anthony Waterer', shiny-leaved, pink-flowered 'Sarah van Fleet', small pure-white 'Schneezwerg' are three more good Rugosas. Two bad ones are both the Grootendorsts, 'F.J.' and 'Supreme', which have common-looking picotee-petalled flowers. (*Rosa rugosa fimbriata*, far older and more *racée*, in the author's opinion, is the only carnation-petalled rose worth growing.) Another disappointment is 'Agnès' – a dull yellow in color, and with flowers which are grudgingly born and poor-looking when they are.

MODERN HYBRID SHRUB ROSES. These are the products of careful hybridizing, and in the process some have lost qualities and gained others. Some are perpetual flowering – but have smaller flowers than some that only flower once. Some are strongly scented – but pale in color. In the short list that follows only the few hybrid shrub roses which seem to have every quality are included.

'*Fritz Nobis*' has a mass of pink, clove-scented flowers and rich foliage. Its hips are russet red and it grows in a full but neat habit. It has sweet briar blood, and even when not in flower scents the air around after rain.

'*Aloha*' is one of the great modern roses, and as good grown as a climber or a shrub. It carries its pink Edwardian-looking flowers all summer, with a rewarding fresh burst in autumn.

'*Frühlingsgold*' and '*Frühlingsmorgen*' are two great German roses – cream and pink flowered respectively. Both are covered with flowers in May, and sometimes later.

'*Nevada*' is one of the best of all the comparatively new roses. Its single, creamy-white flowers weigh down its close-leafed, thornless branches in June. And it flowers again intermittently till the frost. 'Nevada' has the blood of two famous roses, 'Frau Karl Druschki' and 'Madame Edouard Herriot'.

'*Nymphenburg*' has hybrid Musk forbears and is as perpetually flowering as any in the group. Its flowers are salmon-pink overlaid with gold.

'*Raubritter*' has an unusual quality of growing happily downwards, so is ideal for planting on top of a wall or slope. Its shell-shaped flowers are most distinctive and pungently scented. It flowers later than most.

Rosa spinosissima 'Ormiston Roy' has five-petalled golden centred yellow flowers.

SPECIES ROSES. These are the original wild roses which have been collected for Western gardens from all over the world. Most have the single flowers of the true Eglantine and many are as beautiful in autumn as they are at flowering time, on account of their shining hips. Nine of the most desirable species roses are, *Cantabrigiensis* with ferny leaves, large pale butter-pats of flowers; 'Lawrence Johnston', christened by Graham Thomas after the great American gardener who created one of England's loveliest gardens, Hidcote, in Gloucestershire – his rose has yellow flowers and is a strong climber; *R. Moyesii*, for its heraldic crimson flowers and urn-shaped hips ('Eos' and 'Geranium' are other good varieties of this splendid rose); *Rosa rubrifolia* for its pinkish leaves, and *Rosa pteracantha* for its giant, glassy thorns; *Rosa soulieana* for its myriad white flowers, greyish leaves and odd Chinese appearance; and *R. xanthina* 'Canary Bird' for its charmingly descriptive name (*xanthos* is the Greek for yellow), reddish young growth and wreathes of flowers.

CLIMBING ROSES. Twenty-one of the best climbing roses, according to the author's experience, would include the scarlet 'Allen Chandler'; the single pink saucer-flowered 'Cupid'; the golden, hardy 'Elegance'; dark velvet-red 'Guinée'; the old favorite but still wonderful white 'Madame Alfred Carrière'; 'Madame Gregoire Staechlin' – almost best of all, with its rich pink flowers which, unfortunately, only appear for a glorious fortnight in

188

'Shelley heaped roses for his sweetheart's bed,
and for Thomas Moore the last rose of summer was left blooming alone.
Tennyson could scarcely hear the sound of rose petals falling ...'
On the wall Bourbon rose 'Mme Isaac Pereire' with 'Buff Beauty' in front.

June; 'Paul's Lemon Pillar' – white with poetic green shadows; 'Souvenir de Claude de Noyel' – crimson-red flowers; the tender double yellow 'Banksiae' – called after Sir Joseph Banks' widow, and one of the loveliest of roses (it must never be pruned); 'Chaplin's Pink Climber' – a hardier climbing rose; the pink late-flowering 'New Dawn'; and the famous golden, single-flowered 'Mermaid', though this is so fiercely armed that it is rough to handle and so is better grown as a free standing bush.

Three roses which are ideal for growing up old apple trees are 'Wedding Day', 'François Juranville' and 'Emily Grey'. Besides these climbing roses, one might recommend the climbing varieties of such well-known Hybrid Teas as 'Caroline Testout', 'Étoile de Hollande', 'Lady Hillingdon', 'Ophelia', 'Peace' and 'Speks Yellow'.

ROSA FLORIBUNDA. These have been so much improved in the last twenty years that they are now worthy of an important place in any rose garden. The first floribundas were raised in Denmark by the pioneer Dines Poulsen nearly forty years ago – from a cross between the old low-growing, but long-flowering R. polyantha, with a Hybrid Tea. One of the earliest floribundas was

191

Climbing rose 'Caroline Testout' was raised in France in 1901 and has been growing on garden walls ever since.

'Else Poulsen', called after Poulsen's daughter, a good rose, but one which has now been superseded by newer plants which are stronger growing, longer flowering, and more valuable for cutting; and the new floribundas are more resistant to the usual ills which attend most roses, such as black-spot and mildew.

First of the improved floribundas were 'Frensham', with its curiously heraldic red flowers which die more tidily than any other rose, 'Fashion' with flowers of a subtle azalea shade, and the once very popular 'Donald Prior', which has flowers of scarlet. 'Queen Elizabeth', though too tall, provides wonderful flowers for cutting – and can make an attractive screen. Newer floribundas, some of which are already almost too well known – the penalty of any really good plant – are the ubiquitous but still romantic 'Iceberg' (in Germany, 'Schneewittchen', raised by Kordes), the rich Edwardian-looking pink-flowered 'Plentiful'; the golden 'China Town' (a Poulsen introduction in 1962); 'All Gold', and the brilliant 'Rosemary Rose', which has attractive bronze foliage to set off its sculptured carmine flowers. Best of all, and proof that the old firm of Poulsen can still produce prize-winning roses, is the new, deep coral 'Pernille Poulsen'.

The name 'Dorothy Wheatcroft' commemorates the wife of a famous rose-grower of today, Harry Wheatcroft. It is a splendid tall-growing rose which well earned its recent award from the National Rose Society. The flowers of 'Dorothy Wheatcroft' are a warm glowing red.

Pet hates, of the author at least, are the horrid 'Masquerade', which tries to flower in three colors and fails; the grubby looking 'Lavender Pinocchio', and all the new floribundas which have flowers of hot brick red, tinged with yellow, such as 'Korona' and 'Firecracker'.

Recently a clever gardening friend planted a most effective rose border in her garden in Gloucestershire, combining floribundas, in front, and Musk roses and shrub roses of the same color, behind. By doing this she achieved floribunda color for months on end, and shrub-rose scent. In this successful combination, 'Rosemary Rose' echoed the red tones of *R. moyesii*, 'Lavender Lassie' the mauve tints of 'Tour de Malakoff' and 'Iceberg' reflected the cool white of the strongly-scented, white-flowered Musk rose, 'Pax'.

If only the roses mentioned in this chapter, and no others, were planted, they would make an impressive and comprehensive rose garden. Every year new roses appear in the catalogues, though, of these, only a few take their place among the great classic roses. But, should a catalogue of a hundred years ago be studied, few of the roses in it would be listed today; the best-loved faces in the rose garden change slowly – but change they do, and the work of hybridization, to achieve better and more sweetly smelling flowers, goes on –

192   That thereby Beautys rose might never die.

Hybrid Tea rose 'Peace' was raised in France during the dark days of World War II. Its petals have a creamy tinge, evidence of some Austrian Copper blood.

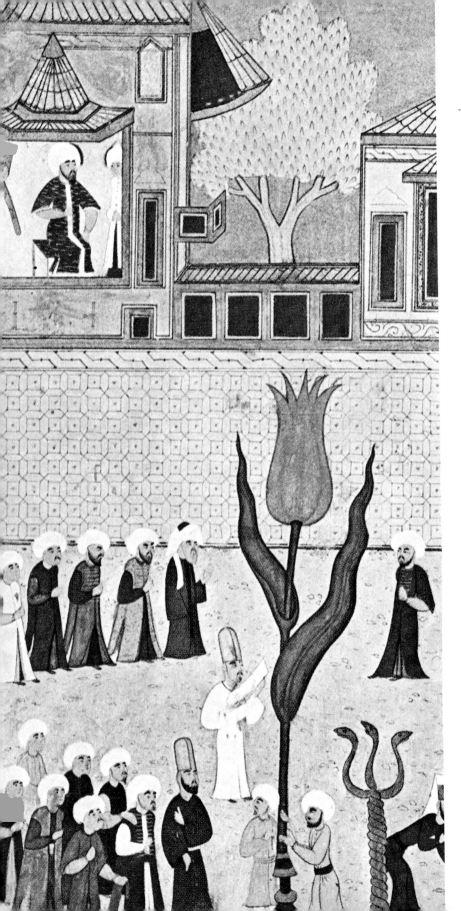

LEFT *A sixteenth-century Turkish painting of a flower festival at the court of Sultan Murad III. Tulips were introduced to the west from Turkey during the reign of Elizabeth I.*

CAROLUS CLUSIUS.
Botanices Professor.

Charles de L'Ecluse, also known as Clusius of Artois (1526–1609) sent the first tulips to England.

One of the earliest pictures
of a tulip is this drawing

by Konrad Gesner in De
Hortis Germaniae Liber,
1561.

Tulip

Flowers unknown in the West
before the reign of Queen Elizabeth I

'Tulipa ... is a strange and forein flower.' And so it was, for John Gerard, writing in 1597: for the first tulips had arrived in England only a few years before; they had been sent from Vienna by Charles de l'Ecluse – Clusius of Artois – who lived from 1526 to 1609. Richard Hakluyt, the Welsh traveller and geographer, records their arrival. 'Within these four years there have been brought into England from Vienna in Austria divers kinds of flowers called Tulipas, and these, and others, procured a little before from Constantinople by an excellent man called Monsieur Carolus Clusius.'

It was the excellent Clusius, founder of the bulb industry in Holland, who sent the first tulip bulbs to England. Furthermore, he was the first botanical writer, in his *Rariorum aliquot stirpium ...* to describe plants themselves rather than explain their medical properties.

Before Clusius' parcel of bulbs arrived in London, tulips had been grown in Vienna from bulbs sent there by Ogier Ghislaine de Busbecq, who was a keen botanist and Ambassador from the Holy Roman Empire to Suleiman the Magnificent, Sultan of Turkey. Tulips had, for many years, been the favorite flower of Turkey, which is the native land of many of the species.

The word tulip stems from the Turkish word *dulband*, a turban, which a brilliantly colored, full-petalled tulip closely resembles. Of this Sacheverell Sitwell has written:

The sumptuary arts of costume have never attained to such a degree of magnificence as in sixteenth-century Turkey. There is even a parallel – or a reflection to be traced between the appearance of their clothes and the shape and form of the tulip. Green silk dresses worn by descendants of the

Prophet are the stem and stalk of the flower, while it can be seen without any further emphasis, that the head of the tulip is the turban. (*Old Fashioned Flowers*.)

In Albert Grandville's *Les Fleurs Animées*, a work which has provided several illustrations for this book, there is a picture of Tulipa, half flower, half woman, who was the favorite of the Sultan Shahabaan. She was the daughter of a Dutch sea-captain, and had been captured by pirates. Tulipa is depicted surrounded by courtiers and eunuchs in tulip-shaped turbans, and her story, as told in *Les Fleurs Animées*, is a short one. Beautiful, but rather a bore, and not nearly animated enough for her pleasure-loving husband, Tulipa was no good at all at 'singing or dancing or making calembourgs'; so Shahabaan soon tired of her, had her sown up in a leather sack, and dropped into the Bosphorus.

The sad story of poor Tulipa is a typical Grandville fantasy, but there was a very real tulip mania in the sixteenth century in Holland, the country which is ever identified with the flower.

Mr Wilfrid Blunt has described this 'most astonishing drama in the whole history of horticulture – the Tulpenwoede or Tulipomania', in his delightful and informative book *Tulipomania*. 'In order to appreciate this gigantic gamble which, like the South Sea Bubble and the Mississippi Company, ended in national disaster, it is necessary to understand something of the botanical nature of the flower.' And Mr Blunt goes on to explain how the bulbs first brought from Constantinople were probably not those of species tulips (that is, tulips that grow in the wild), but of cultivated kinds.

The tulip in Les Fleurs Animées *half flower – half woman became, for a short time, the favourite of the Sultan. The word tulip stems from the Turkish* dulband, *a turban.*

196

These self-coloured tulips are called 'breeders' and they have, unlike almost any other kind of flower, the unique habit of changing or 'breaking' into a variation in which only part of the original color is maintained in streaks, feathering or 'flames'. Gerard observed that 'Nature' seemed 'to play more with this floure than with any other that I do know'. Once this break has occurred, the tulip seldom reverts to its original all-over coloring, and the children-bulbs keep the new colors. It was, notes Mr Blunt, 'in the unpredictability of the break, or freak' that the gambler's chance lay.

The Scottish poet James Thomson noted this unpredictability in his poem *The Seasons* in 1730:

> … then comes the tulip race, where beauty plays
> Her idle freaks: from family diffused
> To family, as flies the father dust
> The varied colours run: and while they break
> On the charmed eye, the exulting Florist marks
> With secret pride, the wonders of his hand.

Tulpenwoede (*woede* is the Dutch word for fury) in its most acute form, when 'exulting florists' who had had lucky 'breaks' sold their newest tulip bulbs for vast sums, lasted only three years, from 1634 to 1637, but high and low indulged in it, and fortunes were won and lost. Estates were exchanged for a simple bulb. One of the most famous flowers, the scarlet and white striped 'Semper augustus', was sold for 5,500 florins (£400 or close to $960). A similar bulb today would cost a shilling, in America perhaps 30 cents. Of this celebrated flower, the historian of the tulip, Nicholas Van Wassenaer, wrote 350 years ago, 'No tulip has been held in higher esteem, and one has been sold for thousands of florins; yet the seller was himself sold (so he said), for when the bulb was lifted, he noticed two lumps on it which the year following would have become two offsets, and so he was cheated of two thousand florins'. 'These offsets', he adds, 'are the interest, while the capital remains.'

The Dutch Van Clipp, the homely father of Grandville's unfortunate Tulipa, as he smoked his pipe on the deck of his ship which was so soon to be captured by Turkish pirates, heard fantastic stories of the speculation in tulips in his native Holland. How one bulb fetched thirty-six bags of corn, seventy-two bags of rice, four fat bullocks, twelve sheep, eight pigs, two tuns of wine, four tuns of beer, two tuns of salt butter, two pounds of cheese and a silver cup. And how a bulb farmer had once eaten a stew which cost him 100,000 florins, when his cook had mistaken some of his rarest tulip bulbs for onions.

By 1637 the craze for tulips, and the speculation in buying and selling bulbs, had burned itself out, and the Dutch reverted to their usual good sense. But tulipomania was an extraordinary footnote to Dutch history, and one which shocked or amused the whole of Europe at the time.

Nearly a hundred years later the same phenomenon occurred in Turkey, and the same 'fury' possessed the Turks as it once had the Dutch. Ahmed III mounted his golden throne in 1702, and it was during his reign that buying and selling tulip bulbs once again became a favorite form of speculation. So great was this that the Sultan had to command the Kaimakam of Istanbul to peg the price of the tulips, and punish profiteers by banishment from the city.

For centuries the Turks used tulips in every kind of decoration, woven into fabrics, burned into the multi-colored surfaces of the tiles used to adorn the *mihrabs* of mosques on the banks of the Golden Horn and in the remote cities of Erzerum and Kars in eastern Turkey. Designs of tulips luxuriously bordered the Sultan's services of porcelain and influenced the shape of ewers and goblets.

In 1850 Alexandre Dumas (Père) made a black tulip the central character of his famous novel, and wove into a rollicking tale of political intrigue the light-hearted love story of the tulip breeder Cornelius Van Baerle who 'in the course of two years, covered his flower beds with such marvellous productions as no mortal man following in the steps of the Creator, except perhaps Shakespeare and Rubens has ever equalled ...' and who at times seemed more enamoured of a tulip than of his fiancée, the beautiful Rosa Gryphus.

The tulip, unlike so many plants, played little part in medicine. Thomas Fuller, in his *Antheologia, or the Speech of Flowers*, underlines this point when he invents a complaint made by an indignant rose on the subject. The rose laments that, since the advent of the tulip, he is 'neglected and contemned and conceived beneath the honor of noble hands'. Good only to grow in the 'gardens of yeomen'. Surely, the rose goes on, not only his color and scent when living wins him first place among flowers, but even more his virtues

OVER PAGE *To prevent the valuable export bulbs being weakened, tulips, as in this Dutch nursery, are decapitated in the prime of their flowering.*

Mixed groups of tulips in the famous garden at the Keukenhof, near Lisse, in Holland.

A spectacular sight every spring and visited by tens of thousands of visitors.

when dead, 'yea – when dead – I am more sovereign than living ... what cordials are made of my syrups. How many corrupted lungs (those fans of nature), sore wasted with Consumption ... are with cordials made of my stamped leaves restored to their soundness againe?' Whereas, disdainfully, 'The Toolip is no more than a well complexioned stink – an ill savour wrapt up in pleasant colors ... as for the use thereof in physic – no physician hath honored it yet with the mention, nor with a Greek or Latin name, so inconsiderable hath it hitherto been accompted.'

The Tulip in Poetry. The tulip, unlike the rose and the lily, has never been the inspiration of poets. Joseph Joubert in his *Pensées* is of the opinion that 'La Tulipe est une fleur sans âme; mais il me semble que la rose et le lys en aient une.'

203

Perhaps, as a flower, the tulip is too coldly perfect, and Humbert Wolfe once wrote:

> Clean as a lady
> Cool as Glass
> Fresh without fragrance
> The tulip was ...

It would be laughable to compare the lips, eyes and bosom of the beloved to a tulip. One's 'love' could never be like a red, red tulip – and no one will ever 'die of a tulip in aromatic pain'. But here and there, in poetry, tulips find a place. Their orderly stiffness inevitably reminds the poet of soldiers. Andrew Marvell nostalgically remembers, while in Cromwell's army,

> Tulips in several colours barred
> Were then the Switzers of our guard...

and Rupert Brooke emphasizes the flower's dutiful nature when he writes:

> Here tulips bloom as they are told;
> Unkempt about those hedges blows
> An English unofficial rose ...

But Victoria Sackville-West, in *The Garden*, acclaims the beauty of the 'Forein Flowers', to which we have become so accustomed.

> So cosmopolitan, these English tulips,
> To cottager as native as himself!
> Aliens, that Shakespeare neither saw nor sang.
> Alien Asiatics, that have blown
> Between the boulders of a Persian hill
> Long centuries before they reached the dykes
> To charm Van Huysum and the curious Breughel,
> And Rachel Ruysch, so nice so leisurely
> That seven years were given to two pictures.

Varieties of Tulips. Before naming just a few of what in the author's opinion are the most rewarding tulips, it is difficult to resist quoting a gentle satire on the names of tulips which Mr Wilfrid Blunt, in *Tulipomania*, suggests was inspired by a piece by Jean de la Bruyère. It appeared in the *Tatler* soon after that magazine had been started by Richard Steele in 1709.

As I sat in the porch, I heard the voices of two or three persons, who seemed very earnest in discourse. My curiosity was raised when I heard the

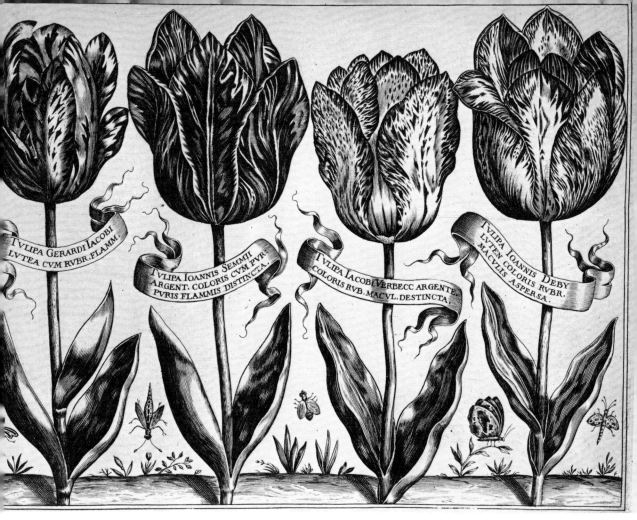

Four tulips from L'Anglois' Livre des Fleurs *published in Paris in 1620.*
The combination of insects and flowers is characteristic of L'Anglois' work.

names of Alexander the Great and Artaxerxes; and as their talk seemed to run on ancient heroes, I concluded there could not be any secret in it; for which reason I thought I might fairly listen to what they said.

After several parallels between great men, which appeared to me altogether groundless and chimerical, I was surprised to hear one say, that he valued the Black Prince more than Duke of Vendôme. How the Duke of Vendôme should become a rival of the Black Prince, I could not conceive; and was more startled when I heard a second affirm, with great vehemence, that if the Emperor of Germany was not going off, he should like him better than either of them. He added, that though the season was so changeable, the Duke of Marlborough was in blooming beauty. I was wondering to myself from whence they had received this odd intelligence: especially when I heard them mention the names of several other generals, 205 as the Prince of Hesse and the King of Sweden, who, they said, were both running away. To which they added, what I entirely agreed with them in, that the Crown of France was very weak, but that the Marshal Villars still kept his colours. At last, one of them told the company, that if they would go along with him, he would show them a Chimney-Sweeper and a Painted Lady in the same bed, which he was sure would very much please them.

To have a flower named for himself is the gardener's final accolade, and flower names, when they commemorate dedicated botanists and horticulturists like Eichler, Gesner or Clusius, are far more fascinating and instructive than when flowers are named for famous people who probably never wielded a trowel in their lives. Though King Alphonso VI of Portugal may be said to be an exception, and well deserves his own flower, for he employed his enforced leisure, while banished to the Island of Terceira, in growing tulips.

The finest tulip garden in the world today is at Keukenhof, near Lisse in Holland, where an unrivalled collection of tulips (and other flowers grown from bulbs) are planted in the vast natural park of the old castle of Jacqueline of Hainault. The garden at Keukenhof, with its flower beds reflected in the surfaces of several lakes, is visited by thousands from all over the world every year. On his last visit the author particularly noted a few of the latest productions of the dedicated Dutch bulb growers – the Van Baerles of today. Three of the most beautiful seemed to him to be the lemon yellow 'Mothers Day', the coral pink 'Fortune's Gift', and the violet 'Van Der Neer'. They were planted two hundred to a bed, and their massed colors fairly made 'the rash gazer wipe his eye'.

Effective as they are planted *en masse*, it happens that tulips are one of the few kinds of flower which can equally well be planted in mixture. Parkinson was of this opinion when he wrote, 'But above and beyond all others the tulips may be so matched, one color answering and setting off another – that the place where they stand may resemble a piece of curious needlework'.

But beds of mixed tulips should be mixed in colors only – double and single tulips, and tulips of different heights, do not look well planted together. *Species Tulips.* Magnificent as the new tulips are, they cannot rival in charm some of the species tulips which have been in cultivation for hundreds of years – tulips which before they grew in gardens, grew happily on the Georgian slopes or on the cool pastures of Azerbaijan.

These are the tulips of which E. A. Bowles wrote in *My Garden in Spring*:

When I speak of Tulipa something or other it is of course more precious to my botanical mind ... I should like to grow every species of Tulipa, even the starry green and white early flowering ones such as biflora ... one of which tries to make a floral display in December ...

Peony flowered tulip 'Mount Tacoma' has luxuriant double flowers of the purest white.

A species tulip which certainly warmed Mr Bowles' heart is *T. kaufmanniana*, usually considered to be the first of all. Its flowers can be gold or brilliant scarlet. *T. kaufmanniana* is one of the most reliable of all tulips: if it is planted a good seven inches deep, and not disturbed, it will flower year after year.

The waxy red and coal-black centred *T. eichleri* from Azerbaijan, named after the careful Wilhelm Eichler, is almost as bright a red as *kaufmanniana*, and a beautiful flower; as is the excellent Clusius' own, parti-colored *T. clusiana* – the Lady tulip, which has flowers of rosy red and cream, striped like a lollipop.

T. maximowicii is another red tulip – a brilliant scarlet with a black marking. This, too, will flower year after year – though experts recommend that it should be lifted every two or three years, and the bulb relieved of its last year's jacket. So many of the early flowering species tulips are red that it is a change to note one that is yellow. This is the unique and perfectly charming *sylvestris* – a tulip which can show several nodding heads on one stem. It is said by some to have been introduced into England by the returning Crusaders; by others it is thought to be an English native. In either case, it is a tulip Shakespeare might have seen, though he mentions no tulip in his plays.

These are just a very few of the species tulips which bring their first cheerful color to the garden in early spring. To name them all would be, in Gerard's words, to 'rolle Sisiphus' stone, or number the sands'; it is impossible to mention, except in passing, a few of the best flowers in more than a handful of the other groups of tulips. First of these are the Darwins, which were introduced in 1899, and have characteristic square-based flowers. Six fine flowerers are the red 'Bartigan', lavender 'Bleu Aimable', well-loved pink 'Clara Butt', creamy 'Niphetos' and dusky 'Tulipe Noire' – which, of course, is not *noire* at all but a dark maroon – prune-juice with a dash of cassis.

Of cottage tulips a good choice of six might include the scarlet 'Grenadier', the gold and bronze 'Bond St', the black-white 'Sorbet' and the old favorite shell pink and ivory 'Zomerschoon'. This is a tulip variety which has been grown for nearly two hundred years. Mr Bowles saw a picture of it in a Dutch book of 1794, and has this to say about it as a flower. 'It is seen at its best in the morning sunlight ... when the first blossoms open I find it hard to tear myself away from them.' A favorite cottage tulip of Victoria Sackville-West was 'Palestrina' – the petals of which she once described as looking like smoked salmon 'if you can imagine smoked salmon sliced so thin that you could see the light through them'.

Three groups of tulips which were admired by Miss Sackville-West were the 'broken' tulips and she did not 'at all resent the idea that their feathery variation should be caused by a virus'.

The Bybloemen, Bizarre and Rembrandt and, most spectacular of all, the ragged, petalled and parti-colored Parrot tulips are the most brilliant group of all. Two good Bybloemens are the huge-flowered 'Bright Interval' which is cherry pink, and the crimson-flecked 'Paljas'. A favourite Bizarre tulip is the yellow, brown-feathered 'Absolom', and the pick of the Rembrandts 'Union Jack' – red and white, but no blue. All the Parrot tulips are irresistible, especially 'Fantasy' (green and pink), 'Firebird' (red and yellow) and the 'Black Parrot'.

Two last tulips which the author has planted in many gardens over the years, and with the greatest success, are the oddly colored 'Artist' – a hybrid of *T. viridiflora*, which is unique with its petals striped and flecked with orange and green; and *T. greigii* 'Plaisir' with petals which are parti-colored in carmine and yellow, and unusual leaves which are variegated green and bronze.

Cultural Notes. Two pieces of advice on tulip growing are useful. All species tulips, almost without exception, originate on hills and slopes – therefore it is essential that they should be given sharp drainage. The second tip is how to tell when bedding tulips can be lifted to make way for summer flowers. As soon as the petals fall the seed pods should be removed; this will stop the flow of sap up the stalk. A week or two more, and as soon as you can twist the stem round your finger without it snapping, it is safe to lift the bulbs and store them for the following year.

There are water-lily flowered tulips, peony flowered tulips, Mandarin tulips with a faintly Chinese look, and a Turkish tulip – *T. acuminata*, which is a really hideous flower with straggling, stringy petals.

Robert Thornton (1768–1837) described tulips as 'The most ravishing beauties of the vegetable world.'

Loveliest of all are surely the tulip-flowered tulips – the tulips the Dutch masters such as Bosschaert and the careful Rachel Ruysch included in their bouquets. No picture of a *Bloempot* could be considered complete without at least one tulip, whatever the flowering season of the other flowers portrayed.

Tulips were described by Robert Thornton in his famous *Temple of Flora* as 'the most ravishing beauties of the vegetable world'. They came to us via the box-bordered gardens of Holland and the marble parterres of Constantinople, from India, Persia and all over the world. In her poem *The Garden* Miss Sackville-West wrote,

> Tulip, dulband, and turban; rare
> Persian that wanders in our English tongue

But as the neglected Rosa Gryphus sighed, fascinating though the subject is, 'one cannot always talk about tulips'.

Viola tricolor *or 'Hartes Ease' from*   *Crispin de Passe's* Hortus Floridus.

Viola

'Come take your due of garlands, violet woven'
Pindar to the City of Athens

Violets, violas and pansies all belong to the botanical family of *violaceae*, a large group of more than four hundred and fifty species. There are violas which originate from almost every country in the world, outside the tropics. Best known, and best loved of the genus in Western gardens are violets and pansies.

The violet was a favorite flower of the ancient Greeks, and as Pindar recognized, it was the emblem of the city of Athens.

Violets grew, and still grow, thickly in the woods round Stratford-on-Avon, and Shakespeare mentions them in his plays no less than fifteen times. Perdita, of course, includes violets in her often quoted catalogue:

> violets dim,
> But sweeter than the lids of Juno's eyes
> Or Cytherea's breath.

And the nodding violet flowered on Oberon's bank 'whereon the wild thyme' blew.

Violets are often described as nodding, and it has been suggested that they hang their heads to protect their pollen from the rain, though this is a habit of growth shared by many plants: and the pollen of numberless upward-looking plants survives unharmed. A more likely explanation is offered by Ruskin in his *Garden of Proserpina*. Violets, he says, grow most happily on banks which face south. They are 'bank flowers, not field flowers'. Field flowers usually raise their faces to the sun, while bank flowers look at the sun from a different angle. But it is a rule to which there are many exceptions. Certainly, all violets

210

do hang their heads, and for the poet and writer they will always nod. Thus they have come to symbolize modesty and shyness; and in *Alice through the Looking Glass*, the violets in the garden of otherwise very talkative flowers hardly uttered a word.

Laertes, in *Hamlet*, twice uses violets as a simile. The first is when he warns Ophelia against Hamlet's protestations:

> For Hamlet and the trifling of his love
> Hold it a fashion and a toy in blood
> A violet in the youth of primey nature
> Forward, not permanent, sweet not lasting
> The perfume and suppliance of a minute,
> No more ...

And Ophelia herself, who according to Anne Pratt, 'colors all nature with the hues of her own sad thoughts', sighs, 'I would give you violets, but they withered all when my father died'. Later, when her pathetic story is over, the devoted Laertes speaks of violets for the second time, hoping that they will one day spring from her grave.

Anne Pratt asks 'which of us could spare the violet from the memories of early life: and how many of us are even now reminded by its passing scent of scenes which may never be revisited, but whose verdure and sunshine make a picture on which the eye of the mind can linger as long as life itself. ...'

One of the most beautiful water-colors by Albrecht Dürer, in the Albertina Collection in Vienna, is of a simple bunch of violets. In *A Gallery of Flowers* Germain Bazin sensitively suggests the artist's feelings for the flower: 'It is as though, in humility before the wonder of nature, he is holding his breath, in order to cease thinking, and be only an eye. ... No artist has expressed, like Dürer, the humility that belongs to this flower. ...'

For the forgotten Victorian poet Willis, violets meant the return of summer:

> I have found violets, April hath come on
> And the cool winds feel softer, and the rain
> Falls in the beaded drops of summer time.

For him they flowered

> ... with such a simple loveliness among
> The common herbs of pasture and breathe out
> Their lives so unobtrusively, like hearts
> Whose beatings are too gentle for this world.

LEFT *Modern hybrid pansies have flowers that are almost round.*

A basket of pansies. By early in the last century they had lost their long viola faces and had become more circular and more richly colored.

Violas drawn by Leonardo da Vinci
(1452–1519), from his manuscript notebooks.

Violets. A water color by
Albrecht Dürer (1471–1528) in the
Albertina Collection in Vienna. 'No artist
has expressed, like Dürer, the humility
that belongs to this flower'.

Violets throughout history were used in medicine – Pliny the Elder recommends them as a cure for headache, and later, Anthony Askham recommends violets, in his *Little Herbal* published in 1550, as a sedative. His instructions run thus: 'For them that may not sleep for sickness, seethe the violets in water, and even let him soak well his feet in the water to the ankles: and when he gets to bed bind of this herb to his temples, and he shall sleep well, by the Grace of God.' The violet had other uses in physic. Joseph de Tournefort recommended them as an efficient laxative for children, Gerard used violets as a cure for ague, and Nicholas Culpeper thought that they made a certain cure for the 'French Pox'.

Pleasanter is it to mention the use that has been made of violets in confectionery and sweets. In the East the flowers were used in the making of sherbet. In salads, the violets were eaten raw, as were the petals of anchusa, scattered on lettuce and sliced onion. Crystallized violets still occasionally appear, on cakes and sweets, and a favorite dish in the reign of Queen Elizabeth I was *Mon Amy* which, it seems, was a cross between bread and butter pudding and trifle; this the cook, as a finishing touch, was advised to 'plant with flowers of violet, and serve forth'.

215

The Madonna with the Violet by Stefan Lochner (1400–51), principal Master of the Cologne School.

L'Unique Pensée
de la France.

A Paris chez Delaunay rue Napoléon Nº9

Napoleon on his way to exile in Elba promised his supporters to 'return with the violets'. Soon he was secretly referred to as Père Violette and violets became the flower of the Bonapartists.

The modest violet had political fame thrust upon it in France during the first Restoration. Napoleon, on his way to exile in Elba, is said to have promised his supporters 'to return with the violets'. At once the violet became the symbol of the Bonapartists, and the Emperor, hitherto referred to mysteriously as 'L'Homme', overnight became 'Père Violette', and prints like the one shown on this page were circulated. *Les vieux moustaches* annoyed the Bourbon Duc d'Angoulême by wearing bunches of violets on parade. The flowers held their popularity and their Napoleonic affiliation long after Waterloo. Violets were favorite flowers during the Second Empire, and the author remembers, while a student in Paris, an operetta set in the days of the Empress Eugénie – *Violettes Imperiales*.

Many of the six hundred wreaths at the funeral of the gallant young Prince Imperial, son of Napoleon III, killed fighting with the British Army in South Africa in 1879, were of violets. Princess Bacciochi, in her memoirs, recalls that the scent of violets in the small church at Chislehurst, where the funeral service took place, was overpowering. And *The Times* of 14 July 1879 noted that the violet wreath of the Princess of Wales, herself a lover of violets, bore a card 'written in Her Royal Highness's own hand' with the words, 'A token of affection and regard for him who lived the most spotless of lives, and died a soldier's death, fighting for our cause ...'. Another tribute was a bunch of violets, 'from the child the Prince last kissed before he left England'. To this day, violets are the flower of the Bonapartes and memories of the First and Second Empires are tinged with their scent.

There is a St Helena violet, which was a favorite flower of Miss Gertrude Jekyll. For her, it smelled sweeter than any other variety. Its color, too, she found particularly delicate, as subtle as the grey-blue tint of the Confederate violet – *Viola priceana*. Did this flower, too, have political connotations, and did the Confederate troops wear buttonholes of this violet when they marched, so confidently, to Gettysburg? I have been unable to find how this violet got its name. An American friend suggests it may be because its color recalls the uniforms worn by the soldiers of the Southern States in the Civil War. On the other hand, like the Virginia Creeper, sometimes called the Confederate Vine, it may just be because it grows wild in Confederate country.

It has been rather austerely suggested that *viola* is the old Latin name used by Virgil and Pliny, and that it is a variant of the Greek word *ion*. A romantic theory suggests that it derives from the ancient legend of Zeus and Io, the daughter of the King of Areus, whom Zeus turned into a heifer when his passion for her aroused the dangerous jealousy of his wife Hera. Concerned that his four-footed love might get bored by an undiluted diet of grass, Zeus arranged that sweeter fare might be provided for her, and so decreed, according to Gerard, that 'the earth brought foorth this foode, which being made for hir, received the name from hir...'.

Varieties of Violet. The species of violets commonly grown in Western gardens are not very many, though the hybrids are now innumerable. First and foremost is *Viola cornuta* – the Horned violet which originates in southern Europe, and has been found in gardens for many centuries. It makes a tight mass of heart-shaped green leaves, above which it shows a mass of flowers which might be likened to a cloud of butterflies. It was from the *V. cornuta* that James Grieve (who gave his name to the famous apple) raised the modern violas, by crossing *V. cornuta* with the British wild pansy, the yellow *V. lutea*. This important alliance took place in the late sixties of the last century.

Viola odorata is the sweet smelling violet of the Greeks and of poets down the ages. It is the wild violet of the countryside, of which Victoria Sackville-West wrote in *Even More For Your Garden*, when writing of plants that seed themselves: 'The violets for instance – I would not despise even our native *Viola odorata* of the banks and hedgerows, whether in its blue or its white form, so well deserving the adjective *odorata*. And how it spreads, whenever it is happy, so why not let it roam ... as it listeths?'

Modern hybrid violets show colors varying from white – *V. odorata alba* – to the delicious pink 'Coeur d'Alsace' – from palest mauve to dark purple – dark enough to be the black violet of Theophrastus, which Gerard describes as having 'a great prerogative above the other violets, because the mind conceiveth a certain pleasure and recreation by smelling and handling its most odoriferous flowers ...'

'The Czar' is a famous species of *V. odorata*, and is the finest blue violet, while 'Princess of Wales', named after Queen Alexandra when she was bride to Edward VII, is the sweetest scented single violet. Queen Alexandra loved violets and was seldom seen without a bouquet of them.

Parma violets are the double form of *V. odorata* and are a pale lavender blue. They, too, were popular in Victorian and Edwardian days.

One interesting species of viola, *V. labradorica*, deserves special mention. It is as hardy as its name would imply, for it comes from the frozen north, and according to the RHS Dictionary it even grows in Greenland. The flowers of *V. labradorica* are unassuming, and it is its leaves that are its chief attraction. They are beautifully wine colored. *V. labradorica* makes excellent ground cover, and if planted in half shade and in good soil will quickly make large spreading clumps which deter all but the most dauntless weeds.

It was a violet growing in a temple garden of Japan which once so fascinated Reginald Farrer that he remembered it ever afterwards, with regret.

> The last violet I have to mention I call upon with lamentation. I have never been able to get hold of it, for all the enthusiasm it aroused in me. It was in the wood above the Temple Tombs at Nikko, where between the vast columnar trunks of three secular cryptomerias, the setting sun cast arrows of gold on the dappled green carpet of herbage round their feet. The trees themselves were fired to ruddy sanguine, great scarlet pillars of a huge cathedral. And here and there on the ground there shone a wonderful violet, fired by the sunset to a blazing amethyst. It had the size, growth, and habit of *Viola pedata*, the same finely cleft foliage; its flower was large and stately, of a vivid lavender. And there, amid the budding lilies and the splashed gold and green of vegetation that covered the bare earth, the violet glowed fierce in the red light. And there, for all I know, it still glows. I cannot obtain it.

That 'excellent violet' as Emily Dickinson described the flowers was never, apparently, to be Mr Farrer's.

Pansies. Pansies (*Viola tricolor*) are the 'pretty pawnce' of Spenser's *Shepherd's Calender*, and are the violet's close relation. They are the loved flowers of all children, and no flower has more names, affectionately bestowed. Pansies were 'Heavenly Heartsease' to the physician William Bulleine, whose *Bulwarke of defence against all sickness, sornes and wounds that dooe daily assault Mankind* appeared in 1562. 'God send thee Heartsease', he wrote, 'for it is much better with poverty to have the same, than to be a kynge with a miserable mind. Pray God give thee but one handful of Heavenly Heartsease which passeth all the pleasant flowers that grow in this worlde.'

Other old names for a pansy were 'Three Faces in One Hood' – from the formation and often different coloring of the upper and lower petals; 'Cull' or sometimes 'Call-me to you', 'Kit run the streets' and 'Pink of my John'. 'Herb Trinity' was another, which shocked the puritan Nicholas Culpeper. In his herbal, published in 1653, during the bleak days of the Commonwealth, he noted disapprovingly, 'Our physicians blasphemously call Phansies or Heartsease, a Herb of the Trinity, because it is of three colors'.

The most charming of all the pansy's many names is surely 'Love in idleness'. This was the 'Little western flower before milk white, now purple with love's wound', the flower on which the bolt of Cupid had fallen. 'Love in idleness' means 'Love in vain' or without serious intention. The pansy flower, it seems, was an important ingredient, in Elizabethan days, in love potions, for Oberon goes on to say:

> The juice of it on sleeping eyelids laid
> Will make a man or woman madly dote
> Upon the next live creature that it sees.

Pansies and Violas. It is complicated, and outside the scope of this book, to define the exact difference between viola and pansy. Ruskin complains that no botanical authority has ever been able to explain it, and goes on to devote four pages of *The Garden of Proserpina* to trying to do so himself, without marked success. Very generally it can be said that the viola's flower is smaller and more compact, and does not show the dark whisker-like markings that have given the pansy's face its endearing expression, since the days when Milton wrote of 'the pansy freaked with jet' to the present day, when a modern strain has been well named 'Felix', from the cat-like appearance and dark whiskering of their flowers.

The year 1810 was an important one in the development of the pansy, for at that time it caught and held the fancy and interest of Mr T. Tomson, head gardener to Lord Gambier, who, like many admirals (he had commanded the Baltic fleet at the bombardment of Copenhagen) took to gardening on his retirement. Lord Gambier's gardener developed the pansy by crossing and re-crossing varieties of *Viola tricolor* with the yellow *V. lutea* and *V. altaica*, a native of the Crimea and Turkestan. Alice Coats records in *Flowers and Their Histories* that by 1816 Mr Tomson was known in the gardening world as the

Lord Gambier (1756–1833) 'like many admirals took to gardening on his retirement'. His gardener, Mr Thomson, by crossing Viola tricolor *with the yellow* V.V. lutea *and* altaica, *produced the modern hybrid pansies.*

'Father of the Heartsease'. The flowers he produced had quite lost their long viola faces and had become more circular and more richly colored. In fact, they had been transformed into the pansies we know today. By 1830 hundreds of new kinds of pansy were on the market, and Henry Phillips, author of *Flora Historica*, is quoted as saying, 'Thoughts are not more numerous than the varieties of this little sportive flower'.

The author remembers an incident in his childhood which surely played a part in stirring his early interest in gardening. Every gardener knows that his show of pansy flowers can be prolonged for months if the dead heads are removed regularly. A gardener was engaged in this work, when he paused and, picking up a faded flower head, showed a very interested small boy its five petals. 'There wurr five sisters', he said in his broad Ayrshire accent, 'and they went to see their granny, who was ill in bed'; while speaking he plucked off the petals one by one, and revealed the little pouch which contains two of the pansy's stamens in the centre. This looked exactly like a figure in bed, with the bed-clothes pulled up. ' "Grand mama", said the wee girls, "You look much better"; "Thank you my dears", replied the old lady, "but just look how thin my legs are",,' and with that the gardener dexterously pinched off the pouch of the pansy, revealing two wispy stamens which did look like two very thin legs indeed. The story was received with delight and has never been forgotten.

Varieties of Pansy. Up till some years ago pansies were available by variety; nowadays they tend to be sold in mixed collections, and very beautiful and varied these are. But it is still possible, with care, to find seedsmen who can provide seeds of the most popular strains of years ago, which have a far, far greater charm than the opulent new creations of the hybridist. A few favorite varieties, most of which have been grown in Western gardens for many years, are the ever popular blue 'Maggie Mott', one of the pansies in her garden singled out for special praise by Gertrude Jekyll, the lavender, sweet-scented 'Kitty Bell', and the gold and yellow 'Royal Sovereign' and 'Bullion', 'Primrose Dame' and the pristine 'White Swan'. One of the author's favorite pansies, which he has been careful to grow in any garden he has ever had anything to do with – even in as remote a one as the garden at the former Viceroy's house in New Delhi – is the enchanting 'Jackanapes'. This indeed merits Henry Phillips' description of a 'little sportive flower', with its dark brown upper petals, bright yellow lower ones and ridiculously mischievous expression.

The seed pod of a pansy (centre) looks 'exactly like a figure in bed, with the bedclothes pulled up'. When the petal spur or pouch is removed, leg-like stamens are revealed.

Blue pansy 'Maggie Mott' growing at the base of climbing roses in the garden of Schloss Mainau on Lake Constance in Germany.

Water lily

Inspiration of the greatest Impressionist painter

Two names that must always be connected with water lilies are those of Claude Monet, the French Impressionist painter, and Bory Latour-Marliac, the great pioneer of water-lily culture.

Monet was particularly inspired by the water lilies in his garden, and he would sit for hours watching the iridescent interplay of sunshine on the water studded with groups of water lilies.

Marliac, in his garden at Temple sur Lot, was 'a wizard with the water lily', according to Frances Perry, an acknowledged expert of today, and it was Marliac who created with painstaking care many of the splendid modern hybrid water lilies. His achievements will be noted later in this chapter.

Water lily in English, 'seeblume' in German, 'nenuphar' in French, 'plomp' in Dutch, 'nymphaea' in Latin – the English name, water lily, though it has come to mean everything that is cool and exquisite, is basically unimaginative, as is the German word; the Dutch is ugly and absurdly unsuitable. As so often, it is the French and Latin names that are the most beautiful and the most descriptive. From where did they come? *Nymphaea* derives from the Latin *Nymphe* – a water nymph, for obvious reasons – and the learned Dr Chaumeton goes further by suggesting that *Nymphe* is another version of the Greek word *Numphe* – a virgin – from the anti-aphrodisiac qualities of the plant attributed to it by the ancient Greeks. *Nenuphar*, it is thought, is a corruption of the Arab name for the plant *nilufar*. and further back still, from the ancient Egyptian Nilotpala, the royal lotus of the Pharaohs. The Egyptians particularly revered the water lily. Ignorant of the phenomena of nature, they saw miracles in everything, and to them it was particularly miraculous that the flowers of some water lilies should emerge from the water at sunrise, and re-enter the water when the sun set behind the Great Pyramid. They decided therefore that there was a mysterious link between the morning star and the *nenuphar*. From this derived the

A canal shaped lily-pond in the garden at Cornbury Park in Oxfordshire.

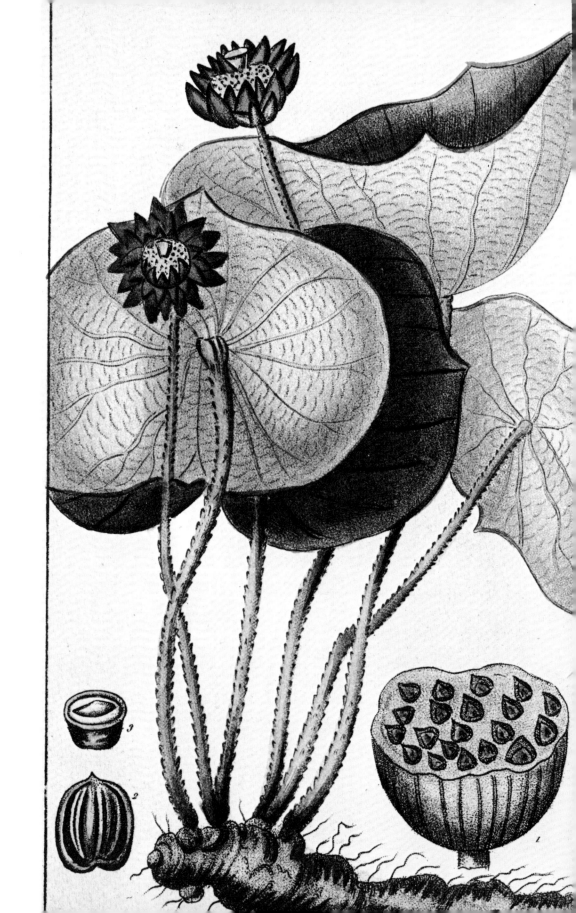

custom of crowning with water lilies the statue of Osiris – whose resurrection after his murder by Set symbolized the rising sun; and afterwards the heads of any king of Egypt to whom his subjects wanted to attribute immortality.

Coldness, purity and chastity are the qualities suggested by the lily of the water, as much, or more, than by the lily of the field.

In Albert Grandville's *Les Fleurs Animées*, the water lily, in the guise of Soeur Nenuphar, presents the very personification of impregnable virtue. The devil, it seems, while in Bruges, overhears the most beautiful singing outside a convent. Because 'il a toujours été dilettant', he slips into the convent to listen more closely. One particular Ursuline nun captures his attention, and then his heart. A close siege of Soeur Nenuphar's virtue follows, with the devil doing his best to distract the nun from her devotions.

First, he takes the form of a dashing cavalier 'frisant sa moustache'. No good. He leaves a novel on the nun's prie-dieu open at the page 'La plus échevelée de l'ouvrage, une scène d'amour pantelante, rutilante, éburiffante'. No good either. Sister Nenuphar glances at the book, yawns, and falls asleep. The devil, 'outré', then tries his most potent aphrodisiac charm. He burns a 'pastille du serail' made from the heart of a young girl who has died of love. No success, and the devil has to admit defeat. Grandville shows signs of sympathy with Satan, and of impatience with the nun, leaving her in her convent with the words, 'La vie monotone et languissante des réligieuses était celle qui lui convenait'.

LEFT *Nenuphar is a corruption of the Arab name 'niluphar,' and further back still from the ancient Egyptian 'nilotpala', the royal lotus of the Pharaohs.*

Nymphaea alba, lutea *and* alba major *from* Hortus Eystettensis. Nymphaea lutea *is the native yellow water lily,* alba *the white.*

Nymphæa lutea.

Nymphæa alba minor.

Nymphæa alba maior.

225

An early and most inadequate description of the water lily occurs in the *Grete Herball*, published in 1529. 'Nenufar is a herb that groweth in water and hath large leaves and a floure in the manner of a rose. The roote thereof is very big' – and of the flowers, 'one is white and another yellow', and that is all.

If water lilies did not inspire the author of the *Grete Herball*, two hundred and fifty years later they certainly made an instant impression on the poet William Cowper, who, in June 1788, wrote to his 'dearest Coz', Lady Hesketh, to tell her the following remarkable story:

> I must tell you a feat of my dog Beau. Walking by the river side, I observed some water-lilies, floating at a little distance from the bank. They are a large white flower with an orange-coloured eye, very beautiful. I had a desire to gather one, and having your long cane in my hand, by the help of it endeavoured to bring one of them within my reach. But the attempt proved vain. ... Beau had all the while observed me very attentively. Returning soon after toward the same place, I observed him plunge into the river, while I was about forty yards distant from him; and, when I had nearly reached the spot, he swam to land with a lily in his mouth, which he came and laid at my foot.

So struck was he by the incident that he committed it to verse in a poem, of which only the first three and the last verses will be quoted:

> The noon was shady, and soft airs
> Swept Ouse's silent tide,
> When, 'scaped from literary cares,
> I wandered on his side.
>
> It was the time when Ouse display'd
> His lilies newly blown;
> Their beauties I intent survey'd,
> And one I wish'd my own.
>
> With cane extended far I sought
> To steer it close to land;
> But still the prize, though nearly caught;
> Escap'd my eager hand.

Cowper then goes on to record how his spaniel Beau

> Prettiest of his race
> And high in pedigree ...

'marked' his 'unsuccessful plans', and determined to help him by jumping into the water and retrieving the lily. Cowper determined that the incident should be made known so,

Charm'd with the sight, The world, I cried,
Shall hear of this thy deed:
My dog shall mortify the pride
Of man's superior breed.

Water Lilies and Claude Monet. Water lilies still float on the waters of the River Ouse near Goosey bridge and though, writes Ann Pratt, 'The gentle poet has long since quitted the scene which his humble pity aroused ... both verse and flower remain to remind us of his simple tastes and pleasures ...'.

Claude Monet's devotion to his garden has already been mentioned. It was a garden unlike others, as Georges Clemenceau, the artist's biographer makes clear in his book *Claude Monet, Les Nymphaeas:*

> ... a quiet lake of water lilies, with a Japanese bridge, hung with wisteria as the only romantic concession. It was there that Monet found his inspiration; he would sit for hours without moving, without speaking, his eyes fixed on the reflections of the clouds and sky between the water lilies' leaves. Looking, for Monet, was to understand; water lilies had a special message for him, a message which his incomparable painting was able to communicate. That is the 'Miracle des nymphaeas ... qui ont quelque chose à nous dire, mais ne nous le diraient pas, sans Monet'.

Victoria Regia. A hundred and thirty years ago a water lily – though certainly not of a variety which could have grown in Monet's garden or in any private garden of today – made a world-wide sensation. This was the giant lily afterwards called the 'Victoria Regia', which first astonished Western eyes in the year of its Royal namesake's accession. It was discovered by the Prussian-born explorer and traveller Sir Robert Schomburgk, floating on the waters of the Berbice river in the South American colony of British Guiana, and one catches something of his enthusiasm and excitement as one reads his report of his discovery.

> It was on the 1st of January, 1837, while contending with the difficulties that Nature imposed in different forms to our progress up the river Berbice, British Guiana, that we arrived at a point where the river expanded and formed a currentless basin: some object on the southern extremity of the basin attracted my attention; it was impossible to form any idea what it could be, and animating the crew to increase the rate of their paddling, we were shortly afterwards opposite the object which had raised my curiosity – a vegetable wonder! All calamities were forgotten. I felt as a botanist, and felt myself rewarded. A gigantic leaf from five to six feet in diameter, salver-shaped with a broad rim of a light green above and a vivid crimson below, was resting upon the water. Quite in character

The lily pond with the Pin Mill building
reflected in it at Bodnant, a
famous garden in North Wales.

with the wonderful leaf was the luxuriant flower, consisting of many hundred petals passing in alternate tints from pure white to rose and pink. The smooth water was covered with the blossoms, and as I rowed from one to the other I always observed something new to admire. The leaf on its upper surface is of a bright green, in form almost orbicular except that on one side it is slightly bent. Its diameter measured from five to six feet; around the whole margin extended a rim from three to five inches high, on the inside light green like the surface of the leaf, on the outside like the leaf's lower surface, of a bright crimson. The ribs are very prominent – almost an inch high, radiating from a common centre.

But it was not until nine years later that seed of the 'vegetable wonder' reached Kew and though the seed germinated and the plant grew, only vast leaves were produced, but no flowers. Joseph Paxton (1801–65), gardener, protégé and friend of the Duke of Devonshire, heard of the failure of the giant lily to flower at Kew. Could he, he wondered, induce it to flower at Chatsworth in Derbyshire – if given the special treatment and conditions which he believed the great greenhouse at Chatsworth could provide? He was determined to try. Dramatically, in *Paxton and the Bachelor Duke*, Miss Violet Markham tells how Paxton proceeded:

In July 1849 he was in treaty with his friend Sir William Hooker for a plant. He writes to say that he is building a tank for the lily at Chatsworth; it will take three weeks to heat and finish properly; he is going to Scotland, but on his return will either send or come for the plant himself.

With the greatest care the infant plant was transported from Kew to Euston

Water lilies prefer to grow in still water.
They do not like the spray of a fountain or being rocked about.

Lith. de E. De Trigne.

Station in London and then by train to Bakewell. The root, from which the giant was to grow, fitted quite comfortably into a small box.

Paxton had exhausted his ingenuity in arrangements for Victoria's comfort at Chatsworth. She was to be deluded into thinking she was on her native waters. A tank, 12 feet square and 3 feet 4 inches deep, had been prepared for her. Five earth-loads of soil had been placed in the centre, and on this mound she was invited to repose. She was to be warmed and lighted – a task less easy – as though she were in the tropics.

A little water-wheel set in the tank kept the water in gentle motion as on her native river. The precious passenger survived the journey without damage or fatigue. She was introduced to her new home and then everyone settled down to an anxious period of waiting and watching. Would she or would she not flower? But Victoria was capable of gratitude. Paxton had done a great deal for her comfort. She made up her mind to reward him. The measure of her gratitude was not niggardly.

Two months later Victoria had spread her leaves – each nearly four feet across and more than ten feet in circumference, and the tank had to be enlarged to give the giant lily more room. Every day she became larger, putting out more and more leaves – was she going to flower? Paxton, though at that time he could not have known exactly how important a part in his life the Victoria lily was going to play, was on tip-toe with excitement. The suspense was almost unbearable. 'No birth of a prospective heir to the throne was ever awaited with keener anxiety.' Every new development was excitedly reported to the Duke of Devonshire, who was in Ireland. The leaves grew even more enormous – was the miracle going to happen? In November, a letter announcing great news reached Lismore Castle from Derbyshire, when Paxton wrote: 'Victoria has shown flower!! An enormous bud like a poppy head made its appearance yesterday. It looks like a large peach placed in a cup. No words can describe the grandeur and beauty of the plant.'

All Paxton's plans were changed – for at this critical moment he could not tear himself away from Chatsworth and his now enormous child. Soon the lily was showing its flower fully open and there were more to come. The sensation in the horticultural world was immense – Paxton wrote to friends in the fraternity saying that the lily was worth coming thousands of miles to see.

The Queen herself was fascinated, and Paxton was sent for on 13 November to present Her Majesty at Windsor Castle with a vast pink flower and one of the giant leaves.

The Duke was enchanted at Paxton's triumph and most impressed. Visitors, the great Sir William Hooker and Dr Lindley, author of *The Vegetable Kingdom*, among them, streamed up to Chatsworth to admire.

The vast 'salver-shaped leaves' which had so impressed Sir Robert 231

The Devil, in J. J. Grandville's Les Fleurs Animées *tries to lead astray the chaste Soeur Nenuphar.*

Sir Joseph Paxton (1801–65) designer of the Crystal Palace. He succeeded in inducing the Victoria Regia *lily to flower in a specially built tank in 1849.*

RIGHT *The* Victoria Regia *lily in flower at Chatsworth, as shown in the* Illustrated London News *of 17 November 1849. An experiment was carried out to test the surprising weight-carrying capabilities of the leaves 'by placing a young lady upon one of them, who was borne up for some time in perfect safety'.*

Schomburgk attracted as much and even more attention than the flowers and it was the leaves and their extraordinary construction which were to give Paxton the idea which was to bring him world-wide fame. Their frame-work of hollow ribs gave each leaf extraordinary buoyancy and enough strength to support considerable weights. On 22 November, Miss Markham records, the carrying capacities of 'Victoria Regia' were put to the test, and Annie – Joseph Paxton's youngest daughter, who was seven years old – was put on one of the leaves by the Duke of Devonshire. Hooker was incredulous on hearing the story, but Paxton wrote to confirm its truth. The leaf was able to sustain a weight of a hundred pounds. The little girl, in crinoline and long drawers, made a pretty picture, and Douglas Jerrold recorded the incident in verse:

> On unbent leaf in fairy guise,
> Reflected in the water,

THE GIGANTIC WATER-LILY (VICTORIA REGIA), IN FLOWER AT CHATSWORTH.

> Beloved, admired by hearts and eyes,
> Stands Annie, Paxton's daughter ...

The scene was reported in the *Illustrated London News* of 17 November 1849. Meanwhile the 'Victoria Regia' lily continued on its glorious way, flowering generously month after month. And Paxton had taken the lesson of her leaves to heart, giving 'Victoria' the credit for his ingenious design for the building for the Exhibition of 1851, when he exhibited to the Fine Arts Society one of the great lily's leaves five feet across

> and pointed out that its underside was a beautiful example of natural engineering. For it possessed ribs like cantilevers radiating from the centre (where they were nearly two inches deep), with large bottom flanges, and very thin middle ribs with cross girders between each pair to keep the   233

middle ribs from buckling. 'Nature was the engineer,' said Paxton, 'nature had provided the leaf with longitudinal and transverse girders and supports that I, borrowing from it, have adopted in this building.'

'No example', writes Miss Markham, 'could be more striking of Paxton's quick eye, and his power of making good his lack of theoretical training as an architects, by gifts of natural observation.' It was thus that the natural formation of a water lily's leaves played a part in the design and construction of the great Crystal Palace, one of the sights of London for nearly a century.

Hardy Water Lilies. Frosts are unknown in British Guiana, and any sudden fall in the temperature would kill the 'Victoria Regia' lily stone-dead – but it is noteworthy how water lilies grown under ordinary conditions in Western gardens react to frost. Indeed, they can act as an efficient frost-warning. It is safe to assume that, once a water lily's leaves appear on the surface of the water in spring, all danger of frosts is over. As summer proceeds, their leaves rise out of the water in glistening tufts. When, in autumn, these tufts sink back to the surface, frost may be assumed to be imminent.

Many of the great modern hybrid water lilies were raised, as has been noted, by Bory Latour-Marliac (1830–1911), who started his great work of hybridization and development in the year 1860. After years of fruitless endeavour he discovered his own unique method of hybridization and from that moment, in 1875, he dedicated his whole garden to aquatic plants. About 1879 he put the first brilliant results of his labours on the market. These were *N. marliacea rosea*, in 1879, and *N.m. chromatella* in 1880.

Mrs Perry takes up the story in *Water Gardening*:

> He crossed and re-crossed the species and varieties at his command, so that it hardly seemed possible he could know them himself and the parentage of many became an enigma. He kept his methods secret, and to all intents and purposes they have passed away with him, but he has bequested to the world a race of hybrids which will live and ever make his name famous and earn the gratitude of all garden lovers.

M. Marliac's daughter married Jean Laydecker, whose name was given to several hybrids, and who is still living – a vigorous eighty-two, carrying on his father-in-law's work. His present efforts are directed to breeding a strain of hardy water lilies from plants originating in the tropics.

Thanks to M. Latour-Marliac and his son-in-law, the simple flower for which the Lady of Shalott
          'left the web and left the loom
          and took three paces through the room
          to see the water lily bloom',
has long since been superseded.

A choice of the new hybrids would certainly include the white-flowered, green-sepalled *richardsonii*, which has the curious habit of lifting its huge cup-shaped flowers high out of the water, like a lotus; the magnificent white and scented *gladstoniana*, and pink *marliacea carnea*, a plant worthy of being named after the master himself. The pale rose-colored *laydeckeri lilacea* commemorates his son-in-law.

Crimson and red varieties of water lilies to choose include the famous 'escarboucle' – most brilliant of all modern hybrid water lilies, with its vermilion petals and feathery crimson-tinted anthers. 'James Brydon' is another good red, as is *sanguinea*. Still the best of all yellow water lilies is another that bears M. Marliac's own name – *Nymphaea marliacea chromatella*. This has, as an added attraction, leaves that are mottled and marbled with brown. Two other good yellow varieties are 'Sunrise', which is scented and has flowers filled with golden filaments, and *N. odorata sulphurea*.

Planting. There is no need, writes Reginald Farrer.

> to trouble with the common white water lily. So much larger, so much stronger, so much more brilliantly white are the big foreigners and hybrids. Between any of these and the others in the matter of vigor, there is nothing at all to choose. For the larger water lilies are of the most weedlike vigor. Plant them in a hamper filled with clay and manure; drop them into a still pool; cut away the trees so that they may have full sun; and then they will grow like rhubarb, and flower like French Marguerites.

Another method of planting is to make a kind of sandwich of two pieces of turf, with the lily root in between, and drop it into the water where it is to grow – but however you plant water lilies, one thought must be kept in mind.

Nearly all aquatic plants dislike running water or at least water that is in too rapid movement – and water lilies dislike it most of all. Every water lily, from the ordinary white or yellow lily of the wild to the newest, largest, most fully double scarlet creation of M. Marliac, will only grow happily in water open completely to the sun, which is untroubled either by a strong current or a fountain's drip. All water lilies resent disturbance or being splashed or rocked about. In a small pool, with an overflow, if it has no natural feeding stream it is best to fix a small permanent jet at one side of the pool, to keep the water fresh and lessen the chances of algae or blanket weed.

M. Georges Clemenceau suggests that water lilies had a mute message for us which only the genius of Monet could pass on. Since Monet painted his almost abstract pictures at Giverny, the character of the garden water lily, thanks to M. Marliac, has materially changed. It could be said that today's more sophisticated and brightly-colored flowers, while losing nothing of their character, have gained new eloquence.

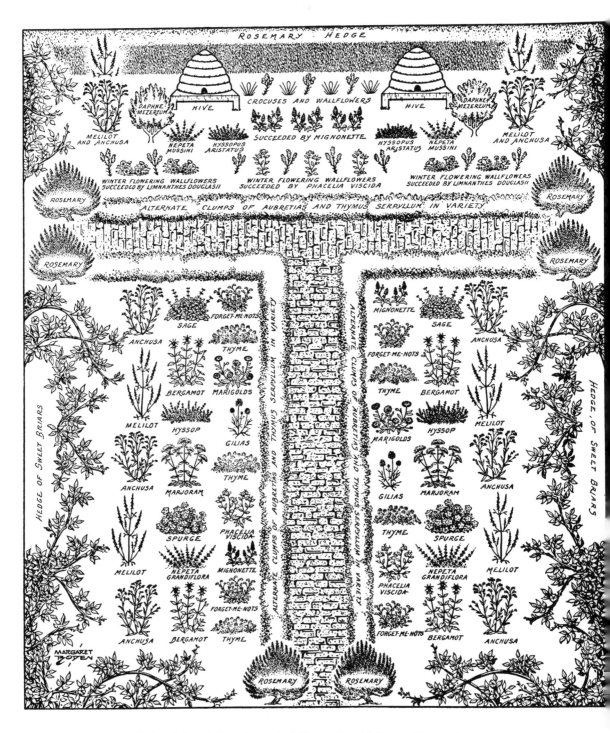

'Herbs ... with their definite habits of growth, different colored foliage and innate character
lend themselves ... to being set out in a pattern of box edged or paved pathways.'
A plan of a herb garden designed by the late Eleanor Sinclair Rohde.

Archangelica officinalis *is one of the most impressive plants in the herb garden, with its architectural leaves and round umbels of flowers.*

According to Du Bartas' Divine Weeks and Works *(1641)* '... *ingendring pestilence infects not those that in their mouths have ta'en Angelica, that happy Counterbane ...*'.

Herbs

'The Lord hath created medicines out of the earth;
And he that is wise, will not abhor them.'

Parkinson opens his *Theatrum Plantorum* with the words, 'From a Paradise of pleasant flowers I am fallen (Adam like) to a world of Profitable Herbs'. The preceding chapters of this book have each dealt with plants most prized for their flowers. This chapter will be devoted to herbs which are rather grown for the value of their leaves and roots.

From the earliest times down to the present day herbs have played a part in medicine, digitalis (foxglove) and Atropa Bella-Donna (Deadly Nightshade) in the form of atropine, are as important in the pharmacopoeia of the most modern American hospital as they were in the apothecary's chest of simples. *Conium maculatum* (hemlock) is as damaging to the nerve system today as it proved to Socrates. Every child is taught that the application of a dock leaf (*Rumex obtusifolius*) will relieve the sting of a nettle, and it is perfectly correct. Rumex contains tannin, a recognized anti-irritant. Thoughtfully, nature has ordered that the two plants usually grow near one another.

If herbs play less part medicinally in all our lives today, it is not because their powers have lessened, but perhaps because the ills they have the power to cure are less in evidence. In the unlikely event of being bitten by a bat, one would rather rely on an immediate injection of penicillin (itself a vegetable growth) than an application of a poultice of tansy. Attacks, these days, of the tetters, are rare – and should one suffer one, mercurochrome would offer a more likely cure than an application of white bryony. Our ancestors were much afraid of the bite of sea hares – whatever they may have been. For this, a piece of angelica, held in the mouth, was a recognized antidote, as it was for 'frenzies in the night'. But today, an anti-tetanus injection is prescribed for the bites of most animals. And though sleeplessness is as prevalent now as it

237

was two hundred years ago, a sleeping pill would act more quickly than a pillow stuffed with hops.

Herbs fascinated the ancients, who attributed to them almost human qualities. They studied their habits, personal likes and dislikes, as well as their properties: and they thought that herbs entertained strong friendships and 'enmities' between themselves.

Pliny was of the opinion that rue disliked basil but that 'rue and the figtree are in a great league and amitie' together: that alissanders (a kind of celery) 'loveth to grow in the same place as rosemary, but the radish is at enmitie with hyssop'. Sage and onions apparently get on as well together in the border as in the company of roast duck, while coriander, dill, mallows, herb patience (*Rumex patientia*) and chervil 'love for company to be set or sowne together'. Francis Bacon, who had strong ideas about gardening and composed his most famous essay on the subject, is inclined to scoff at these ancient fancies, and suggests that some plants will thrive in each other's company simply because the composition of the soil suits them: 'Wheresoever one plant draweth such a particular juice out of the earth, as it qualifieth the earth, so as that juice which remaineth is fit for the other plant: there the neighbourhood does good ... because the nourishments are contrary or several: but where two plants draw much the same juice, there the neighbourhood hurteth ...' Sound sense.

Apart from their medicinal values, herbs were valued for their scent. And in religious services, both pagan and Christian, incense has always played a part. In the May 1880 issue of *The Nineteenth-Century Magazine* it was suggested that the gods of God, being spirits, 'neither required nor desired solid offerings, but that the aetherial nature of the ascending fragrance was gratifying and sustaining to them'.

Fortunatus, the Bishop of Poitiers, has left a poem suggesting how flowers and herbs should be used to decorate churches in spring.

> When winter binds the earth with ice, all the glory of the field perishes with its flowers. But in the spring-time when the Lord overcame Hell, bright grass shoots up and buds come forth ... Gather these first-fruits and ... bear them to the churches and wreath the altars ...

What is a herb garden? It has been the custom for centuries to set aside one part of the garden for culinary and medicinal herbs. In the fifteenth century herbs were grown on raised banks of earth fronted with stone or brick and planted at the top, an excellent practice as nearly all herbs like a position in full sun which is sharply drained.

Part of a herb garden's charm must always lie in its design as outlined by its paths; and herbs themselves with their definite habits of growth, different colored foliage and innate character, lend themselves better than most plants to being set out in a pattern of box-edged or paved pathways. Bacon, in his celebrated and often quoted essay, suggested paths planted with low growing herbs such as 'Burnet, Wild Thyme and Water Mints. Therefore you are to set whole alleys of them, to have the pleasure when you walk or tread.'

Thyme grows between the flagstones of one of the most beautiful herb gardens in England, that of Victoria Sackville West at Sissinghurst Castle in Kent, of which there is a picture on page 248. Here, besides all the better known herbs, grow such unusual plants as woad (*Isatis tinctoria*) and costmary (*tanacetum*) 'that so likes the cup' because in medieval times it was often put in beer or negus. In one corner of the herb garden at Sissinghurst there is a stone bench, with the seat itself set with thyme, a delightful conceit – and one of which Bacon would surely have approved. Such a fragrant sitting place could well have found a place in Stephen Hawes' 'Knotte of Marveylous Greatness' where there were 'Rampande Lyons – made all of herbs – and dragons, of marvelous liveness, of divers fleures, made full craftily'.

An even craftier herb garden than Stephen Hawes' sixteenth-century plot was the garden devised by the great Linnaeus, where there was a sundial made of flowers and herbs which marked the passing hours by the opening and shutting of their flowers. Salsify, it seems, is an early starter, as its yellow flowers open at 3 a.m. punctually, and shut as punctually at midday – hence its colloquial name of Jack-Go-to-Bed-at-Noon: but chickwood (*trientalis*) does not show signs of life till the comparatively late hour of a quarter past nine, though then it stays open for exactly twelve hours.

Andrew Marvell, who wrote with such feeling of plants and the pleasures of nature, included in his poem *The Garden* some lines describing such a floral sundial:

> How well the skilful gardener drew
> Of flow'rs and herbs this dial new;
> Where, from above the milder sun,
> Does through a fragrant zodiac run,
> And, as it works, the industrious bee
> Computes its time as well as we,
> How could such sweet and wholesome hours
>   Be reckon'd but with herbs and flow'rs?

It is only recently that herb gardens have come back into popularity. Perhaps the revival of interest is due to the growing attention to the subtleties and lore of plants, rather than the search for a show of color. A hundred years ago herb gardens were practically unknown. In the *Quarterly* for June 1842 a writer complains: 'The olitory or herb-garden is a part of our horticulture now comparatively neglected, and yet once the culture and culling of simples was as much a part of female education as the preserving and tying down of "rasps and apricocks" '. And he goes on to say that once there was not 239 a garden owner in the country that did not know how to make dill-tea from herbs of their own planting; and that there was a charm, usefulness, as well as beauty, about thyme, sage, mint and marjoram which should earn them a place in the garden where their decorative qualities may be appreciated. And he adds the suggestion that:

> A strip for a little herbary half-way between the flower and vegetable garden would form a very appropriate transition stratum and might be the means, by being more under the eye of the mistress, of recovering to our soups and salads some of the comparatively neglected herbs of tarragon, and French sorrel and purslane and chervil and dill, and clary, and others whose place is now nowhere to be found but in the pages of the old herbalists. This little plot should be laid out, of course, in a simple, geometric pattern; and having tried the experiment, we can boldly pronounce on its success.

This quotation is one of many to which the author was introduced by Lady Rosalind Northcote, whose *The Book of Herbs*, published in 1912, he has found a mine of the most useful and fascinating information. The advice on the design of a herb garden quoted by Lady Rosalind holds as good now as it did fifty years ago: and at least two of the herbs mentioned, tarragon and dill, are no longer the strangers to cooking that they seem to have been in 1842. Both will be included among the better-known herbs to be described in this chapter. And, as herbs will for ever be connected in our minds with cooking as well as with medicine, it will not be out of place if reference is made, here and there, to some special dishes which owe their success to the inclusion of herbs.

Lady Rosalind Northcote (1873–1950) was an authority on herbs and wrote The Book of Herbs *in 1912, a book rich in information on the subject.*

Bastard Bawme with White Floures, or Melittis, as illustrated in Gerard's Herball.

ANGELICA (*Archangelica officinalis*) has always been credited with every good quality, though actually its medicinal powers are few. It is one of the most handsome plants of the herb garden and strikes an impressive attitude in any border where it is planted. Its leaves are a rich green and deeply cut, and if sown in July angelica will grow into a good plant by the following year, and make a fine show of almost spherical flower heads, which are the delight of bees. In ancient times angelica, if held in the mouth, was supposed to drive away infection. In Joshua Sylvester's translation of the French soldier and poet, Guillaume Du Bartas' *Divine Weeks and Works*, published in 1641, this property of the plant was noted,

> Contagious aire, ingendring pestilence,
> Infects not those that in their mouths have ta'en,
> Anglica, that happy Counterbane.

Angelica was considered, even by the unsuperstitious Gerard, to be the counterbane, too, to witchcraft and enchantment, as well as being useful as food. In his *Herball*, he tells us that angelica 'grows in an Island in the North called Island [Iceland]. It is eaten of the inhabitants, the bark being pulled off, as we understand by some that have travelled into Island ... and they report that it hath a good and pleasant taste', but he qualifies his statement by adding, '... to them that are hungry'; though Parkinson declared that the whole plant 'both leafe, roote and seede is of an excellent comfortable sent, savour and taste'.

Angelica was once much used in making sweets; now it is seldom seen, except candied, on the top of cakes. It is used for the flavoring of the liqueur chartreuse.

Angelica is one of the few herbs which prefers to grow in a damp situation, and it needs a rich soil to attain its full fine architectural form.

BALM (*Melissa officinalis*) was once used with angelica as an ingredient of a cordial called Carmelite Water. It is one of the most clean-smelling and refreshing of all herbs and Ann Page, in *The Merry Wives of Windsor*, seems to have suggested it as a kind of furniture polish when she tells her companions:

> The several chairs of order look you scour
> With juice of balm and every precious flower ...

Melissa's attractive name derives from the Greek for bee, as it is a herb that bees particularly like. Gerard notes that 'the hives of bees being rubbed with the leaves of bawme, causeth the bees to keep together and causeth others to come unto them', and adds, 'bees are delighted with this herbe above others, where upon it has been called apiastrum'. The very word 'balm' suggests soothing, and Macbeth describes sleep as 'balm of hurt minds – great nature's 241 second course'. Dioscorides claims that balm is a cure for mad dogs' bites, insects' stings, toothache and breathlessness. It was also – according to John Aubrey (1627–97) the antiquary and folklorist, whose curious and credulous *Miscellanies* was published in 1696 – a successful remedy for consumption.

Melissa makes a neat green bush two to four feet high and shows white and yellow labiate flowers in June. There is a variegated kind, *Melissa aurea*, which has green leaves streaked with gold, and is an attractive plant. All varieties of balm are strong-growing and inclined to be rampant spreaders. One plant dug up in March, when it is beginning to show leaf, pulled into pieces and replanted, will make a broad clump six feet across within a few months. BASIL (*Ocimum basilium*), a herb seldom grown in English gardens, has a very special magic; it is not hardy, and presents some difficulty in culture. The best way of raising basil in northern gardens is as a pot-herb, and this is how it is usually grown even in such warm southern countries as Greece and Italy.

A pot of basil will always have a special significance – thanks to Keats' famous poem *Isabella or The Pot of Basil*. In this sad story Isabella, daughter of a rich merchant of Florence, falls so much in love with the poor Lorenzo that:

> They could not sit at meals but feel how well
> It soothed each to be the other by.

Lorenzo was a shy lover and dared not disclose his feelings

> Until sweet Isabella's untouched cheek
> Fell sick within the roses just demain.

Finally Lorenzo spoke, but the proud brothers of Isabella were so furious at the thought of their sister marrying the humble Lorenzo, that they murdered him and buried his body in a nearby forest. Isabella pined away until, in a vision, her lover appeared to her, and told her where he was buried. Isabella found the body, and concealed Lorenzo's head in

> A garden pot, wherein she laid it by
> And covered it with mould, and o'er it set
> Sweet basil, which her tears kept ever wet.

Keats had adapted his poem from an old tale of Boccaccio, and Isabella and her Basil pot were the subject of a famous picture by Holman Hunt which was first exhibited in 1867.

Basil is said to benefit, though it is difficult to explain why, from the touch of a human being. Norman Douglas held that it should never be cut, but have its leaves picked by hand. These are certainly pleasant to handle, for they give off a strongly aromatic scent.

In ancient times basil had the curious reputation of breeding scorpions. This is probably explained by the fact that, as basil is so often grown in

242

Isabella or the Pot of Basil – by Holman Hunt (1827–1910). Isabella, in Keat's poem, concealed her dead lovers head in a pot '… and o'er it set sweet basil, which her tears kept ever wet'.

containers which are regularly watered, the ground underneath provides a cool retreat for scorpions, as for other insects.

Culpepper was suspicious of basil, writing:

> This is the herb which all authors are together by the ears about and rail at one another (like lawyers). Galen and Dioscorides hold it not fitting to be taken inwardly, and Chrysippus rails at it with downright Billingsgate rhetoric; Pliny and the Arabians defend it. Something is the matter, this herb and rue will not grow together, no nor near one another, and we know rue is as great an enemy to poison as any that grows.

Certainly there is nothing poisonous about basil. If there was, the author of this book would have suffered long ago – for he considers 'pomodoro con basilico' (tomatoes with basil) and a vinaigrette dressing one of the best of all salads. Another most appetizing way of using basil in cooking is in 'pesto' – the sauce made of basil, garlic, pine-nuts and grated cheese, which is so popular in the north of Italy. 'Pesto' is difficult to make for owners of northern gardens as pine-nuts are difficult to come by, though ground walnuts can be used instead. CAMOMILE (*Anthemis nobilis*) is a herb which drew one of Thomas Culpepper's most telling shafts. The ancient Egyptians, he records, dedicated the lowly camomile to the sun 'because it cured agues' but then 'they were the arrantest apes in their religion'. Camomile might well be one of the plants that Francis Bacon had in mind when he advised setting alleys of herbs to make paths that smelled sweetly when walked on. For camomile (the name derives from the Greek word meaning 'apple of the earth', and the scent camomile gives off when trodden rather recalls the fragrance of apples) is a masochistic plant – it thrives on ill treatment, and actually seems to enjoy being walked over, as Bacon advised. Falstaff (in *Henry IV*, part 1) says of it, 'the more it is trodden on, the faster it grows', adding philosophically, 'yet youth, the more it is wasted, the sooner it wears'.

Recently experiments have been made with lawns planted entirely of camomile, and there is one in the garden of Buckingham Palace. Victoria Sackville-West described, in *Even More for Your Garden*, a camomile lawn she had seen in London, which fully lived up to Falstaff's simile, for it was walked over daily by hundreds of people, and stood up well to the wear. Another advantage of a camomile lawn is that it needs mowing less often than a conventional lawn of grass.

Closely kin to camomile is the feverfew, a charming old-fashioned plant still found growing in cottage gardens. Its name stems from febrifuge and it was once used as a remedy, like camomile, for agues and fevers. The gold-leaved feverfew is a beautiful little plant, and its new tufts of bright leaves shine bright against the dark earth in the last dim days of winter. Its colloquial and most descriptive name is Golden Feather.

244

CHERVILS and CHIVES (*Anthriscus cerefolium Allium schaenoprasum*). William Langland, in his *Vision Concerning Piers Plowman*, written in the fourteenth century, sets us an example by coupling these two favorite herbs and wrote of 'Chibolles and chervelles and ripe chiries manye' (the French for chives is *ciboulette*). Of all herbs chervil was the favorite of John Evelyn, who surely grew it in his 'Garden of Curious Greenes'. 'It should never be wanting in our Sallets', he declares, 'as it is exceeding charming to the spirits'.

Gerard records that the Dutch used chervil as an important ingredient for 'a kinde of loblolly or hotchpot, which they do eat ...' and he praised it for its 'wholesomesse for the cold and feeble stomach' and for its ability to cheer 'old people that are dull and without courage; it rejoiceth and comforteth the heart and increases their lust ...' Useful properties.

Chervil makes an attractive plant, with its white umbels of flowers and delicate lacy foliage which goes pink in July. This is the sign that the seed is ripening and must soon be gathered and re-sown. If left till the following spring, or even for a month or two, germination will be poor. That is the clue – sow chervil seed as soon as it is ripe, and you will have all of the herb you want the following summer.

Chives are known to everyone and hardly need to be described. Lady Rosalind Northcote describes chive leaves well as miniature rushes which 'would serve admirably for elfin hautbois'. Chives have always been popular in the West. Linnaeus' favourite pupil, Peter Kalm (after whom he named the kalmia), was impressed with the many vegetables, chives among them, grown under glass and tucked up under straw matting every night, which he saw in the nursery gardens near London. In Chelsea, particularly, he noted that there was 'scarcely anything else than either orchards or vegetable market gardens'.

As a plant chives have every quality – they are excellent to mix with cream cheese and for sprinkling on cold vichyssoise soup. Furthermore, chives, with their mauve heads of flowers, can make a good-looking border in the herb or kitchen garden. For city-dwellers they will grow amiably in pots, if kept well watered and placed in as sunny a window sill as can be found. Curiously enough, when Lady Rosalind wrote her book, chives were going through a brief period of disfavor and she writes, 'the chief purpose for which I have heard them required is to mix with the food for young guinea fowls and chickens'. Chives have certainly gone up in the social scale since 1912.

DILL (*Anethum graveolens*) is an annual and should be sown each year in spring where it is to grow, and the young plants thinned out to about a foot apart. By July it will have made a four-foot-high, graceful feathery-leaved plant, not unlike fennel in appearance. Its name, dill, is supposed to come from the Scandinavian word to dull – as dill water has always been given to children to make them sleep, and its calming properties are recognized.

Dill is supposed to be a sure antidote to witches spells.

> Here holy vervayne and here dill
> 'Gainst witchcraft much availing ... (*The Muses' Elysium*)

Perhaps it is because witches are comparatively rare these days that dill is now so seldom grown, except by those few who have discovered how good it is with fish. Dill is a favorite flavoring in its native Sweden where, in Stockholm, crayfish festivals are held every summer, and the consumption of dill sauce must be enormous. Three hundred years ago, 'Gerckens muriated with the seed of dill' were favorites of John Evelyn, and before him Parkinson considered that dill gave 'pickled cowcumbers a prettie, spicie taste'.

FENNEL (*Faeniculum vulgare*). It is an odd fact that fennel has always been connected with flattery – both in England, and also in Italy where 'Dare finocchio' (to give fennel) means to pay false compliments. All the flowers in Ophelia's catalogue are supposed to have a special significance, and to her brother Laertes, who has just been offered the crown of Denmark by an irresponsible crowd, Ophelia mockingly offers fennel. In Ben Jonson's play *The Case Altered*, Christopher flatters another character in the play by addressing him as 'My good Lord' and gets the reply, ' "Your good Lord"! Oh, how this smells of fennel.'

The connotation survives down to the present day in the Cockney word for flattery – 'flannel'.

As well as with flattery, fennel is connected by some mysterious, long lost link, with sorrow: 'Sow fennel sow sorrow' is an old proverb which has crossed the Atlantic and is still occasionally heard in New England.

In cooking, fennel is still often used with fish and Parkinson notes that it 'is of great use to trim up and strowe upon fish, as also to boil or put among fish of divers sorts ...' In some parts of Italy, in Tuscany in particular, *finocchio* is used as a stuffing for *porchetto*, the ever popular sucking-pig.

In the mixed border fennel makes a tall handsome plant some five feet high with feathery airy leaves and yellow heads of flowers. The bronze fennel is a particularly good-looking plant and associates well with other late summer flowers such as dahlias and Michaelmas daisies. But it is a prolific seeder and can become a nuisance if not kept in check.

LAVENDER (*Lavendula spica*) and LAVENDER COTTON (*Santolina chamycyparissus*). Though these two very well-known herbs bear similar names there is no relationship between them. Lavender is little used in cooking, but it has always played an important part in the household. 'Hot lavender' comes first in Perdita's catalogue and references to lavender in literature are legion – one rather delightful one occurs in Izaac Walton's *Compleat Angler*, when Piscator leads his companions to an 'honest ale house, where we shall find a cleanly room, lavender in the windows and twenty ballads stuck about the wall'. Earlier, Piscator refers to a mysterious herb, benione, which, if hung over a stream, will frighten away otters, and so improve the fishing.

Lavandula stoechas *has strongly aromatic leaves and is a native of the Stoechades or Iles de Hyéres. Its old English name was Stickadove.*

Gerard van Spaendonck, c. 1800.

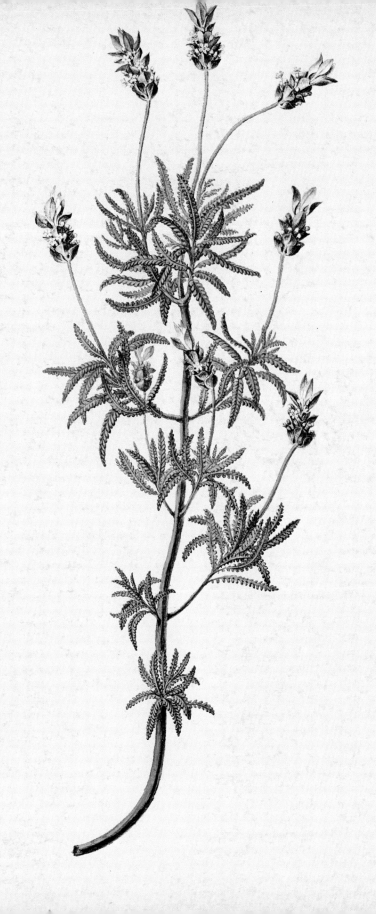

Gerard quotes Virgil 'in the fourth of his Georgickes, where he intreateth of chusing of seats and places for bees, and for the ordering thereof, he saith thus

> About them set such lavender and store of
> wild time with strong savorie to floure.'

He then goes on to recommend the use of lavender for many of the ailments, such as headaches and 'migram', for which lavender water is still used today.

White lavender is an attractive plant and only differs from ordinary lavender in the colour of its flowers. Gerard says, 'This plant bringeth milke white floures: and the other blewe, wherein especially consisteth the difference.'

There has always been a tradition that white lavender was the favorite flower of Queen Henrietta Maria, wife of Charles I. Perhaps it is true – perhaps it is a legend which dates from a Parliamentary Survey published by Oliver Cromwell after the final defeat of the Royalist party in the Civil War. By November 1649, the King had been executed. The Lily Queen was in exile and her possessions were put up at auction at the sale of her Manor at Wimbledon, 'parcel of the possessions of Henrietta Maria, the relict and late Queen of Charles Stuart, late King of England'. Even the plants in the garden were disposed of, too. Among them were 'very great and large borders of ... white lavender, and great varieties of excellent herbs'.

The most usual lavender grown is *Lavandula spica vera*, the Old English lavender which has darker and narrower leaves than the equally popular Dutch lavender (*L. vera*) with its silvery leaves and a compact bushy habit of growth.

Common Fennel, Chervil, Tarragon, and Wilde Marjorome of Candy from Gerard's Herball.

249

LEFT *It has been the custom for centuries to set aside one part of the garden for culinary herbs. A corner of the herb garden at Sissinghurst Castle in Kent.*

The Hidcote variety (*L. atropurpurea nana*) has the deepest blue flowers of any lavender and makes a neat low-growing grey-leaved plant. It gets its name from a famous garden in Gloucestershire which was originally planned and planted by a great American gardener, Lawrence Johnston, one of the first gardening friends of the author of this book. Not only is there a Hidcote variety of lavender but there is a Hidcote hypericum and a Hidcote rose. Hidcote will always be a famous name in gardening.

One last lavender, and a not completely hardy one, *L. stoechas*. This is a perennial, but worth growing for its curiously strong aromatic leaves. Its uninspiring name derives from its natural habitat – the Stoechades Islands (the Iles de Hyères) off the south coast of France. It has several other old names – such as stickadove or cassidonie. The last is simplified, by Gerard, into cast-me-down.

Cotton lavender or *Santolina chamaecyparissus*, though one of the most strongly pungent of herbs, like lavender, is not used in cooking. Thomas Tusser includes it in his list of 'Strewing Herbs' and it is easy to imagine that cotton lavender, like ordinary lavender laid in cupboards and chests, would be an effective deterrent to moths – hence the old French name for the plant, *Guarde-Robe*. It is one of the most decorative of all edgings for a herb garden, and, if clipped hard back in early spring, makes matt grey cushions of foliage which are very effective. The green-leafed variety, *viridifolia*, which is less often seen, can also be treated in this way. Though spring clipping prevents santolina from producing its bright golden buttons of flowers, these are no great loss. It is the leaves that are the chief beauty of the plant.

MINT (*Mentha*), is one of the very few herbs that everyone knows, and its two present uses in cookery, with lamb or cooked with green peas, are the same as its uses centuries ago. Pliny says that mint excites the taste to 'a greedy desire of meat', while in Parkinson's day mint was added to 'Pease that are boyled for pottage'.

Besides the mint usually grown for the kitchen – *Mentha viridis* – there are several other kinds of mint which are grown for their decorative leaves or different tastes and scents. Pineapple mint has strongly fragrant leaves, and apple mint grows taller than the type, and has longer leaves. It makes the best mint sauce of all. Lemon mint, *Mentha citrata*, called also bergamot mint and is the source of a strongly scented oil. *Mentha variegata* has leaves which are splashed with light green and white, and is a decorative, though invasive, border plant. Sometimes some of the leaves of *M. variegata* are pure white all over, which gives the plant an odd and pleasing effect.

Mentha pulegium is Penny Royal, a prostrate creeping plant with pale mauve flowers which, according to Gerard, 'rather lieth downe than standeth up'. When real tea was still a luxury for the rich, Penny Royal was used to make a comforting infusion by the very poor.

Catmint (*Nepeta cataria*) is one of the most familiar of herbaceous plants, and it is really not a mint at all, in spite of its name. Its pungent leaves are said to be beloved by cats. But Gerard includes 'Nep', an old name for it, in his list of mints and quotes 'later Herbarists' referring to it as 'Herba catti' 'because cats are very much delighted herewith ... that they rub themselves upon it, and wallow or tumble in it'. This would only seem to apply to newly set young plants – not to nepeta which has been grown from seed, for an old rhyme runs:

> If you sett it, the catts will eat it
> If you sowe it, the catts won't know it.

Last and least of mints is *Mentha requienii*, after the French botanist Esprit Requien, who in the last century made a study of the flora of Corsica. *M. requienii* forms a thin moss-like mat which is strongly peppermint scented when trodden on. Like all mints, it prefers damp ground and some shade.

Mentha is said to have been named for Minthe, a naiad, who became the mistress of Hades, son of Kronos. Their love incurred the jealousy of Persephone, who, according to the Greek historian Strabo, trampled Minthe underfoot, whereat she was transformed into the plant named after her, 'which smells the sweeter for being trodden on'.

ROSEMARY (*Rosmarinus officinalis*) is a herb which might have a whole book to itself, so great a part does it play in legend and history.

First, its Latin name, *rosmarinus*, means 'Dew of the Sea' which well describes its sea-blue flowers. It is thought that the plant was introduced by the Normans into England, but though rosemary doubtless played its part in the festivals of the Roman gods, there is something un-pagan about the plant. In spite of the real meaning of its name, one connects it unconsciously with the Virgin Mary; and there is a legend that Mary, on the flight into Egypt, cast her blue cloak over the white flowered rosemary, whose flowers henceforth were blue in memory of the honour conferred on them. Another legend holds that no plant of rosemary will ever grow higher than Christ; and it is certainly one of the few shrubs which might show a flower or two at Christmas.

Rosemary was a favorite plant of Sir Thomas More, who said of it: 'As for Rosmarine, I lett it runne all over my garden walls, not onlie because my bees love it, but because it is the herb sacred to remembrance, and therefore to friendship; whence a sprig of it hath a dumb language'. Rosemary has always been connected with remembrance – Ophelia's mention of it being only one of many, and Gerard quotes the 'Arabians and other Physitions' as being of the opinion that rosemary was actually good for the memory. Banckes wrote in his *Herball* that even to smell the pungent leaves of rosemary kept one 'youngly'.

Rosemary was used as decoration for festivals, but also for funerals. Friar Laurence suggests strewing rosemary on Juliet's 'Fair corse', and Robert

Herrick, in his poem *The Garden*, writes of rosemary as one might write today of white lilies.

> Grow it for two ends, it matters not at all
> Be't for my bridall or my buriall...

Though the stories and legends connected with rosemary are legion, there are comparatively few varieties of the plant in cultivation. The best known variety is *R. officinalis* – the shrub which Thomas More used to cover his walls, the shrub, which, true to the legend, seldom grows higher than a man, and which can bear its flowers for many months of the year. Miss Jessup's variety of *R. officinalis* is fastigiate, and makes a neat upright growing little bush. *R. officinalis aureus* is a rosemary with variegated foliage; it is fairly uncommon, and has attractive sparkling foliage, which recalls the days of the Tudors, when branches of rosemary were gilded and used as Christmas decoration. 'Corsican Blue' is a newly introduced kind of rosemary which makes a smaller, more compact bush than the type, but has brighter flowers. More than others of the family it needs shelter from cold winds, and well-drained soil. All rosemaries like growing by the sea.

Now and then, regrettably, one sees rosemary plants which have been clipped like lavender or box. This should never on any account be done, for the plant's two great beauties are its blue flowers, lost if the bush is cut back,

LEFT Rosmarinus officinalis *or rosemary is one of the best known of all herbs. Here it grows on either side of an old garden door in Kent.*

Even in frosty weather the blue glaucous leaves of Ruta graveolens *retain their unusual color. 'Jackman's Blue' is the most striking variety.*

and its loose graceful growing habit with its lighter green, upward-pointing new shoots.

RUE (*Ruta graveolens* – meaning strongly scented, as the leaves of all rues are). This is the herb which Perdita coupled with rosemary: two herbs which 'keep seeming and savor all the winter long', and it was for the gardener in *Richard II* a 'Sour herb of grace; rue, even for ruth'.

The wise Canon Ellacombe, in his *Plant lore and garden craft of Shakespeare*, suggests that:

> Ruth was the English name for sorrow and remorse, and to rue was to be sorry for anything or to have pity, ... and so it was a natural thing to say that a plant which was so bitter, and had always borne the name Rue or Ruth must be connected with repentance. It was therefore the Herb of Repentance, and this was soon transformed into the Herb of Grace.

The practical use of rue has always been connected with fumigation, and a hundred and fifty years ago court rooms were strewn with rue as a protection from jail fever. In Sardinia its pungent leaves are scattered in the room in which a body awaits burial; there it is firmly regarded as a plant connected with death, and therefore unlucky. The author discovered this, when he attempted to establish a particularly bright blue-leaved rue in a garden in

253

Sardinia, and found every morning that it had been pulled up and thrown away.

Recently a very beautiful new variety of rue has been raised by Messrs Jackman, 'Jackman's Blue'. This form of *Ruta graveolens* has leaves which are a really brilliant color, and the plant has leapt to popularity since the war. Like the rarer varieties of hellebore it is a plant for the connoisseur. But to go one further – for those who would like to 'wear their rue with a difference' – there is an even newer, variegated form, unusual certainly, but far less decorative. For the blue of the leaves of Jackman's rue provides one of the most striking leaf colors in the garden.

SAGE (*Salvia officinalis*). In the annals of the celebrated school of medicine at Salerno there runs a passage, 'Cur morietur homo cui salvia crescit in horto?' (How can a man die who grows sage in his garden?). Sage has always been credited with the most beneficent powers. Its name, *salvia* in Latin, is akin to salve, and Culpepper records that it is 'held of most' to be a cure for such divers ills as the 'pricking of the fishe called in latine Pastinaca marina whiche is like unto a flath with venomous prickes about his tale'. And not only, it appears, did an application of sage cure harm from stingrays, but it was a general cure for all 'woundis'. It was also an excellent dye for the hair, and, according to Banckes, good for revitalizing the lethargic. John Evelyn, after a eulogy of the plant's 'noble properties', ends his praise with the words, 'In shorte, it is a plante endued with so many and wonderful properties, as that the assiduous use of it is said to render men immortal'.

If this supposed quality extended to the immortality of the soul, it may explain why sage was sometimes planted on graves. In April 1662 Samuel Pepys notes in his *Diary* that, 'Besides my lord Southampton's park and lands, where in one view we could see £6,000 per annum, we observed a little churchyard where the graves are accustomed to be all sowed with sage'.

Most animals dislike the scent of sage, though toads are an exception to this rule, and their liking for the plant has been noted by several writers, including William Turner. But it is doubtful whether the staider toad behaves in the aromatic shade of a sage bush as do frogs, as Bulleine informs us, in that of scabious, where, apparently, they will 'shadow themselves from the heate of the daye, puppying and playing under the leaves which to them is a pleasant tent or pavilion'.

There are numerous kinds of sage in cultivation. Most common is *Salvia officinalis*. This makes a low rounded bush with olive green, slightly tomentose leaves. More colorful – in fact one of the most valuable colored-leaved plants in the garden – is *S. officinalis atropurpurea*, with rich purple foliage which contrasts well with grey or silver leaved plants. Most spectacular of all sages is the variegated kind – the 'Painted Sage' – which has leaves which are splashed, as with paint, in different colors of purple, gold and pink. The

golden sage, *S. aurea*, is also a striking plant.

As this is a chapter on herbs, these are the sages which should find a place in the well-planted herb garden. There are, however, other members of the salvia family which it would be neglectful to pass over. The annual *Salvia bicolor* is an excellent plant, with its leaf tips (not flowers) of purple, pink or white, as is the brilliant blue *S. patens* – surely the bluest blue of any flower. The reddest red is provided by salvias such as 'Harbinger' or 'Fireball': horrible plants which have become a by-word – 'Red salvias' the cognoscenti exclaim in horror – and yet bright red salvias can, if thoughtfully placed, look most effective.

Another effective salvia is *Salvia sclarea* – of which the colloquial name, 'Clary' (Clear Eye), tells us for what medicinal purpose it was once used. The modern form of this beautiful plant is known as *S. turkestanica*, and of this the 'Vatican' type is the best. It should be planted in every mixed border. Not only is it a visual delight from the first moment its leaves unfold – downy and opalescent – in spring, but the plant looks well all through the summer, when its handsome silvery mauve flower heads persist for several weeks. *Salvia turkestanica* is not truly herbaceous and it is best treated as a biennial; that is, it should be sown in July to flower the following year.

A true herbaceous salvia is *S. virgata nemerosa* ('Twiggy' and 'woody') now more simply known as a *S. superba*. This is a plant which entirely lives up to its new name and its many spires make a fine show of rich purple in the border in late June. Like *S. turkestanica* it looks well far into autumn, and, with its shrubby compact growth, it makes the perfect underplanting for lilies – which, as is noted elsewhere, like to be planted with their roots shaded and their flowers in the sun.

Another herbaceous salvia, very seldom grown but a great personal favorite, is *S. uliginosa* (growing in wet ground). This grows taller than *S. superba*, and makes a graceful plant four feet high. Its flowers are of a particularly attractive pale blue. As its name implies, it likes a damp situation.

TARRAGON (*Artemisia dracunculus*). In Gerard's day tarragon was 'cherished in gardens' and Parkinson describes its taste as 'not unpleasant' but 'somewhat austere'. Why and how tarragon – in French *estragon* and in Latin *dracunculus* – (little dragon) achieved its dragon connotation is not known. Tarragon originates in Russia. There are several varieties and the one known as French tarragon, sometimes difficult to find, is the best for cooking purposes. This has smooth bluish green leaves as opposed to the Russian tarragon (*Artemisia dracunculoides*), which is much less strong in taste and has leaves which are rougher, though of a brighter green. The Russian plant, unfortunately, is the more vigorous grower. Tarragon likes to be grown in a well-drained, sunny position and in deep, not too damp, soil. Wet in winter can easily kill it. Unlike most herbs, tarragon as a plant is not particularly attractive to look at, but it is of the greatest value in cooking – as anyone who has eaten well-prepared *Poulet à l'estragon* will agree.

Closely related to the culinary herb are the silver-leaved artemisias which are such decorative additions to the mixed border. In fact it could be said that a well-planned border would be incomplete without them. Of these *A. palmeri* is the most often grown, but least satisfactory, as it is too rampant and spreading. Better plants are the tall, feathery (but not quite hardy) *A. arborescens*, the almost white-leaved *A. ludoviciana* and the excellent new 'Lambrook Silver'. But none of these silver-leaved artemisias are herbs in the true sense of the word.

Rudyard Kipling once wrote:

> Excellent herbs had our fathers of old
> Excellent herbs to ease their pain
> Alexanders and Marigold
> Eyebright, Orris and Elecampane
> Basil, Rocket, Valerian, Rue
> (Almost singing themselves they run)
> Vervain, Dittany, Call-me-to-you
> Cowslip, Meliot, Rose of the Sun.
> Anything green that grew out of the mould
> Was an excellent herb to our fathers of old.

In this chapter many 'excellent herbs' have been omitted. It would have been instructive, for instance, to note that the seed of Coriander is likened to manna in the Bible (Numbers, XI, 7) but that according to William Turner, if you swallow too many you are in 'greate jeopardie of madnesse'.

It would have been pleasant to digress on the legend of Elecampane (*Inulus helenae*) which Gerard tells us 'sprang from Helen's tears'. It might, too, have been useful to tell how Lovage (ligusticum) can be used to season meat, and the pretty golden marjoram (origanum), pizza. And how the little known fenugreek (*Trigonella foenum graecum*) can be used to physic horses.

There is no space to describe the use of sorrel (rumex) in a soup or in a salad, to which John Evelyn thought it supplied 'so grateful a quicknesse ...'. Nor is there space to do more than mention one of the sweetest of all herbs – thyme – of which Parkinson describes eleven kinds including one which sounds tantalizingly desirable – the 'gilded or embroidered' thyme.

Lady Rosalind Northcote ends her note on thyme by quoting John Abercrombie, 'an upright man and cheerful companion', in *Everyman His Own Gardener*. His information, Lady Rosalind tells us, 'is always given in a concentrated form'. Thyme, to him was no more than 'an ever green, sweet scented, fine flavored, aromatic undershrub, young tops used for various kitchen purposes.'

256

A path of weathered brick is hedged on either side with silver-leaved
Santolina chamaecyparissus or Cotton Lavender.

Acknowledgements

The author and publishers would like to express their gratitude to the following
for permission to quote from their works.

Germain Bazin *A Gallery of Flowers* Thames and Hudson;
Professor Bergström *Dutch Still Life Painting in the Seventeenth Century* Faber and Faber;
Wilfred Blunt *Old Garden Roses* Rainbird;
Georges Clemenceau *Claude Monet Les Nymphéas* Librairie Plon;
Alice Coats *Garden Shrubs and their Histories* Vista Books;
Jack Drake Inshriach Nursery, Aviemore, Inverness;
Frank Elgar *Van Gogh; A Study of His Life and Work*, Thames and Hudson (F.A.Praeger, New York);
Executors of the late Violet Markham, *Paxton and the Bachelor Duke* Hodder and Stoughton;
Roy Genders *Garden Pinks* John Gifford Ltd;
Geoffrey Grigson *The Englishman's Flora* Phoenix House;
Michael Haworth Booth *Effective Flowering Shrubs* Collins;
Edward Hyams *Lilies* Nelson;
M.J.Jefferson Brown *The Winter Garden* Faber and Faber;
Kenneth Lemmon *The Golden Age of Plant Hunters* Phoenix House;
Nigel Nicolson For permission to quote from his mother The Hon. V.Sackville-West's poem
                The Garden and other books;
Frances Perry *Water-Gardening* Country Life;
Sir Sacheverell Sitwell *Old Fashioned Flowers* Country Life;
Geoffrey Taylor *The Victorian Flower Garden* and *Some Nineteenth-Century Flower Gardeners* Skeffington;
Neil Treseder *Royal Horticultural Society Journal.*

The author's gratitude is also due to Princess Jean De Caraman Chimay and the Viscount de Noailles for
information about M.Soulange-Bodin and M.Latour-Marliac.
To the Earl of Iddesleigh for information about Lady Rosalind Northcote.
To Mr David Carritt, to M. H.P.Gourry, to M. and Mme Arpad Plesch, to Mr Andrew Blakely,
to the Countess of Rosse and to Mr Patrick Synge. And he owes a special debt of thanks
to Mr Peter Stageman of the Royal Horticultural Society Library and the staff of the Botanical Library
of the British Museum.

The photographs on pages 102 and 215/1 are reproduced by gracious permission of Her Majesty the Queen. The author and publishers wish to thank the following people and museums for permission to reproduce illustrations from their collections:

Allwood Bros: 53; Dobies of Chester: **212**; Duke of Devonshire: 232;
J.E.Downward, F.I.B.P.: 20, 42, 49, 110, 118/2, 120/2, 175/1, 185/1, 188; John Hadfield: **87**; Antony Hail: **38**;
Illustrated London News: 233; Nigel Nicolson: 40; *The Times*: 236; Lady Ann Tree: **58**.

Albertina Museum, Vienna: 215/2; British Museum: 11/1, 11/2, 13/1, 14/1, 14/2, 17/1, 17/2, 21, 22, 35/1, 52, 56, 74, 84, 99, 101, 106/1, 108, 118/1, 121, 132/1, 140, 143, 145, 152, 155/2, 161, 163, 166–7, 180/2, 194/2, 196, 205, 210, 225, 249;
Castelvecchio, Verona: **171**; Hallsborough Gallery: 24; Harris Museum and Art Gallery, Preston: 124;
Kunsthalle, Bremen: 86; Laing Art Gallery, Liverpool: 243; Louvre, Paris: **125**; Mauritshuis, The Hague: **28**;
Metropolitan Museum, New York: 92; Natural History Museum, London: 43, **47**, **116**, **126**, **135**, **172**;
National Gallery, London: **26–7**; National Portrait Gallery, London: 12, 31/1, 31/2, 35/2, 175/2;
Osterreiches Museum fur Angewandte Kunst, Vienna: 64; Osterreiches National Bibliothek, Vienna: 133;
Royal Academy, London: 51, Slavisches Institut, Munich: 194/1; Teylers Stichtung, Haarlem: 198;
Uffizi Gallery, Florence: **25**; Victoria and Albert Museum, London (Crown Copyright): 15, **153**;
Windsor Castle: 102, 215/1.

Photographs were kindly supplied by the above-mentioned museums and collections and by the following (colour plates are shown in **bold type**):
Cecil Beaton: 40; Bulloz: 55/2; Kerry Dundas: 127, 131/1, 196, 203, 209, 224; Elliot and Fry: 240/1;
J.R.Freeman: 2, 4, 11/1, 11/2, 13/1, 14/1, 14/2, 17/1, 17/2, 21, 22, 34/1, 34/2, 35/3, 43, 50, 52, 56, 65, 74, 76, 84, 91/1, 91/2, 99, 101, 106/1, 118/1, 121, 132/1, 140, 143, 145, 152, 155/2, 161, 163, 166–7, 180/2, 194/2, 196, 205, 210, 225, 229; Richard Green: **199**; Hirmer Verlag: 85; Mansell Collection: 13/2, 55/1, 96, 219;
Mi-Collime Fayetteville: 60; Philpson Studio: 243; Radio Times Hulton Picture Library: 62, 134, 138/1, 155/1, 173;
Rheinisches Bildarchiv: 214; Patrick Rossmore: **136**, 177; Scala: **25**, **171**; Edwin Smith: 69/1, 160, 191, 223, 228;
Harry Smith: **67**, **88**, 90, 105, 144, **154/1**, 180/1, **211**, **248**.

The following photographs were taken by the author: 8, 18, **37**, **38**, 41, 59, 63, **68**, 69/2, 71/2, 73, **77**, 79, 81/1, 81/2, 82/1, 82/2, 95, **97**, **98**, 106–7, 111, 113, **115**, 117, 118/3, 120/1, 131/2, 132/2, 138/2, 151, **154/2**, 159, 182–3, 185, **189**, **190**, 193, **202**, 221, 222, 229, 237, 252, 253, 257.

Index

References to plates are italicised